A HISTORY OF REGULATING WORKING FAMILIES

Families in market economies have long been confronted by the demands of participating in paid work and providing care. Across Europe the social, economic and political environment within which families do so has been subject to substantial change in the post-World War II era and governments have come under increasing pressure to engage with this important area of public policy. In the UK, as elsewhere, the tensions which lie at the heart of the paid work/unpaid care conflict remain unresolved, posing substantial difficulties for all of law's subjects both as carers and as the recipients of care. What seems like a relatively simple goal – to enable families to better balance care-giving and paid employment – has been subject to and shaped by shifting priorities over time, leading to a variety of often conflicting policy approaches. This book critiques how working families in the UK have been subject to regulation. It has two aims:

- To chart the development of the UK's law and policy framework by focusing on the post-war era and the growth and decline of the welfare state, considering a longer historical trajectory where appropriate.
- To suggest an alternative policy approach based on Martha Fineman's vulnerability theory in which the vulnerable subject replaces the liberal subject as the focus of legal intervention. This reorientation enables a more inclusive and cohesive policy approach and has great potential to contribute to the reconciliation of the unresolved conflict between paid work and care-giving.

A History of Regulating Working Families

Strains, Stereotypes, Strategies and Solutions

Nicole Busby
and
Grace James

•HART•

OXFORD • LONDON • NEW YORK • NEW DELHI • SYDNEY

HART PUBLISHING

Bloomsbury Publishing Plc

Kemp House, Chawley Park, Cumnor Hill, Oxford, OX2 9PH, UK

1385 Broadway, New York, NY 10018, USA

29 Earlsfort Terrace, Dublin 2, Ireland

HART PUBLISHING, the Hart/Stag logo, BLOOMSBURY and the Diana logo are trademarks of Bloomsbury Publishing Plc

First published in Great Britain 2020

First published in hardback, 2020
Paperback edition, 2022

A catalogue record for this book is available from the British Library.

Library of Congress Cataloging-in-Publication Data

Names: Busby, Nicole, author. | James, Grace, 1972- author.

Title: A history of regulating working families : strains, stereotypes, strategies and solutions / Nicole Busby and Grace James.

Description: Oxford ; New York : Hart, 2020. | Includes bibliographical references and index.

Identifiers: LCCN 2020012533 (print) | LCCN 2020012534 (ebook) | ISBN 9781849465571 (hardcover) | ISBN 9781509904617 (Epub)

Subjects: LCSH: Social legislation—Great Britain—History—20th century. | Working class families—Law and legislation—Great Britain—History—20th century.

Classification: LCC KD3000 .B87 2020 (print) | LCC KD3000 (ebook) | DDC 344.4103/282—dc23

LC record available at https://lccn.loc.gov/2020012533

LC ebook record available at https://lccn.loc.gov/2020012534

ISBN: HB: 978-1-84946-557-1
PB: 978-1-50994-345-6
ePDF: 978-1-50990-460-0
ePub: 978-1-50990-461-7

Typeset by Compuscript Ltd, Shannon

To find out more about our authors and books visit www.hartpublishing.co.uk. Here you will find extracts, author information, details of forthcoming events and the option to sign up for our newsletters.

PREFACE

As academics with an established interest in the legal regulation of families, caregiving and paid work, our motivation for writing this book was to gain a better understanding of how and why UK governments have chosen to regulate working families in the way they have. Embarking upon this project, we began with a solid conviction, as has long been recognised by many, that in order to understand our present we need to engage with our past.

The process of researching and writing the book provided us with an original and valuable opportunity to take a longer view and to consider legal and policy approaches with the added benefit of hindsight. Although sometimes difficult to contain, this project was a joy to research. It took us out of our comfort zones and was both fascinating and humbling. Fascinating because it enabled us to locate and ponder transitions, movements and pressure points in our history when certain policy approaches established, promoted or challenged particular discourses that have become dominant in a range of related legal fields. The process was humbling because we were confronted with evidence of centuries of hardship and poverty, often unrecognised or forgotten, endured by so many families over a long time period.

As is always the case with research projects of this scale, there are many people to whom we are indebted. We are grateful for the team at Hart Publishing for their unwavering support and patience. The road to publication has been a long one as progress was stalled several times for a variety of reasons including maternity leave and general workload (paid and unpaid) fatigue. Our thanks go to our colleagues and friends who have supported us and helped to shape our thinking, read drafts and participated in related projects that have helped us (re)formulate our views – in particular Thérèse Callus, Rachel Horton, Paul Almond, Eugenia Caracciolo di Torella, Michelle Weldon-John and Rebecca Zahn.

We are particularly grateful to Professor Martha Albertson Fineman, whose vulnerability theory provides the critical lens through which we assess the UK's law and policy framework. Martha kindly met with us to discuss the book and our engagement with vulnerability theory. She was generous with her time and in sharing her thoughts and offered some much-needed encouragement at the final stages of writing up.

Finally, families are at the heart of this project and, as always, we thank ours – Calum, Eve, Eleanor and Màiri and Richard, Chris, Alex and Harry – for their consistent and unconditional love and support. We don't take them, or our privileged existence, for granted.

CONTENTS

1

Introduction

I. Scope and Aims

The notion of explicitly regulating working families is a very modern concern, yet families worldwide have long been confronted by the practical, financial and emotional demands of participating in paid work *and* providing care for their dependent members. This book traces and critiques how laws, and labour laws[1] in particular, have helped or hindered working families in the UK. An historical perspective provides a useful vantage point from which to assess the variety of, and similarities within, legal approaches favoured over time and allows us to reflect upon the differing strains and stereotypes that have challenged the lives of working families. We shed light on conflicts and tensions, constructed and real, between the needs of working families and other institutions or within families themselves during any given period. The critical identification of prominent stereotypes, such as the 'single mother' or 'the elderly relative', is useful in this assessment as they have, in different ways at different junctures and depending upon the objectives of the policy discussed, been used to both justify and restrict particular legal approaches. Relatedly, an historical perspective provides an opportunity, with the advantage of hindsight, to (re)consider potential strategies and solutions adopted in relation to working families. This can include consideration of policies that are adopted at specific points in history or that are shelved. Indeed a deliberate lack of political engagement can be significant in this context as non-engagement or neutrality as a strategy has consequences for all concerned: as Herring suggests, 'it is impossible for the state to take a neutral stance towards forms of caring'.[2] We comment upon strategies and solutions in order to demonstrate how they shape, promote or challenge the very strains and stereotypes that we identify.

We aim to map and critique a particular journey in the UK's legal history and, in doing so, seek explanations regarding, for example, why regulators engaged, or failed to engage, with the difficulties faced by working families and why the

---

[1] Labour law is concerned with the wider relationship between organised groups (eg workers, unions, employers) and institutions (eg the market, families and the state). Employment laws focus more on the regulation of individual employees and whilst the particular legislation directed at working families is part of the latter – this critique as a whole is interested in the regulation of working families in a broader sense.

[2] J Herring, *Caring and the Law* (Oxford, Hart Publishing, 2013) 89.

work–family balance (WFB) framework came to be constructed in the way that it did. Importantly, we consider whose interests have been, and continue to be, promoted by the adoption of particular strategies and solutions. Of equal, if not greater, significance is our examination of whose interests have been, and continue to be, sidelined or ignored. We also consider what alternative constructions might have offered and could, in the future, offer working families. Overall, we demonstrate that the transformations in the UK vis-à-vis the regulation of working families, especially over the past five decades, have either promoted or sidelined a myriad of interests which are diverse and often competing: transformations that have huge consequences for, and have resulted in the (re)positioning of, care work and labour market activities. The need to fundamentally re-examine our approach to the legal regulation of working families is situated in the realities of this transformation and the interests and values it embodies: interests and values that, as we argue, need to be revealed and challenged in order to better support working carers and the recipients of their care going forward.

Before discussing the broader context for our particular focus and outlining the methodology and structure of the book, it is necessary to define our specific interpretation of key terms, namely 'the family', 'care work' and 'dependency', and to outline the core theoretical perspective – vulnerability theory – and the main themes from that perspective that facilitate and influence our critique.

II. Key Definitions

A. The Family

Definitions of 'the family' are undoubtedly subjective and, as Herring notes, 'family forms have varied enormously over the ages and ... the notion of what a family is or what family life involves changes between generations and societies'.[3] For many years marriage, sexual relationships and parenting have provided the main focus for definitions of the family and this institution is often thought to be permanent and principally responsible for care work: 'Family is wrongly assumed to be unchanging, an essentialized institution, natural in form and function, that is the repository for dependency'.[4] Such views have fortunately been challenged by those who want a more inclusive and flexible definition that better reflects the functions of family life today rather than the form of the family,[5]

---

[3] ibid, 195.

[4] MA Fineman, *The Autonomy Myth: A Theory of Dependency* (New York, New Press, 2004) 155.

[5] See, eg, discussion in F Williams, *Rethinking Families* (London, Calouste Gulbenkian Foundation, 2004) and L Murray and M Barnes, 'Have Families been Rethought? Ethic of Care, Family and "Whole Family" Approaches' (2010) 9 *Social Policy and Society* 533; and see Silva and Smart, who usefully comment that 'families are what families do' (EB Silva and C Smart (eds), *The 'New' Practices and Politics of Family Life* (London, SAGE Publications, 1999) 5.

and seek to avoid emphasis on the sexual relationship, as well as biological and heteronormative bias.[6]

In this book we reject the traditional heteronormative conception of the family and our definition includes all types of family arrangements. In addition, we welcome calls for a better understanding of the implications of constructing the family as 'separate' and 'private': 'The family', as Fineman asserts, 'is contained within the larger society, and its contours are defined as an institution by law'.[7] We recognise the symbiotic relationship between the family and other social institutions noting that 'it is very important to understand the roles assigned to the family in society – roles that otherwise might have to be played by other institutions, such as the market or the state'.[8] We, as do Fineman and others, call for more emphasis on relationships of care[9] when designing social policies relating to the family. Moreover, as will become evident in the substantive chapters that follow, we berate any inability to grasp the profound, and often undervalued, effect of families 'on the success and failure of policies created for the market and the state'.[10]

Whilst most of the discussion around definitions of 'the family' have centred on, and been developed within the context of, family law, there are clear implications for our project. This book is concerned with laws and policies that aim to support working families. Hence, if 'the family' is defined too narrowly for this purpose then care work that is undertaken by workers who fall outside the definition will be excluded. For this reason it is crucial that we remain sensitive to any assumptions that are made within adopted definitions of families over time: we also agree with Murray and Barnes's view of 'the practices of family' as 'predicated on shared and situated relationships of care'[11] and with Silva and Smart's view that 'families remain a crucial relational entity playing a fundamental part in the intimate life of and connections between individuals'[12] and, we would add, other institutions – such as the market and the state. How far and in what ways these connections are supported is considered in the book, where we use the broad terms of 'familisation' and 'defamilisation' to help us unpack and critique where responsibility for care work is situated at any given time: the former denotes a strategy that, consciously or not, places care as a private familial concern.

---

[6] See, eg, C Pateman, *The Sexual Contract* (London, Polity Press, 1988); J Probert, 'Family Law – a Modern Concept?' (2004) *Family Law* 901; S Cretney, *Same Sex Relationships, from 'Odious Crime' to 'Gay Marriage'* (Oxford, Oxford University Press, 2006); N Barker, *Not the Marrying Kind* (London, Palgrave, 2012).

[7] Fineman, *The Autonomy Myth*, above n 4, xviii.

[8] ibid.

[9] See Herring, *Caring and the Law*, above n 2, ch 6; Fineman, *The Autonomy Myth*, above n 4; Murray and Barnes, 'Have Families been Rethought? Ethic of Care, Family and "Whole Family" Approaches', above n 5.

[10] MA Fineman, 'Cracking the Foundational Myths: Independence, Autonomy and Self-Sufficiency' (2000) 8 *The American University Journal of Gender, Social Policy and the Law* 13, 15.

[11] Murray and Barnes, 'Have Families been Rethought? Ethic of Care, Family and "Whole Family" Approaches', above n 5.

[12] Silva and Smart (eds), *The 'New' Practices and Politics of Family Life*, above n 5, 2.

The latter refers to a process of moving care from the private into a public place – with greater responsibility for the state.[13]

B. Care Work

Unpaid work involving the care of children is being undertaken within tens of millions of families across the UK. In addition, over 8 million people provide care for adults who are ill, frail or disabled and that figure is predicted to rise.[14] An estimated 1.3 million care for both children and parents.[15] The extent of unpaid care work being undertaken on a daily, and often nightly, basis is staggering and provides a blunt reminder that most of us will be cared for and provide care for someone close to us at some point in our lives. The importance of such care work is fundamental but difficult to measure, especially as it has historically gone unrecognised in any material sense. Most will agree that such relationships are crucial to the daily existence and wellbeing of millions of recipients of care:[16] it is also an essential component of our humanity that enhances the quality of our lives.[17] Although the nature of care work will have altered in many ways, this basic fact is not specific to any time or place in history.

For the purpose of this book, we define care work as domestic/private[18] and unpaid work that involves taking care of others – usually family members – including children, older people in need of care and those who are disabled or

---

[13] See discussion in Herring, *Caring and the Law*, above n 2, 110–15. Of course, the state has increasingly contracted out much care service provision in recent years so the reality has become more complex.

[14] The Census puts this at just under 6.6 million, but using Carers UK's definition (which includes providing emotional support and the work involved in arranging and facilitating care), the figure is much larger – see Carers UK (2019) *Juggling Work and Unpaid Care Report*. See also G James and E Spruce, 'Workers with Elderly Dependants: Employment Law's response to the Latest Care-giving Conundrum' (2015) 35 *Legal Studies* 463.

[15] Known as 'sandwich carers', this growing cohort is also experiencing higher levels of mental ill health, feeling less satisfied with life and struggling financially, when compared with the general population (see ONS, *More Than One in Four Sandwich Carers Report Symptoms of Mental Ill-Health* (London, ONS, 2019).

[16] Note that for some, the term 'recipient' of care and care 'provider' are viewed as problematic because they fail to reflect the networks of care that we live in and the fact that we all fall into both categories – see Herring, *Caring and the Law*, above n 2, 31.

[17] This generalisation is well founded but, of course, poor quality care can be damaging and the unequal dynamics between carer and recipient ought not to be underestimated. Moreover, the lack of literature from the perspective of recipients of care has been described by Herring as an 'embarrassment': Herring, *Caring and the Law*, above n 2, 30.

[18] We focus here on *unpaid* care work as opposed to the work undertaken in millions of homes across the UK by paid care workers. Care work can be 'contracted out' but we are mostly concerned in this book with the type of care that is non-transferable: the care work that is a personal part of a reciprocal caring relationship, usually undertaken by a family member. Such care work might be supported by third party interventions, indeed such interventions might be part of the 'solution' to the care work/paid work conundrum offered by the state, but that work per se is not the focus of this book.

sick. Care work can involve physical, mental and emotional labour.[19] It can be mundane and repetitive, can be incredibly stressful and exhausting but can also be life-enhancing, pleasurable and mutually rewarding.[20] Although the nature and scope of care work is clearly context-specific and changes over time[21] and within individual relationships, the skills involved should not be underestimated.[22] Moreover, it is important to recognise the impact of this unpaid labour upon a carer's wellbeing. This impact can also shift over time[23] and is dependent upon, for example, her/his own health, the age and wellbeing of the recipient of her/his care, the support network available to the individual and family, as well as particular workplace cultures and expectations. In relation to the latter, Carers UK have found that many carers of older dependants feel that they have little choice but to reduce working hours or leave paid employment altogether because of the lack of support available to them: an estimated 600 people give up paid work every day for this reason.[24]

Although our focus is on private and unpaid care work, often termed 'informal' care, participating in paid work is in many ways an act of care, in that it provides financial support for all family members: by defining care work as unpaid private/domestic labour and excluding *paid* work it is not our intention to negate this contribution to the family or to underestimate the symbiotic relationship that exists within families where responsibilities for work (paid and unpaid) might be negotiated and re-negotiated across time between the parties.[25] Nor does our focus on the paid work/unpaid care equation mean that we wish to exclude carers who do not or cannot undertake paid work alongside their care commitments. Such individuals are worthy subjects of labour law, but our overriding aim is to explore the effects of state attempts to rebalance the relationship between paid work and caregiving and the place of law and policy in achieving this.[26] Importantly, making a distinction between unpaid private (care) work and paid work enables us to unpack the gender inequalities that exist in how labour is divided: unpaid (and

---

[19] See D Bubeck, 'Justice and the Labour of Care' in E Feder Kittay and EK Feder (eds), *The Subject of Care: Feminist Perspectives on Dependency* (Lanham, Rowman & Littlefield, 2002); N Busby, *A Right to Care? Unpaid Care Work in European Employment Law* (Oxford, Oxford University Press, 2011) 43.

[20] See Herring, *Caring and the Law*, above n 2.

[21] It is noteworthy that what is regarded as 'care work' has itself developed over time: as Herring notes, clothing production is now regarded as economic production but used to be a domestic chore: Herring, *Caring and the Law*, above n 2, 89.

[22] Indeed, failure to recognise the various skills involved in care work has been at the heart of much of the injustice that has plagued this area of paid employment – see L Hayes, *Stories of Care: A Labour of Law* (London, Palgrave, 2017).

[23] On the temporality of care see Busby, *A Right to Care? Unpaid Care Work in European Employment Law*, above n 19, 43–44.

[24] See ch 5 below and Carers UK, *Juggling Work and Unpaid Care* (London, Carers UK, 2019).

[25] See ch 4 below.

[26] This is a concern raised by the government in its Industrial Strategy – HM Government, *Industrial Strategy: Building a Britain fit for the Future* (London, The Stationery Office, 2017), which highlighted the 'productivity challenge' of a growing number of workers engaging in care work of this nature.

paid) care work has always been predominantly undertaken by women and as a consequence of this, women have either been excluded from or marginalised within labour markets,[27] a fact that is explored further in chapter two and which resonates throughout the book.

C. Dependency

Dependency is a multi-layered concept[28] that can mean different things to different people at different times. We often speak of young children or the frail elderly as 'dependent' upon caregivers and such dependence is often termed 'inevitable',[29] because we have all been dependent as children and will all be dependent again at the end of our lives. This can be contrasted with women's economic dependency on men, which is socially constructed and hence an alterable social condition, one that has attracted much feminist critique.[30] The extent and nature of dependency is specific to time and place and often culturally and historically sensitive: for example, it is interesting that many working class families were, especially prior to the twentieth century – as will be discussed in chapter four – financially dependent upon the paid employment of their children for day-to-day survival; a fact that challenges modern constructions of children as the family members who are most and 'inevitably' dependent.

Despite variations in our experiences of dependency, one aspect is fairly constant: dependency is not, and never has been, a core concern of policymakers[31] and is 'largely rendered invisible within the family'[32] – an observation that is of particular relevance to our historical investigation of law's engagement with working families because it highlights how the care work that dependency requires is often 'comfortably and mistakenly assumed to be adequately managed for the vast majority of people'.[33] This lack of attention from policymakers entrenches 'derivative dependency', a term coined by Fineman to explain how those who undertake care work, mostly women, are often themselves dependent. Derivative dependency is not a

---

[27] See S Fredman, *Women and The Law* (Oxford, Oxford University Press, 1997). See further discussion in ch 2.

[28] See Fineman, 'Cracking the Foundational Myths: Independence, Autonomy and Self-Sufficiency', above n 10 and discussion in E Feder Kittay and EK Feder (eds), *The Subject of Care: Feminist Perspectives on Dependency* (Lanham, Rowman & Littlefield, 2002).

[29] E Feder Kittay and EK Feder (eds), *The Subject of Care: Feminist Perspectives on Dependency* (Lanham, Rowman & Littlefield, 2002) 2.

[30] See, eg, C Smart, *The Ties That Bind: Law, Marriage and the Reproduction of Patriarchal Relations* (London, Routledge and Kegan Paul, 1984); C Smart, *Feminism and the Power of Law* (London, Routledge, 1989); E Feder Kittay and EK Feder (eds), *The Subject of Care: Feminist Perspectives on Dependency* (Lanham, Rowman & Littlefield, 2002); Pateman, *The Sexual Contract*, above n 6.

[31] But see Herring, *Caring and the Law*, above n 2, 90, who suggests that the state has increasingly accepted the social value of care work.

[32] MA Fineman, 'The Vulnerable Subject: Anchoring Equality in the Human Condition' (2008–09) 20 *Yale Journal of Law and Feminism* 1, 11.

[33] ibid.

universal experience[34] and there are economic and structural dimensions to it.[35] The former is concerned with the unpaid or poorly paid nature of care work, the fact that it has a negative impact upon an individual's income generation and results in savings to the state because of the 'hidden' care work undertaken on a daily basis within families. Evidence from Carers UK suggests that financial hardship is prolific amongst those with adult caregiving responsibilities with many cutting back on essentials like food and heating and/or encountering debt in order to survive.[36] Care work can severely impact upon an individual's ability to undertake paid work, not least because 'it saps energy and efforts from investment in career or market activities'.[37] In addition, care work – when it impacts on paid work – penalises the state and its citizens. The former loses potential tax income,[38] which has a knock-on effect in terms of supporting the welfare state[39] which, as stated above, is a fundamentally significant component of the effective regulation of working families. The irony of this economic impact is that whilst the cost of care work is clearly borne by individuals, the benefits are distributed throughout society.[40] Hence, the structural dimension of derivative dependency concerns the 'social factors that affect and are affected by the care work'[41] including the impact of care work upon labour market participation and vice versa. Derivative dependency, as will be highlighted in the following chapters, is both socially constructed and historically gendered, but can be systematically reinforced by legal frameworks that fail to recognise the extent, nature and implications of unpaid care work for carers and fail to either value this work or, ultimately, to support it.

III. Theoretical Underpinnings: Vulnerability

Whilst theories of dependency provide a useful means of critiquing experiences of working families, as Fineman argues, 'vulnerability' can offer an even

---

[34] In fact, as Fineman points out, 'many people in our society will escape the burdens and costs that arise from assuming a care-taking role, perhaps even freed for other pursuits by the caretaking labour of others': Fineman, 'Cracking the Foundational Myths: Independence, Autonomy and Self-Sufficiency', above n 10, 21.

[35] See discussion in T Mattsson and M Katzin, 'Vulnerability and Ageing' in A Numhauser-Henning (ed), *Elder Law: Evolving European Perspectives* (Cheltenham, Edward Elgar, 2017) 113, 124.

[36] Carers UK, *State of Carers Survey* (London, Carers UK, 2013) discussed in James and Spruce, 'Workers with Elderly Dependants: Employment Law's response to the Latest Care-giving Conundrum', above n 14; Carers UK, *Caring For Your Future: The Long Term Financial Impact of Caring* (London, Carers UK, 2018).

[37] Fineman, 'Cracking the Foundational Myths: Independence, Autonomy and Self-Sufficiency', above n 10, 20.

[38] Age UK estimates a cost of £5.3 billion a year to the economy in lost earnings and tax revenue and additional benefit payments: Age UK, *Care Crisis Wipes Over £5.3 Billion From the Economy* (London, Age UK, 2012).

[39] L Pickard, *Public Expenditure Costs of Carers Leaving Employment*, LSE Health and Social Care Blog (London School of Economics and Political Science, 2012) cited in Age UK, *Later Life in the United Kingdom* (London, Age UK, 2013) 13.

[40] Feder Kittay and Feder (eds), *The Subject of Care: Feminist Perspectives on Dependency*, above n 29, 3.

[41] Mattsson and Katzin, 'Vulnerability and Ageing', above n 35, 124.

more powerful theoretical tool. For her, 'vulnerability is – and should be understood to be – universal and constant, inherent in the human condition' and she favours a legal framework that places the 'vulnerable subject' at its core.[42] Although Fineman argues that the term reflects the fact that we are all susceptible to 'an ever-present possibility of harm, injury and misfortune from mildly adverse to catastrophically devastating events, whether accidental, intentional or otherwise',[43] vulnerability is not defined solely through a negative narrative, in terms of victimhood or dependency or deprivation. Fineman is keen to emphasise that 'human beings are vulnerable because … we experience feelings such as love, respect, curiosity, amusement, and desire that make us reach out to others, form relationships, and build institutions'.[44] Individuals will experience (negative and positive) vulnerability to differing degrees throughout their lives and these experiences are shaped by social institutions and the quality and quantity of resources available at any given time – in this sense vulnerability is particular as well as universal: 'We have different forms of embodiment and also are differently situated within webs of economic and institutional relationships. As a result, our vulnerabilities range in magnitude and potential at the individual level. Vulnerability, therefore, is both universal and particular; it is experienced uniquely by each of us'.[45]

A vulnerability approach differs from one centred on dependency because vulnerability is less episodic and is institutional as well as individual:[46] indeed, for Fineman it is crucial that, in order to better recognise unpaid care work, we reconsider the roles of the state, market and the family.[47] Building upon this, the theory is deeply concerned with the promotion of resilience in the face of harms and risks that can arise during the life-course, and clearly places responsibility for building resilience upon institutions and the state.

Fineman's critique is focused on the US system, one that is strongly premised upon values of self-sufficiency and independence and perceives vulnerability as a negative trait that is the result of 'poor life choices', whereas the UK and other European countries are often presented as more paternalistic because of their welfare state traditions. However, as the changes outlined below testify, the UK (and most of Europe[48]) has moved away from the core welfare state tradition that

---

[42] Fineman, 'The Vulnerable Subject: Anchoring Equality in the Human Condition', above n 32, 2.

[43] ibid, 9.

[44] MA Fineman, '"Elderly" as Vulnerable: Rethinking the Nature of Individual and Societal Responsibility' (2012–2013) 20 *The Elder Law Journal Vol 71*, discussed further in ch 5 below.

[45] MA Fineman, 'The Vulnerable Subject and the Responsive State' (2010) 60 *Emory Law Journal* 251, 269.

[46] Fineman, 'The Vulnerable Subject: Anchoring Equality in the Human Condition', above n 32, 11.

[47] Fineman, 'Cracking the Foundational Myths: Independence, Autonomy and Self-Sufficiency', above n 10.

[48] See A Numhauser-Henning, 'The Elder Law Individual Versus Social Dichotomy – A European Perspective' in A Numhauser-Henning (ed), *Elder Law: Evolving European Perspectives* (Cheltenham, Edward Elgar, 2017) 70, 102.

once inspired a generation of citizens and has increased privatisation, drastically cut social spending and favours a neo-liberal approach to governance.[49] Given this shift, the vulnerability approach is appealing because it challenges traits that have long been at the heart of US policies and, as becomes evident in the following chapters, have now become explicit within the UK and EU – traits that at best hinder and at worse marginalise care relationships.

Overall, this approach challenges divisive societal categorisations that can facilitate and promote unnecessary and often corrosive competition. Such divisions are often perpetuated by media representations and political discourse which suggests and includes narratives that position working carers against non-caregiving workers, fathers against mothers (eg in terms of who has the most comprehensive 'right' or 'moral duty' to care) and the young generation against the older generation (eg in terms of who should access state benefits in society). A vulnerability approach offers, instead, 'an integrated approach to society, not one of either separate spheres or competing generations'.[50] A vulnerability approach recognises that we have all needed care at the early point in our life course and that we are all likely to need care again at some future point. As a result it requires acceptance that there is a societal responsibility to support care work, whether or not we undertake that work ourselves. Vulnerability theory is an approach that has become increasingly popular – it offers a fresh insight that allows us to ensure that, drawing on Conaghan's useful phrase, 'our ideas do not go stale, that our frameworks do not entrap us, that we do not render ourselves "deaf" to the noise that is all around'.[51] In the following critique we draw upon vulnerability theory because it offers a conduit for re-evaluating the relevant dominant legal discourses and frameworks that have developed over time. Vulnerability theory is not a blueprint but a means of revealing and dislodging assumptions that permit certain power structures and gendered norms. Our original contribution is evident in the way that we investigate the regulation of working families within the UK over time and draw upon vulnerability theory to reveal flaws in established discourses and frameworks to help us reimagine an approach that better values care relationships. Three aspects of the theory have proved particularly key in this endeavour: they arise throughout, and are discussed further within, the substantive chapters: the importance of (i) placing the 'vulnerable subject'[52] at the heart of our analysis, (ii) remaining attentive to the role of institutions and relationships and (iii) a responsive state.

---

[49] ibid, 91.

[50] Fineman, '"Elderly" as vulnerable: Rethinking the nature of individual and societal responsibility', above n 44.

[51] J Conaghan, 'The Discipline of Labour Law' in J Conaghan and K Rittich (eds), *Labour Law, Work, and Families: Critical and Comparative Perspectives* (Oxford, Oxford University Press, 2005) 26.

[52] See MA Fineman, 'Vulnerability and Social Justice' (2019) 53 *Valparaiso University Law Review* 341, 357; see also, eg, Fineman, 'The Vulnerable Subject: Anchoring Equality in the Human Condition', above n 32; Fineman, 'The Vulnerable Subject and the Responsive State', above n 45.

A. The Vulnerable Subject

The vulnerability approach challenges the myth of an 'autonomous and independent subject', often found at the heart of the legal regulation of working families. The liberal self which represents the 'desirable and achievable ideals of autonomy, independence and self-sufficiency'[53] is, according to Fineman, only 'one of a range of developmental stages that an actual human individual passes through in the course of a "normal" lifespan.'[54] Any institutional or legal frameworks that focus only on this potential developmental stage of their subjects therefore risk excluding, or indeed vilifying, other stages within the life course. This myth of autonomy can often be perpetuated within labour law frameworks – for example, through laws that fail to challenge procedures and traditions that promote an ideal 'unencumbered' worker, encapsulated in the normative standard worker model (see further chapter two), thus excluding those with caregiving responsibilities.[55] Hence, the approach facilitates critique of our historical engagement with working families by gauging the extent to which certain approaches or strategies or particular laws promote and valorise, explicitly or otherwise, autonomy, independence and self-sufficiency. It allows us also to consider the potential ramifications of a legal framework which has the vulnerable subject, the polar opposite of the liberal subject, at its core: 'when we place the vulnerable subject at the center of our theorizing, it becomes clear that there is a collective, or social, injury that inevitably arises from a state unresponsive to the universal and constant human condition of vulnerability and dependency.'[56]

B. Institutions and Relationships

Vulnerability theory also requires us to be more attentive to the roles of institutions and relationships: 'Because we are embodied creatures, we are also dependent on societal institutions and relationships throughout life.'[57] The welfare state, legal systems, labour markets, families are all relied upon over the life course, and they can reproduce inequalities and perpetuate damaging norms but are also vital in any attempt to transform society. It is essential that social institutions and relationships are devised and regulated so that they 'respond to the realities of the human condition.'[58] In addition, institutions – such as the family, state or the market – ought to be assessed from this perspective, not least because they can promote

---

[53] Fineman, '"Elderly" as Vulnerable: Rethinking the Nature of Individual and Societal Responsibility', above n 44, 87.

[54] ibid, 88.

[55] See chs 2 and 3 below in particular.

[56] Fineman, 'Vulnerability and Social Justice', above n 52, 357.

[57] Fineman, 'Vulnerability and Social Justice', above n 52, 358.

[58] ibid, 359.

resilience, which ought to be a key aim of any (vulnerable) society. For example, 'employment systems ... develop the human being, impart assets and allow participation in the market and, thus, facilitate the accumulation of material resources that help bolster individuals' resilience in the face of vulnerability'.[59] This requires a very different approach from the one that is currently promoted – one that transcends the appeal of attending to individuals and particular cohorts but which has a concern for intergenerational justice, a broader sense of a collective responsibility and which fosters resilience.[60]

C. A Responsive State

At the heart of vulnerability theory is the need for a responsive state: 'The nature of human vulnerability forms the basis for a claim that the state must be more responsive to that vulnerability. It fulfils that responsibility primarily through the establishment and support of societal institutions'.[61] If adopted, a vulnerability approach encourages states to be more responsive to, and responsible for, the well-being of their citizens. Unlike dependency, which is often viewed as a temporary stage – such as childhood, illness or old age – it is less easy for governments to ignore because human vulnerability is 'universal, inevitable and enduring'.[62]

To be clear, the role of the state is not to alleviate vulnerability – that is not possible as vulnerability is a constant feature of our humanity. Indeed, it defines 'what it means to be human'.[63] Instead, the state has a role in mediating, compensating or lessening any negative consequences of our collective and individual vulnerabilities. This ultimately means promoting greater resilience in individuals and institutions. As noted by Mattsson and Katzin, 'comparisons should not be made between individuals based on how vulnerable they are, but between states and institutions based on how good they are at providing us with resilience to our shared vulnerability'.[64]

Accepting a role for the state as a resilience-builder allows us to reimagine its activities and obligations to interrogate institutional practices that (re)produce inequalities. From the perspective of working families, this approach would encourage states to assess structural and institutional arrangements that have developed, over many years, as a means of perpetuating disadvantage: 'it brings institutions – not only individual actions – under scrutiny, redirecting attention to their role in providing assets in ways that may unfairly privilege certain groups,

---

[59] Fineman, 'The Vulnerable Subject: Anchoring Equality in the Human Condition', above n 32, 14. In discussing resilience, Fineman draws on the work of Kirby: see P Kirby, *Vulnerability and Violence: The Impact of Globalisation* (London, Pluto Press, 2006).

[60] Fineman, 'Vulnerability and Social Justice', above n 52.

[61] Fineman, 'The Vulnerable Subject and the Responsive State', above n 45, 255.

[62] Fineman, 'The Vulnerable Subject: Anchoring Equality in the Human Condition', above n 32, 8.

[63] Fineman, 'The Vulnerable Subject and the Responsive State', above n 45, 266.

[64] Mattsson and Katzin, 'Vulnerability and Ageing', above n 35, 117.

even if unintentionally'.[65] This offers a far superior approach than sole reliance upon anti-discrimination laws and individual legal action to remedy inequalities that exist: policies and laws provide a useful gauge of how far a state is willing to challenge institutional and structural norms and we return to this throughout the book. Indeed, the state – through its implementation and enforcement of relevant employment regulation and policies – can play an important role in bridging the potential divide between employers, often reluctant to facilitate care relationships, and working families. In terms of an historical assessment, this provides a useful means of assessing the effectiveness of legal interventions across time – a framework's effectiveness can be measured by its ability (or not) to foster and promote resilience.[66]

IV. Context

Having outlined the key concepts and theoretical underpinnings that will be drawn upon and discussed throughout the book, in this section we highlight broader contexts within which our discussion of the legal regulation of working families is located. The abilities of working families to manage care and paid work have been affected, in a variety of ways and to varying degrees over the years, by legal developments in related contexts, some of which have broader and longer trajectories. These include laws that have been implemented and developed in order to protect against health and safety abuses at work,[67] unfair dismissal[68] or discrimination.[69] Also relevant to our discussions are the evolution of dispute resolution procedures and policies,[70] the introduction of funded childcare,[71] changes to social security

---

[65] Fineman, 'The Vulnerable Subject: Anchoring Equality in the Human Condition', above n 32, 18.

[66] What is less clear, given that individuals and institutions (such as workplaces) are each defined as vulnerable within this approach, is what happens (or ought to happen?) when the needs of the individual (in terms of bolstering his/her resilience in the face of vulnerability) conflict with needs of the workplace (to maintain its ability to employ and provide material wellbeing)? Fineman deals with this dilemma suggesting that whilst open to scrutiny these institutions are also resource providers and emphasises the importance of their interdependence: Fineman, 'The Vulnerable Subject: Anchoring Equality in the Human Condition', above n 32, 18.

[67] Examples of relevant legal interventions include the Factory Acts which were enacted from 1833 onwards, the Health and Safety at Work Act 1974 and Management of Health and Safety at Work Regulations 1999, and the ongoing EU agenda relating to workplace health and safety.

[68] The right to claim unfair dismissal was introduced under the Industrial Relations Act 1971.

[69] Introduced through a variety of pieces of legislation over the years (key for us being the Sex Discrimination Act 1975) and consolidated in 2010 under the Equality Act. This area of law has attracted much jurisprudence and has been shaped by EU law: see, for an overview, A McColgan, *Discrimination, Equality and the Law* (Oxford, Hart Publishing, 2014).

[70] For a discussion of this evolution see G Morris, 'The Development of Statutory Employment Rights in Britain and Enforcement Mechanisms' in L Dickens (ed), *Making Employment Rights Effective: Issues of Enforcement And Compliance* (Oxford, Hart Publishing, 2012).

[71] For an interesting overview see A West and P Noden, *Public Funding of Early Years Education in England: An Historical Perspective* (London, LSE, Clare Market Papers, 2016), 21.

laws that impact on labour market participation,[72] state support for adult social care[73] and various relevant austerity measures put in place in times of economic downturn.[74] The core WFB framework we recognise today, which is largely associated with New Labour reforms,[75] is thus part of a wider wave of interconnected policies and regulations, each of which has been developed over time and has its own distinct tensions and dynamics.

In addition to these particular legal contexts, four broader, interrelated, socio-economic shifts have, over time and in different ways and with different implications, unsettled or entrenched traditional thinking around responsibilities for care work. **The first is a growth in the acceptability of statutory intervention in employment relationships.** Freedom of contract has long been at the core of formal employment relationships but, as Fredman notes, nineteenth-century liberal ideals were challenged by the 'relentless exploitation of workers, be they men, women or children'[76] and two methods of legal regulation emerged in relation to the labour market as a result: statutory provision and collective bargaining. The latter was, for a long time, the most prevalent means of intervening. As Morris has commented, 'historically, the brake on the exploitation of workers which a "freedom of contract" model could produce came not from legislation but from collective bargaining'.[77] Indeed, from the end of the nineteenth century, and certainly from the end of the First World War, government policy supported collective bargaining as the preferred method of determining workplace conditions.[78] Examples of early statutory interventions do, however, exist – including the various Factory Acts, which sought to modify the extremes of poor behaviour amongst employers but which were plagued by weak enforcement mechanisms.[79] It is only in more recent times, certainly in the post-war era, that we really witness significant regulation through statute. Key interventions include the introduction in 1963 of a right to a written statement of terms and conditions, the right to statutory redundancy pay in 1965 and the right not to be unfairly dismissed in 1971. By the 1980s, as part of the Conservative government's deregulation agenda, statutory intervention had become the norm in terms of regulating workplaces. This was part of a deliberate strategy to undermine the role of trade unions and played a crucial part

---

[72] For an overview see D Fraser, *The Evolution of the British Welfare State: A History of Social Policy Since the Industrial Revolution* (London, Red Globe Press, 2017).

[73] See, for discussion, Herring, *Caring and the Law*, above n 2, ch 4.

[74] For discussions of the impact of austerity on working families see S Lewis, D Anderson, C Lyonette, N Payne and S Wood (eds), *Work-Life Balance in Times of Recession, Austerity and Beyond* (London, Routledge, 2017).

[75] Outlined more fully in ch 3 below.

[76] Fredman, *Women and The Law*, above n 27, 67.

[77] Morris, 'The Development of Statutory Employment Rights in Britain and Enforcement Mechanisms', above n 70, 7. For a critique of collective laissez-faire and how it has impacted on the gendered division of labour, see ch 3 below.

[78] ibid.

[79] Discussed in ch 4 below.

in their demise,[80] not least because it promoted the promise of improved conditions through individually enforceable rights. It was during this period that several key statutory employment rights were also introduced including time off work for ante-natal care, maternity leave and pay and the right to return to work after leave for childbirth, basic provisions that were consolidated, re-packaged and added to under New Labour and subsequent governments from 1997 onwards.[81]

The growth of an individual-rights-based approach is in many ways a reflection of a larger post-war shift in the predominance and functioning of the UK labour market[82] and a reconceptualisation of the purpose of labour law, away from a focus on workers' needs to a means of managing the economy and economic policy more specifically.[83] This development – from laissez-faire to a preference for collective bargaining, albeit though a system of collective laissez-faire, through to a system that favours statutory rights enforceable by individuals and a focus on employment laws as a mechanism for the regulation of the economy – is an important backdrop for consideration of the evolution of the contemporary WFB framework that we critique in this book. As our analysis shows, this development was not necessarily the most beneficial for working families and it cannot be assumed that it provided an easy passage for legal reform in this area. Although the development of employment rights through legislative intervention is now the norm, it still rests upon a deeply held historical reluctance, and one that has had a tendency to re-surface, to intervene *at all* in the employment relationship. New employment regulation or extensions of existing rights and protections are often still resisted and depicted as a 'burden on business' so that many of the tensions inherent in work–family arrangements, despite this growth in acceptance of statutory regulation, still remain.[84] This deep-seated tension, as we shall argue throughout the book, provides an uneasy foundation for promoting frameworks that help rectify unequal distributions of wealth, power and opportunity, all of which are key to supporting working families with caregiving responsibilities in the long term.

---

[80] The coverage of collective bargaining radically declined in the Thatcher years: see Morris, 'The Development of Statutory Employment Rights in Britain and Enforcement Mechanisms', above n 70, 10.

[81] For a discussion of the earlier provisions see J Lewis and M Campbell, 'UK Work/Family Balance Policies and Gender Equality 1997–2005' (2007) 14 *Social Politics* 4.

[82] All characteristics of what was termed the 'new economy' – see J Conaghan, R Fischl and K Klare (eds), *Labour Law in an Era of Globalization: Transformations, Practices and Possibilities* (Oxford, Oxford University Press, 2002). As a result it has been argued that the employment relationship has become more precarious and intense (see J Fudge and R Owens (eds), *Precarious Work, Women, and the New Economy: The Challenges to Legal Norms* (Oxford, Hart Publishing, 2006) and R Crompton, *Employment and the Family: The Reconfiguration of Work and Family Life in Contemporary Societies* (Cambridge, Cambridge University Press, 2006)).

[83] See A Davies, *Perspectives on Labour Law* 2nd edn (Cambridge, Cambridge University Press, 2009) ch 1.

[84] Whether invisible because they are not deemed worthy of statutory attention or constructed as private 'choices' beyond the realm of state intervention: see, eg, R Crompton, 'Gender Restructuring, Employment, and Caring' (2001) 8 *Social Politics* 266, 269.

A second key, related, pre-cursor to the development of the WFB framework that we recognise today has been **the increased participation of women in the labour market and shifts in terms of the scope and nature of the paid work that women (and men) undertake**. Women have always undertaken paid work, often in private alongside unpaid care work, although class divisions have long been a significant factor in determining the extent and nature of that work, and it has ebbed and flowed over time, often determined by social and economic requirements in general. Whilst we have witnessed a clear increase in the number of women participating in the formal (public) labour market, equally important and related changes have occurred in the scope and nature of the paid work undertaken by women (and men). These changes have been driven by broad shifts in the growth of capitalist industrialism from the late eighteenth century onwards. Fuelled by technical innovations, industrialisation modified the nature of paid employment increasing the demand, and capacity, for productivity and consumption and, for some, wealth. The nature and scope of this productivity has modified and extended in response to the interrelated growth of the capitalist market economy, furthered by technological and transportation innovations and the opportunities and increased competition provided by globalisation. The UK labour market has truly been transformed over the decades and its ongoing development continues to have repercussions for its organisation, production and regulation and, importantly, the roles and experiences of its workers.[85] Of particular relevance to this study is the fact that female labour, which has historically been cheaper, more flexible and often viewed as disposable in times of recession or austerity,[86] has been pivotal in supporting key transformations in social and economic structures: for example, women workers made a significant contribution to the industrial revolution,[87] fuelled the war effort when male labour was in short supply[88] and have been viewed as essential in the 24/7 'new economy'.[89] Herein lies one of the central and constant tensions inherent in any historical critique of working families: whilst the contribution of female labour to the growth

---

[85] See, eg, Fudge and Owens (eds), *Precarious Work, Women, and the New Economy: The Challenges to Legal Norms*, above n 82; Conaghan, Fischl and Klare (eds), *Labour Law in an Era of Globalization: Transformations, Practices and Possibilities*, above n 82.

[86] See M Karamessini and J Rubery (eds), *Women and Austerity: The Economic Crisis and the Future for Gender Equality* (London, Routledge, 2013); J Rubery and A Rafferty, 'Women and Recession Revisited' (2013) 27 *Work, Employment and Society* 414; J Rubery, 'Austerity and the Future for Gender Equality in Europe' (2015) 68 *Industrial and Labour Relations Review* 715. See also Lewis, Anderson, Lyonette, Payne and Wood (eds), *Work-Life Balance in Times of Recession, Austerity and Beyond*, above n 74.

[87] For an early account, first published in 1930, of this contribution see I Pinchbeck, *Women Workers and The Industrial Revolution 1750–1850* (Abingdon, Frank Cass and Company, reprinted in 1977). See also ch 2.

[88] See R Wall and J Winter, *The Upheaval of War: Family, Work and Welfare in Europe 1914–1918* (Cambridge, Cambridge University Press, 1988).

[89] J Conaghan, 'Women, Work, and Family: A British Revolution?' in J Conaghan, R Fischl and K Klare (eds), *Labour Law in an Era of Globalization: Transformations, Practices and Possibilities* (Oxford, Oxford University Press, 2002).

of the economy has been recognised and despite the fact that they have increasingly been 'encouraged' to undertake paid work,[90] women continue to bear the brunt of unpaid and undervalued domestic care work. Explored specifically in chapter three, the inability of legal engagement to rectify this unequal distribution of care work along gender lines is a persistent concern that we return to throughout the book.

A third important context for the development of the legal framework and approach adopted in the UK is **the establishment and evolution of our welfare state**. The beginning of the welfare state is most commonly pinpointed as July 1948, when schemes of medical care and insurance, outlined in the Beveridge Report of 1942, came into operation.[91] It was, however, the result of a longer history of social regulation, established through a number of reforms between 1906 and 1914 but greatly extended over a 40-year period. Key early measures included the introduction of a pension for the over 70s in 1908, a minimum wage for certain low-wage industries in 1909 and, in the same year, the establishment of a Labour Exchange to help people find employment. The National Insurance Act of 1911 also introduced sick pay and free medical treatment, benefitting some 13 million workers at the time.

Despite these early legal interventions, it is generally perceived that the ethos of a 'liberal'[92] welfare state was only fully embraced after the Second World War – a period that Fraser refers to as 'The Classic Welfare State', when 'for some 30 years there was a social democratic political consensus which sustained the Welfare State, which involved full employment, Keynesian economic policy, growing affluence and active state intervention'.[93] Having experienced widespread devastation and, significantly, an unprecedented intensity of state control, citizens were encouraged to trust the government to improve their lives. Within this context, the Beveridge Report of 1942 recommended a universal flat rate insurance scheme which would fund health care and unemployment and retirement benefits. Labour's victory pledge following the 1945 general election, to provide for the people 'from cradle to grave' offered a mandate to strengthen the welfare state provision: in 1945 family allowance was established which provided financial support for low-income families and national insurance was introduced in 1946.

Although not devoid of challenges, the welfare state developed between 1940 and the 1970s provided a platform for supporting citizens who were in need of support but it also had the potential to redistribute wealth and promote education, health and employment for the benefit of all in society. Although not necessarily

---

[90] During wartime, women were recruited into the workplace by the use of propaganda films and more recently, for example, through welfare policies that link state financial support to job seeking, a National Child Care Strategy and Working Families Tax Credit.

[91] See discussion in Fraser, *The Evolution of the British Welfare State: A History of Social Policy Since the Industrial Revolution*, above n 72, ch 1.

[92] Esping-Andersen famously categorised the UK regime as 'liberal' – other regimes were categorised as either conservative-corporatist or social-democratic in nature: G Esping-Andersen, *The Three Worlds of Welfare Capitalism* (Cambridge, Polity Press, 1990).

[93] Fraser, *The Evolution of the British Welfare State: A History of Social Policy Since the Industrial Revolution*, above n 72, 14.

fuelled by purely altruistic concerns, the establishment of the welfare state is a monumentally significant milestone in UK history. A core underlying ethos of the welfare state is that a person's wellbeing is not only the responsibility of that individual, but part of a collective endeavour.[94] The implications of the state demonstrating concern for and accepting responsibility for the wellbeing of its citizens in this way is huge, especially within the context of what had gone before. It did, however, come at a cost and expenditure rose beyond anything that the architects of the core provisions anticipated. Indeed, the political consensus upon which the classic welfare state was founded 'fragmented under the pressure of economic crisis in the 1970s'.[95]

Since 1979 the welfare state has been in crisis, challenged by cuts in social spending and an increase in unemployment as well as growing support for, and absorption of, a neoliberal ideology that favours autonomy and more individualised, as opposed to community-focused, solutions to the social problems that the welfare state was originally created to support. This has undoubtedly hindered its potential as a means of promoting collective responsibility and is a core theme to which we return in this book when critiquing the regulation of working families across time. The welfare state has always attracted criticism, but increased marketisation has provided the greatest threat to its existence: a 2016 report of the House of Commons Work and Pensions Committee, assessing the impact of self-employment and the growth of the collaborative or 'gig' economy, declared that 'how the welfare state adapts to the changing labour market is one of the greatest issues of our time'.[96] The decline of the welfare state comes at a time when the need for the state to retain and deepen its responsibility for the welfare of its citizens is arguably greater than ever.

The final context that has had a significant impact on the way UK governments have engaged with working families, albeit in comparatively recent times, is **the European Community/Union**. Established in 1957, in the wake of the utter devastation caused by the Second World War, the core aim of the European Economic Community (EEC as it then was) was to establish a common market through which inter-state co-operation and economic advantage could grow. Over the years it widened in geographical scope and deepened in terms of legal competence, creating a union that began to develop a social as well as an economic policy agenda, albeit that the former was viewed as a necessary adjunct to the latter rather than a separate focus.[97] Underpinned by social democratic principles, the

---

[94] This relates to the discussion of vulnerability theory above, and advanced throughout this book, favouring such an approach. It might be compared to Fineman's discussion of Franklin Roosevelt's 'fair deal' of which Fineman notes that 'attainment of a fair deal was not designated to be only, or even primarily, an individual responsibility': see Fineman, 'Vulnerability and Social Justice', above n 52, 345.

[95] Fraser, The Evolution of the British Welfare State: A History of Social Policy Since the Industrial Revolution n 72, 14.

[96] House of Commons Work and Pensions Committee, *Self Employment and the Gig Economy* (London, House of Commons, 2016) 1.

[97] As has been stated elsewhere, the Treaty of Rome was 'market making' not 'market correcting': E Caracciolo di Torella and A Masselot, *Reconciling Work and Family Life in EU Law and Policy* (London,

European Social Model became of central importance in the promotion of workers' rights and gender equality,[98] helping to improve the lives of working families across Europe. Social policy initiatives of particular relevance to working families have included its equal pay and equal treatment provisions, leave provisions, regulation of working time and a care strategy.[99] However, as we have argued elsewhere, the EU's engagement with working families has, historically, been disjointed with its influence dwindling in recent years.[100] More recently, however, the EU's activity in this field has undergone a potential revival through its 'New Start' initiative, launched in April 2017. Of particular note is the European Commission's Directive for Work–Life Balance of Parents and Carers, which was endorsed by the EU member states' representatives in the Council of the EU in February 2019 and has since been adopted.[101] Although details of implementation are left to Member States, who will have three years to implement the legislation, this Directive will amend the parental rights regime, introduce a right to request flexible working, paid paternity leave and carers' leave and has re-energised this area of EU social policy.[102]

In June 2016 the UK voted marginally (52 per cent) in favour of leaving the EU. The UK left the EU on 31 January 2020. Membership of the EC/EU has proved, with the benefit of hindsight, to be of fundamental importance to the UK's regulation of working families, specifically the development of a WFB framework[103] of legal rights in the UK and across Europe. For example, two core Directives and a host of purposive rulings by the Court of Justice of the European Union (CJEU) have altered the way in which pregnant workers' and (new) working

---

Palgrave Macmillan, 2010), 25: Busby, *A Right to Care? Unpaid Care Work in European Employment Law*, above n 19; C McGlynn, *Families and the European Union: Law Politics and Pluralism* (Cambridge, Cambridge University Press, 2006).

[98] See C Fagan and J Rubery, 'Advancing Gender Equality Through European Employment Policy: The Impact of the UK's EU Membership and the Risks of Brexit' (2018) 17 *Social Policy and Society* 297.

[99] See Caracciolo di Torella and Masselot, *Reconciling Work and Family Life in EU Law and Policy*, above n 97; Busby, *A Right to Care? Unpaid Care Work in European Employment Law*, above n 19, esp ch 5. See also N Busby and G James, 'Regulating Working Families in the European Union: A History of Disjointed Strategies' (2015) 37 *Journal of Social Welfare and Family Law* 295.

[100] N Busby and G James, 'Regulating Working Families in the European Union: A History of Disjointed Strategies' (2015) 37 *Journal of Social Welfare and Family Law* 295. See also L Hantrais, 'Assessing the Past and Future Development of EU and UK Social Policy' (2018) 17 *Social Policy and Society* 265, who argues that the maintenance of unanimous voting and the subsidiarity principle in a large number of social domains, the shift towards soft law and a wide resistance amongst Member States to tighter social integration has restricted growth in this field. See, however, Numhauser-Henning's view that, despite the fact that its social dimension is often threatened by an increased bias toward marketisation, the EU has still not 'given up on its social ambitions': Numhauser-Henning, 'The Elder Law Individual Versus Social Dichotomy – A European Perspective', above n 48, 111.

[101] Directive (EU) 2019/1158 of the European Parliament and of the Council of 20 June 2019 on work–life balance for parents and carers and repealing Council Directive 2010/18/EU.

[102] For comment see N Busby, 'The Evolution of Gender Equality and Related Employment Policies: the Case of Work–Family Reconciliation' (2018) 18 *International Journal of Discrimination and the Law* 104.

[103] Although termed work–family 'reconciliation'; E Caracciolo di Torella, 'An Emerging Right to Care in the EU: A 'New Start' to Support Work–Life Balance for Parents and Carers' (2017) 18 *ERA Forum* 187.

mothers' rights are regulated.[104] The EU has also been proactive in improving legal protection available to part-time workers,[105] the majority of whom are working mothers trying to facilitate unpaid care alongside paid employment. It has also attempted to encourage gender-neutral care through the promotion of parental leave provisions.[106] Beyond legislation, the EU also provides an unprecedented formal setting for knowledge exchange and sharing of good practice. Post Brexit, we can only hope that advances in this area are mirrored, if not surpassed, in the UK but legitimate concerns have been raised about the future legal protection of workers.[107]

V. Methodology and Structure

In fulfilling the objectives described above we seek to analyse the relevant provisions of law and policy by considering the way that these have been framed[108] across time in the UK. Changing economic, demographic and attitudinal developments impact upon policy priorities, so that the work-family debate – or relevant aspects of it – will never be framed, debated or approached in the same way at any one point or place in history. Nor, for the same reasons, will this 'unsolved conflict'[109] ever be completely resolved. However, what matters is *how* the 'problems' and the 'solutions' – no matter how incomplete and specific to times and places in history those problems and solutions are – are framed. Much work around framing considers the processes within social movements and media

---

[104] The Equal Treatment Directive 76/207/EEC (now part of the Recast Directive 2006/54/EC) and Pregnant Workers Directive 92/85/EEC. For a discussion of this aspect of EU law see, eg, Busby and James, 'Regulating Working Families in the European Union: A History of Disjointed Strategies', above n 100.

[105] The Part-Time Work Directive (Council Directive 97/81/EC of 15 December 1997, OJ 1997 L 14/9).

[106] Parental Leave Directive 96/34/EC, which was subsequently replaced by a revised Directive 2010/18/EU. For further discussion of this development, see ch 3.

[107] See, eg, C Fagan and J Rubery, 'Advancing Gender Equality Through European Employment Policy: the Impact of the UK's EU Membership and the Risks of Brexit' (2018) 17 *Social Policy and Society* 297; R Guerrina and A Masselot, 'Walking into the Footprints of EU Law: Unpacking the Gendered Consequences of Brexit' (2018) 17 *Social Policy and Society* 319; M Weldon-Johns, 'Brexit and Work–Family Conflict: A Scottish Perspective' in M Dustin, N Terreira and S Millns (eds), *Gender and Queer Perspectives on Brexit* (London, Palgrave Macmillan, 2019) 305.

[108] Framing refers to processes by which policies and laws have been created and shaped and includes consideration of the extent to which various actors have (or have not) influenced relevant laws and policies. The process of framing involves generating or constructing an issue, problem or solution in a way that shapes subsequent interpretations of it. For discussion see M Smith, 'Framing Same-sex Marriage in Canada and the United States: *Goodridge, Halpern* and The National Boundaries of Political Discourse' (2007) 16 *Social & Legal Studies* 5; RM Entman, 'Framing: Towards Clarification of a Fractured Paradigm' (1993) *Journal of Communication* 51.

[109] M Barbera, 'The Unsolved Conflict: Reshaping Family Work and Market Work in the EU Legal Order' in T Hervey and J Kenner (eds), *Economic and Social Rights under the EU Charter of Fundamental Social Rights: A Legal Perspective* (Oxford, Hart Publishing, 2003) 139.

engagement, although it has been usefully adopted to help illuminate wider cultural processes – such as the emergence of a new understanding of health and safety policy formation,[110] LGBT claimants' struggles in same-sex marriage cases,[111] women's employment rights,[112] sexual harassment at work,[113] the disability movement[114] and climate change litigation.[115] In what follows, the notion of framing provides a useful vehicle to help unpack historical legal engagement with working families. We examine how the legal framework relating to paid work and families has been shaped and consider how laws and policies have evolved as a result. We also evaluate the impact of particular choices regarding legal interaction or inaction on relevant constituencies, especially working carers and the recipients of their care. The challenge for policymakers within our context is often, as Lewis suggests, reconciling a multitude of interests, some of which compete[116] and this is where 'framing' provides a useful insight, because it allows us to question social reality. As Almond states, through framing 'a social reality is constructed which works to shape subsequent interpretation of that particular issue',[117] interpretations that can then be challenged.

In seeking to understand how legal and policy responses to lived experiences of reconciling paid work and family life in the UK have been, and are being, framed, and to analyse the likely and preferred future trajectory of this engagement we explore that development from an historical perspective. Along with thematic structuring (see below), this enables us to provide an original dissection of the subject matter – one that encourages reflection on legal regulation in this area. Moreover, by viewing the incremental development of the relevant complex contemporary framework though an historical lens, we reveal the impact of certain features on this evolution, such as conceptualisation of 'the family' and 'work' in this context, legal constructions of motherhood and changing perceptions of fatherhood, the relevance of demographic realities such as an ageing society and delayed procreation, attitudinal changes towards care, technological advances and broader legal/policy changes in terms of health and safety protection, EU membership, welfare and social security law.

---

[110] P Almond, 'Revolution Blues: The Reconstruction of Health and Safety Laws as "Common Sense" Regulation' (2015) 42 *Journal of Law and Society* 202.

[111] M Smith, 'Framing Same-sex Marriage in Canada and the United States: *Goodridge, Halpern* and the National Boundaries of Political Discourse' (2007) 16 *Social & Legal Studies* 5.

[112] N Pedriana, 'From Protective to Equal Treatment: Legal Framing Processes and Transformation of the Women's Movement in the 1960s' (2006) 111 *American Journal of Sociology* 1718.

[113] AM Marshall, 'Idle Rights: Employees' Rights Consciousness and the Construction Of Sexual Harassment Policies' (2005) 39 *Law and Society Review* 83.

[114] L Vanhala, *Making Rights a Reality? Disability Rights Activists and Legal Mobilization* (Cambridge, Cambridge University Press, 2011).

[115] C Hilson, 'UK Climate Change Litigation: Between Hard and Soft Framing' in S Farrall, T Ahmed and D French (eds), *Criminological and Legal Consequences of Climate Change. Oñati International Series in Law and Society* (1) (Oxford, Hart Publishing, 2012) 47.

[116] J Lewis, *Work-Family Balance, Gender and Policy* (Cheltenham, Edward Elgar, 2009) 10.

[117] Almond, 'Revolution Blues: The Reconstruction of Health and Safety Laws as 'Common Sense' Regulation', above n 110, 207.

The importance of considering wider normative, political and economic contexts and the manner of their development is now widely recognised: it is important 'to let knowledge of the past work on the experience of the present'.[118] Viewing law's engagement with working families in an historical perspective encourages us to take an original, longitudinal view of how relevant laws and policies have been (re)shaped over time. In terms of timescale and jurisdictional scope, the main focus of our book is the post-war development of policies in the UK,[119] although the exact point of entry for discussion will depend upon the specific context of the topic under consideration in each chapter.

The chapters are structured in a thematic way so as to allow for analysis of the development of specific policy and laws relating to the needs of particular stakeholders although, as we will argue throughout the book, the strains, stereotypes, strategies and solutions discussed are relevant to everyone in society regardless of gender, age, life stage, physical or mental health. There is inevitable overlap between these stakeholders or cohorts and consideration of them in this somewhat dissected way is not meant to detract from the functional, often mutually supportive, interdependency of the family (whatever its form). It does, however, allow us to explore law's interaction, impact and potential to support the various and changing needs of individuals, institutions and society as a whole and to examine the connectivity between them. This is especially important given the theoretical underpinnings of the book: vulnerability theory is underscored by the conviction that we are all vulnerable throughout our lives and this structure of analysis reflects that premise by promoting, from a variety of perspectives, consideration of the consequences of law's engagement upon the very young, the dependent elderly, and those adults who care for them. Each of the core chapters focuses on the particular ways in which the laws and policies relevant to the specific issue under review have been framed over time, a central line of inquiry being the extent to which particular claims and needs have expanded demands for recognition, rights and/or the redistribution of responsibilities in relation to paid work and unpaid care.

Chapter two considers the interaction between women's paid work and their unpaid care commitments and shows how the relevant policies and laws have shaped and been shaped by this interrelationship over time. As this analysis reveals, the fact that most women are required to balance high levels of care with

---

[118] M Foucault, *The Birth of Biopolitics: Lectures at the Collège de France, 1978–1979*, M Senellart (ed), G Burchell (trans) (Basingstoke, Palgrave Macmillan, 2008) 30. Or, as Crompton has suggested: 'in order to understand the present, we have first to understand the past': R Crompton, *Employment and the Family: The Reconfiguration of Work and Family Life in Contemporary Societies* (Cambridge, Cambridge University Press, 2006) 1.

[119] The focus of the book is the UK. Whilst recent employment regulation is, for the most part, the same in all four nations of the UK we do appreciate that in devolved policy areas, notably health and education, different approaches and provisions exist in Scotland, Wales, England and Northern Ireland. The nuances of these different approaches have not always been captured in our analyses because we have had to adopt a broad-brush approach in our historical critique.

paid work has been instrumentalised by policymakers at various times as a means of responding to broader social and economic concerns.

Chapter three focuses on parenthood and outlines how, why, and with what implications the care needs of mothers and fathers have been included within the WFB framework. In contrast to the focus on women's relationship with paid work as a means of meeting specific policy goals, men's relationship with care has been largely avoided as the subject of targeted regulation. This results from the state's tendency to preserve the traditional dichotomisation of the public and private realms of work and family which is currently under pressure in the move towards gender-free care and parenting at least as an aspiration at the household level.

Chapters four and five examine the significance of child welfare and eldercare respectively. Both chapters provide strong narratives that underscore how recipients of care, albeit in different ways and with various repercussions, have often been ignored in law's engagement with working families. The reasons for this are explored and the nuances of the historical developments examined in order to deepen our understanding of the framework that is adopted. In these four core chapters the potential of vulnerability theory is discussed. The concluding chapter then draws together the arguments, presented throughout, for an alternative perspective that is more closely attuned to and influenced by vulnerability theory. What becomes apparent through the detailed discussions within each chapter is that the needs of individuals within working families, and of families themselves – whatever form they may take – have consistently been under-researched and misconceived, with caregiving consistently undervalued. This, as we consider in the final chapter, is symptomatic in part of an unwillingness to acknowledge the interdependency of our lives and the universality of vulnerability throughout the life course.

2

Women and Work

I. Introduction

Any discussion of the targeting of law and policy as a means of improving the unresolved conflict between paid work and family will inevitably focus disproportionately on women. Of course, men also grow up in families and go on to have families of their own. However, men's paid work is unlikely to be directly affected by the arrival of children or the need to balance it alongside high levels of unpaid care for children, elders and others in the way that women's ability to engage with paid work and the arrangements for doing so are undoubtedly impacted. Indeed, because ideologies of motherhood are so strongly embedded in our consciousness, a woman does not actually need to have children in order to be affected by women's collective potential for doing so. It is thus impossible to decouple the historical development of work and family policy from the corresponding story of women's relationship with paid work.

This chapter will thus explore how women's participation in paid work in the post-war era has shaped and been shaped by UK law and policy aimed at regulating work and families. We aim to show how the policy discourse has been framed by the state at different stages relating to the political, social and economic contexts in which claims and resulting challenges have emerged. The influence of social movements concerned with equality and civil justice will be identified, as will the resulting political narratives and specific policy responses and outcomes. The overall objective is to show how the dual processes of claim-staking and policy framing have shaped the implementation and outcomes of legal intervention in the area of women's paid work over the past 70 years. As this analysis demonstrates, the resulting framework has, to varying degrees and in different contexts, instrumentalised women through their dual role as paid workers and carers in order to serve various social and economic goals. The focus will be on women's work – both paid and unpaid – rather than on motherhood. Of course, the two are inextricably linked and so reference will be made to the effects of family formation and family-based care on women's work throughout this chapter. Motherhood, more specifically its relationship – and contrast – with fatherhood, will be the focus of chapter three, which will explore the shifting identities and dominant ideologies attached to both through lived experience and policy provision.

As this chapter shows, despite women's continued participation in paid work and the visible growth in their employment rates during the post-war era, despite much legal intervention over the years aimed at tackling poor working conditions and discrimination, despite calls from the women's movement, in all its various forms, and individual battles for equal pay and treatment, women still do not have substantive equality within workplaces. By exploring the development of relevant and related areas of law and policy, we seek to uncover why this is the case. As this analysis reveals, none of the legislative intervention or policy provision that we present in the chapter has challenged the status quo; there has been no sustained political commitment to disrupt the established gender ordering. The effect of this in the contemporary setting is that when women enter paid work, they carry with them decades of disadvantage perpetuated by assumptions regarding their place in the world which are imbued with ideas about motherhood and caregiving.

Terminology is particularly important in this context as, when applied to women, the terms 'work' and 'employment' acquire particular meanings. As Fudge has noted, the phrase 'women's work' carries with it an ambiguity that simply does not apply to the expression 'men's work'.[1] The reasons for this are interrelated: the term encapsulates unpaid care work, the physical, mental and emotional[2] demands of which most women are confronted with, often alongside paid work. In addition, even within the confines of the labour market, women's work is characterised by high levels of occupational and hierarchical segregation, with women far more likely than men to work in certain occupations, primarily within the service and related sectors, and to be confined to work which is low-skilled, low-paid and often precarious.[3] Such features are subject to further division along the lines of class, race and age so that, although much of the paid work performed by women shares certain common features, women's homogeneity cannot by any means be assumed in this respect with wide diversity evident in working patterns, aspirations and attainment depending on the personal characteristics of individual women and, due to the effects of child bearing and rearing on labour market attachment, over the life course.

Despite such diversity, however, the story of women's paid work and its relationship with law and policy is inextricably linked to the state's varying approach to the provision of care, most notably for children, and associated welfare benefits. Women's paid employment outside of the home has risen substantially in the UK in the post-war era, largely due to changes in the employment behaviour of mothers who have increasingly remained in or returned to paid work following childbirth. Nonetheless the patterns and nature of women's paid work continues

---

[1] J Fudge, 'Women Workers: Is Equality Enough?' (2013) 2 *Feminists@law* 2, https://journals.kent.ac.uk/index.php/feministsatlaw/article/view/63/183.

[2] AR Hochschild, 'Emotion Work, Feeling Rules, and Social Structure' (1979) 85 *American Journal of Sociology* 3, 551; AR Hochschild, *The Managed Heart: Commercialization of Human Feeling* 2nd edn (California, University of California Press, 2012).

[3] J Fudge and R Owens (eds), *Precarious Work, Women, and the New Economy: The Challenges to Legal Norms* (Oxford, Hart Publishing, 2006).

to be shaped by parenthood in ways that men's work is not. As the chapter shows, although successive governments may have adopted different approaches to the apparent conflict between paid work and unpaid care, there is continuity in the paucity of the state's provision of childcare despite decades of attempts to encourage and retain mothers' labour market participation. This reveals much about the state's reluctance to intervene in the unpaid care component of the paid work/unpaid care equation which arises from mainstream political attitudes to gender relations and an enduring tendency to preserve the status quo. This has largely been achieved by the state's manipulation and purposeful shaping of women's paid work through its relationship with the demands of unpaid care which continues to be placed, for policy purposes, within the nuclear family model. The resulting instrumentalisation of the relationship between women's productive and reproductive work has not taken a linear path, being subject to twists and turns depending on the political ideology, wider social concerns and related economic objectives of the day. However, the key policy aims have rarely been targeted at the attainment of gender equality as a policy goal in itself but, rather, have been focused on other concerns such as full employment and/or reductions in welfare spending.[4] The overall effect is that women's relationship with paid work has been shaped and directed by successive generations of policymakers with very little strategic and sustained thinking about how to reconcile it with the competing demands of unpaid care.[5]

In presenting a chronology of relevant policy development, this chapter (along with chapter three) outlines the various historical contexts and resulting laws which have led and shaped women's participation in paid work over the past two centuries. This is a complex task: the lack of an identifiable single law and policy framework makes it necessary to cast a relatively wide net over a range of interrelated provisions. Much of the chapter's focus is thus on the anti-discrimination framework and associated state action in areas such as childcare, and policy-based strategies aimed at influencing the balance between welfare and work, for example, through the provision of working age benefits. Given the wide scope, discussion of each area will be necessarily brief. What is intended is a broad-brush representation of the historical development and general thrust of the state's approach to women's paid work over time rather than a definitive guide to law and policy in any one area or specific timeframe.

The chapter is structured as follows. In section II we consider how women's work came to be defined by its social, economic and political contexts in the eighteenth and nineteenth centuries. As this analysis reveals, divisions concerning the private realm of home and the public world of paid work which emerged following the

---

[4] J Lewis and M Campbell 'Work/Family Balance Policies in the UK since 1997: A New Departure?' (2007) 36 *Journal of Social Policy* 3, 365.

[5] N Busby, *A Right to Care? Unpaid Care Work in European Employment Law* (Oxford, Oxford University Press, 2011).

Enlightenment consigned women to the role of wife and homemaker with limited legal status. This division was further entrenched by the valorisation of (productive) paid work and the undervaluing of (reproductive) care work following the industrial revolution which saw the emergence of the standard (male) worker model. In section II we consider the impact of war on women's paid work experiences and show how, in order to enable the mobilisation of women into jobs vacated by men serving in the Second World War and to further the war effort, state-provided nurseries were made available which were swiftly closed down again at the advent of peace. Women's work during the First and Second World Wars, as explored in section III, was marked by continuity and change driven largely by wider economic and social goals: women's participation in paid work was encouraged and facilitated as a means of filling labour shortages yet the state's desire to preserve social stability during the post-war era meant that women's place in the home was paramount. This resulted in the differential treatment of women's paid work, which attracted fewer legal protections than men's and which was viewed as secondary to women's primary responsibilities in the home. Law's response to the workplace inequality endured by women in comparison with their male counterparts is considered in section IV, in which we chart the introduction of anti-discrimination law in the 1960s and 1970s. As our analysis shows, despite the substantial gains made to women's paid work experiences by legal intervention, the limits of the formal equality approach have severely restricted law's impact on the reconciliation of paid work and unpaid care. This restrictive approach is further illustrated by the shift to a flexible workforce and the growth in part-time jobs for women during the 1980s and 1990s, explored in section V. Whilst providing a means of facilitating care commitments, part-time and other forms of 'atypical' work further differentiated women's paid work from men's, reaffirming and exacerbating its poor quality and insecurity and giving rise to a permanently precarious largely female workforce. In section VI, we consider the birth of 'family-friendly' employment policy introduced by the New Labour government during the late 1990s, notable for its recognition that workplaces should explicitly accommodate workers' care responsibilities. This change in approach has sustained until the present day and, although welcome, its early promise has been stymied by its attachment to pre-existing arrangements and co-option by other, largely economic, policy goals. This point is illustrated by our consideration, in section VII, of the impact of austerity policies introduced by the Coalition and Conservative governments between 2010 and the present day. The cuts to public services and welfare benefits were implemented as a reaction to the global banking crisis and resulting financial crash of 2008. In the UK women have undoubtedly paid the highest price through loss of income and reductions in services and employment opportunities revealing the fragility and temporality of the gains made in the drive for women's economic independence over the past two centuries.

In section VIII we consider the future of women's paid work, reimagining a policy framework predicated on the recognition of our shared vulnerability rather than the valorisation of our (fictive) autonomy. As an historical analysis shows, although 'the feminisation of employment'[6] may have been led by an increase in the *quantity* of jobs performed by women, this has not necessarily been matched by improvements in the *quality* of such jobs which continue to be low-status, low-paid and precarious. In offering an explanation as to why women's social and economic activities continue to be valued so differently from those of men, Fineman's vulnerability theory draws on the contrast between the liberal subject,[7] in its contextual guise as the paradigmatic 'standard worker', and the vulnerable subject.[8] As the application of a vulnerability approach in section VIII reveals, a reorientation of the target of policy intervention, away from the liberal subject and towards the vulnerable subject, has the capacity to shift the risk associated with bearing responsibility for (or being assumed to bear responsibility for) both paid work and unpaid care away from female workers so as to enable its equitable redistribution across all of law's subjects including relevant institutions.[9] The recognition of vulnerability as the universal human condition has the potential to enable us all to engage in whatever form and balance of (paid/unpaid; productive/reproductive) work is necessary as either provider or beneficiary/recipient at various stages of the life course regardless of gender, class, race, age or other personal characteristic.[10]

II. Private Work, Public Work and the Standard Worker Model

Any analysis of women and work must start with a consideration of the legal frameworks intended to regulate relationships within workplaces and homes and the relevant institutions supporting such relationships which have their roots in the eighteenth-century Enlightenment. This is the vantage point from which contemporary law and policy originates and which consequently colours all provision. As the following analysis shows, the resulting framework is primarily concerned with the accommodation of care requirements within the pre-existing arrangements surrounding paid work rather than vice versa. The effect of this has been to reaffirm and further entrench already rigid ideas about how and when paid work should be performed and what sort of individual is best suited to its performance.

---

[6] According to Fudge and Owens, the term has a double meaning referring both to 'the increased labour market participation of women and the proliferation of forms of employment historically associated with women, that is, jobs that are part-time, temporary, poorly paid, and lacking benefits and collective forms of representation' – see Fudge and Owens (eds), *Precarious Work, Women, and the New Economy: The Challenges to Legal Norms*, above n 3, 12.

[7] MA Fineman, 'The Vulnerable Subject: Anchoring Equality in the Human Condition' (2008–09) 20 *Yale Journal of Law and Feminism* 1.

[8] ibid.

[9] Including, but not confined to, the family, employing organisations, the labour market, the welfare state, civil society and the state more generally.

[10] MA Fineman, 'Vulnerability and Inevitable Inequality' (2017) 4 *Oslo Law Review* 3, 133.

The unencumbered standard worker has long been the paradigm against whom other workers are measured so that anyone unable to conform with the full-time, permanent model regulated by the employment contract is 'othered' or accommodated rather than being considered the target of regulation. The process of othering is present within the current contractual framework by which employment relations are regulated, is reaffirmed by the language used to describe 'alternative' working arrangements – '*atypical*', '*non*-standard', '*part*-time' – and provides the very basis by which discrimination law seeks to provide equal treatment to those who do not conform to more traditional ideas of how paid work 'should be' performed. As this chapter will demonstrate, the result is a compensatory approach intended to provide recompense for treatment that arises because of the worker's difference on the grounds of her sex (or other personal trait), which is categorised as a 'protected characteristic' under the Equality Act.[11] The alternative offered by Fineman's notion of the vulnerable subject[12] recognises the limitations of this approach and seeks to counter it by focusing on vulnerability as *the* human condition rather than as a personal trait intrinsic to individual identity. When it is applied to the context of UK workplace regulation, the vulnerability approach highlights the need for a radical rethink requiring, as the following overview shows, the displacement of centuries of interlinked ideology, tradition and practice which underpin the current regulatory framework.

A. The Sexual Contract[13]

In William Blackstone's 1765 treatise, *Commentaries on the Laws of England*, the relationships that existed between master and servant, father and child and wife and husband were characterised as paternalistic and dependent.[14] The poor law entrenched married women's economic dependence upon their husbands, denying them full access to poor relief on their own account.[15] Industrialisation resulted in a move away from master and servant as the central relationship by which labour was regulated and its replacement with contract. However, as Deakin and Wilkinson[16] explain,

> the result of this process of change was not a general model of the contract of employment which was capable of being applied to all wage-dependent workers, but instead

---

[11] Equality Act 2010 s 4. The others are: age; disability; gender reassignment; marriage and civil partnership; pregnancy and maternity; race; religion or belief; sexual orientation.

[12] MA Fineman, 'The Vulnerable Subject: Anchoring Equality in the Human Condition' above n 7.

[13] C Pateman, *The Sexual Contract* (London, Polity Press, 1988).

[14] W Blackstone, *Commentaries on the Laws of England* (1809) Book I, ch XV (Oxford, Oxford University Press, 2016).

[15] S Deakin and F Wilkinson, *The Law of the Labour Market: Industrialization, Employment, and Legal Evolution* (Oxford, Oxford University Press, 2005), ch 3; S Fredman, *Women and the Law* (Oxford, Oxford University Press, 1997), chs 2 and 3.

[16] Deakin and Wilkinson, *The Law of the Labour Market: Industrialization, Employment, and Legal Evolution*, above n 15, 107.

a hierarchical model of service, which originated in Master and Servant Acts and was gradually assimilated into the common law.

This hierarchical approach eventually gave way to a more equitable system of labour regulation heralded by collective bargaining and the origins of social legislation during the 1940s. The 'private' domain of the household, the site of reproductive labour, and the 'public' workplace, in which productive labour was performed, were separated with waged labour becoming the means by which income was achieved for those without property. As Fudge states, 'This process of marketisation simultaneously undermined older forms of protection and emancipated workers from paternalism.'[17]

The development of the market relied heavily on contractual principles, both as an organising tool and as a process of regulation,

> The gradual extension of civil rights to propertyless men in the eighteenth century enabled them to enter into contracts and to enforce their promises. The employment contract became the primary means for men to obtain access to the means of subsistence. However, married women were incapable of entering into contracts.[18]

Under the legal doctrine of coverture, marriage rendered husbands and wives as 'one person in law'[19] so that the woman's legal existence was suspended during the marriage, or 'at least incorporated and consolidated into that of the husband'[20] deeming her to be 'a *feme-covert*'.[21] Like the household and family, the woman was placed under the patriarchal control of her husband. Her ability to make contracts was severely restricted with the effect that she was unable to own property in her own name.[22]

The separation of the private and public realms of reproductive and productive work was further entrenched through the increasing importance of the employment contract as the principal regulatory tool by which the latter was governed. The emergence of the social contract emancipated men but did little to disturb the gender order. Carole Pateman's concept of the sexual contract underpins the social contract and entrenches men's political domination over women as well as men's right of access to women's bodies,[23] both of which are legitimated by the marriage contract. Thus, contracts made in both the private and public realms were, and continue to be, informed by and imbued with patriarchy. By focusing

---

[17] J Fudge, 'A New Vocabulary and Imaginary for Labour Law: Taking Legal Constitution, Gender and Social Reproduction Seriously' in D Brodie, N Busby and R Zahn (eds), *The Future Regulation of Work: New Concepts, New Paradigms* (London, Palgrave Macmillan, 2015) 12; N Fraser, 'A Triple Movement? Parsing the Politics of Crisis after Polanyi' (2013) 81 *New Left Review* 119.

[18] Fudge, 'A New Vocabulary and Imaginary for Labour Law: Taking Legal Constitution, Gender and Social Reproduction Seriously', above n 17.

[19] Blackstone, *Commentaries on the Laws of England*, above n 14.

[20] ibid.

[21] ibid.

[22] For a fuller account of the legal effects of Coverture, see Fredman, *Women and the Law*, above n 15, 40–49.

[23] Pateman, *The Sexual Contract*, above n 13, 2.

on the public sphere and production within the social and economic construct of the 'labour market', contemporary understandings of contract obscure this basic patriarchal relationship and mask the dependency of the market on the reproductive work performed within the private sphere.[24] Furthermore, as not everyone can participate equally in its creation,[25] the idea of the contract as an expression of freedom is false,[26] as is the conceptualisation of the liberal subject through a rhetoric of the 'individual as owner of oneself',[27] which promotes the idea that all contracts involving property in the person are free.[28] Pateman's analysis reveals the deeply flawed nature of the social contract tradition due to its predication upon and failure to address the sexual contract. Nonetheless, it is the basis on which institutions and relationships in both the private and public realms were grounded and continue to be shaped and reproduced.

B. The Industrial Revolution

The late eighteenth century saw the growth of collective action as a means of improving the conditions in which waged labour was performed. This movement prioritised men's work in the public sphere casting women into the shadows, excluded by their confinement to the private sphere of the household and their responsibility for domestic labour.[29] The distinction between paid work outside the home and unpaid work within it originates from the time of the industrial revolution. Prior to the concentration of labour in factories, the division between different forms of work had been largely obscured by the prevalence of subsistence agriculture and the various forms of craft work emanating from cottage industries. With the growth of industrialisation, married women's participation in paid work outside of the home actually declined from 25 per cent in 1851 to 8.7 per cent in 1921.[30] Moreover, 'as wages became the dominant mode of recognising and rewarding labour, women's unpaid domestic contribution began to disappear as real work'.[31] Coverture was abolished in the late nineteenth century, but the intensification of production and the advent of 'Taylorist' labour processes made it increasingly difficult for women to combine childbearing and childrearing with

---

[24] ibid, 4, 11.

[25] ibid, 6.

[26] ibid, 8.

[27] ibid, 8; In Foucauldian terms, the 'entrepreneur of the self', see M Foucault, *The Birth of Biopolitics: Lectures at the Collège de France, 1978–1979* (M Senellart (ed), G Burchell (trans)) (Basingstoke, Palgrave Macmillan, 2008) 240.

[28] Pateman, *The Sexual Contract*, above n 13, 14–17.

[29] ibid, 17.

[30] S Atkins and B Hoggett, *Women and the Law* (Oxford, Blackwell, 1984) 18–19, excluding the boost in numbers during the war effort – see below.

[31] W Seccombe, *A Millennium of Family Change: Feudalism to Capitalism in Northwestern Europe* (London, Verso, 1992) 244.

paid work.[32] Legislation and policy governing work outside of the home and social security were shaped by the experiences and perceptions of the unencumbered (male) worker and their operation further entrenched related conceptualisations of work and contribution.[33]

This vicious circle of women's economic dependency upon men and men's absolute reliance on the provision of reproductive labour by women was led, reinforced and entrenched by law and policy. The prioritisation of the unencumbered standard worker as the paradigm subject of the employment contract resulted in specific practices aimed at controlling women's ability to engage in paid work including the marriage bars that excluded married women from certain occupations. Legally sanctioned sex discrimination[34] underscored ideas that married women who did engage in paid work did so for 'pin money' rather than to make a necessary contribution to the household wage or to satisfy any personal need for economic independence.[35]

III. Women's Work in Wartime

Despite many women's inability to participate in paid 'productive' work and the exclusion of their reproductive labour from law's reach, women have always worked, be it inside or outside of the home or both. Policymakers' engagement with this dual workload in the first half of the twentieth century is marked by both continuity and change depending not on any desire to free women from the social and economic constraints imposed on them, but on the wider political circumstances of the time. Following the post-Industrial Revolution move towards a market economy, women's primary responsibility for childcare and homemaking impacted on their employment opportunities with ideological and practical constraints preventing their engagement in paid work outside of the home. However, the twentieth century saw women's participation in the paid workforce increase substantially, catalysed initially by participation in wartime and auxiliary industries.

Women's employment rates increased during the First World War, although it is difficult to quantify by exactly how much as domestic workers were excluded from the official figures and many women workers moved from domestic work

---

[32] Fudge, 'A New Vocabulary and Imaginary for Labour Law: Taking Legal Constitution, Gender and Social Reproduction Seriously', above n 17, 13.

[33] ibid,14; Fredman, *Women and the Law*, above n 15, chs 2 and 3.

[34] The Sex Disqualification (Removal) Act 1919, which forbade discrimination in employment against married women, was limited by the wide exception allowing women's exclusion by regulation from the civil service and foreign service and by restrictive judicial interpretation; see Fredman, *Women and the Law*, above n 15, 80–82.

[35] See S Harkness, S Machin and J Waldfogel, 'Evaluating the Pin Money Hypothesis: The Relationship between Women's Labour Market Activity, Family Income and Poverty in Britain' (1997) 10 *Journal of Population Economics* 2, 137.

into the jobs created by the war effort.[36] Estimates range from 23.6 per cent of the working-age population in 1914 to between 37.7 per cent and 46.7 per cent in 1918.[37] Married women's employment rates increased sharply, accounting for nearly 40 per cent of all women workers by 1918.[38] Historical analyses differ in their accounts of how much this sudden increase in their employment rates impacted on the lives of women in post-war Britain. Braybon has highlighted the enduring narrative in which the war is characterised as a watershed moment for women who acquired new skills enabling them to enter new sectors of employment and occupations, gaining the 'reward' of partial enfranchisement in 1918.[39] Angela Woollacott recounts the regression in women's status following its temporary enhancement in the wartime workplace.[40] However sustained the effect was and regardless of class differences, women's ties to the private realm of the home and the constraints imposed on them by the pervasive conceptions of motherhood were never far away. In her study of women welfare supervisors in munitions factories during the war, Woollacott[41] sums up the compromise struck by women professionals regarding their engagement in the public realm and traditional notions of maternalism thus:

> At the end of the nineteenth century and in the first decades of the twentieth, the dominant cultural views concerning women's social roles laid heavy stress on them as mothers. Anxiety about the declining birth rate, concern about and investigations into the health of the working class (much of which was based on Britain's need for a fit imperial race), and the challenges presented by the feminist movement all precipitated this clamant emphasis. Women who were active in the public sphere during this era, as moral reformers, suffragists, teachers, nurses and social investigators, frequently invoked the maternal qualities of women, their supposed moral purity and nurturing instincts, to justify their own activities and demands.

A. Paid Work and State Childcare

The need for women munitions workers prompted the limited establishment of state-funded day nurseries so that by 1917 there were 100 nurseries across the

---

[36] G Braybon, *Women Workers in the First World War: The British Experience* (London, Barnes and Noble, 1981) 49.

[37] ibid.

[38] ibid.

[39] G Braybon (2003) 'Winners or Losers: Women's Symbolic Role in the War Story' in G Braybon (ed), *Evidence, History and the Great War: Historians and the Impact of 1914–18* (Oxford, Berghahn, 2003).

[40] A Woollacott, *On Her Their Lives Depend: Munitions Workers in the Great War* (London, University of California Press, 1994).

[41] A Woollacott, 'Maternalism, Professionalism and Industrial Welfare Supervisors in World War I Britain' (1994) 3 *Women's History Review* 1, 29. Welfare supervisors were generally middle-class women employed in factories, whose job it was 'to attend to the facilities, uniforms, health, efficiency and general welfare of the greatly expanded number of women in industry' (at 32).

country. Following the 1918 Education Act, local authorities could apply for grants to assist with funding nursery education for children aged 2–5 years if they wished to make such provision available.[42] The take-up was not high, with resources focused on a range of other priority areas deemed necessary to aid the nation's recovery from the devastation wreaked by the war. Throughout the inter-war years, government policy on how many places should be provided was open to interpretation, so that there was no obligation on local authorities to make any provision. By 1938 there were only 118 nursery schools providing care for 9,504 children between 9 am and 3.30 pm.[43] Additional state-funded childcare places for under-fives were provided by the Ministry of Health's day nurseries for the children of working women. However, to qualify, the mother had to be the sole adult wage-earner and her work deemed 'necessary' for the family's income so that places were limited to the children of unmarried, separated or widowed women. Provision was scant, with only 104 day nurseries available in 1938 across England and Wales, offering places for 4,291 children,[44] and 118 nursery schools.[45]

The onset of the Second World War once more saw an increase in women's employment rates. Between 1939 and 1943, 1.5 million women joined the 'essential industries', including the manufacture of munitions, and the number of women working in engineering rose from 97,000 to 602,000.[46] There was a shift in the marital status and age of women in factory work, with a greater proportion of those aged between 35 and 44 and married women now working.[47] From 1940 the Minister of Labour, Ernest Bevin, requested the setting up of nurseries to facilitate the recruitment of married women. These were provided by local authorities and funded by the Ministry of Health, with numbers increasing in 1941 following pressure from, among others, the Trade Union Committee Women's conference.[48]

Places were not provided free of charge but were subsidised, with mothers expected to furnish their children with necessary items such as nappies and a change of clothes.[49] From the outset, disagreement regarding the purpose and need for childcare abounded. The Treasury took the view that the purpose of this expansion in provision was primarily to support the flow of female labour so that 'existing theories of nurseries as educational or beneficial to child health were

---

[42] A West and P Noden, Public funding of early years education in England: an historical perspective, *Clare Market Papers 21* (London, London School of Economics and Political Science, 2016).

[43] P Summerfield, *Women Workers in the Second World War: Production and Patriarchy in Conflict* (Abingdon, Routledge, 2012) 20.

[44] East End Women's Museum (2018), Women, Babies and Bombs: How Day Nurseries Contributed to Working Women's Lives During World War II, available at https://eastendwomensmuseum.org/blog/2018/8/7/women-babies-and-bombs-how-day-nurseries-contributed-to-working-womens-lives-during-wwii.

[45] D Riley, 'War in the Nursery' (1979) 2 *Feminist Review* 82, 83.

[46] Summerfield, *Women Workers in the Second World War: Production and Patriarchy in Conflict*, above n 43.

[47] ibid.

[48] East End Women's Museum, above n 44.

[49] ibid.

secondary'.[50] An active nursery school movement accorded with this approach, whereas the Ministry of Health unsurprisingly maintained that child welfare and health were part and parcel of early years care.[51] The Ministry actively resisted expansion, arguing that increases in demand were overstated, with the gradual increase in supply owing much to campaigns and deputations by community and women's organisations.[52]

By September 1944, there were 1,450 full-time nurseries providing care for children from birth to age 5 and, for 2–5 year olds, 109 part-time nurseries and 784 school-based nursery classes.[53] During the Second World War, nurseries were estimated to have provided places for 59,000 children, including 18,000 under the age of 2.[54] However, as Riley has noted, at the end of the war,

> The war nurseries closed down at speed. The Exchequer's grant to the local authorities was halved after 1945 and responsibility handed over to the local authorities; requisitioned buildings returned to their peacetime uses.[55]

In her exploration of the reasons for the swift and unequivocal withdrawal of day care following the Second World War, Riley cautions against assumptions that the state's action was fuelled largely by psychologist John Bowlby's studies related to child welfare being best served by maternal care.[56] Social and economic forces, Riley argues, had just as much to do with the closure of the day nurseries, which did not in fact occasion a mass return to the home by wartime women workers.[57]

B. Women's Paid Work in the Post-war Era

Although women were demobilised in large numbers from paid work to make way for returning servicemen in the immediate aftermath of the Second World War, the sustained economic growth which would endure throughout the 1950s soon called for the urgent expansion of the labour force. By the late 1940s the government had launched a campaign to encourage the recruitment of women in certain types of paid employment and was actively seeking the increased migration of workers from the (former) British Colonies to fill labour shortages.[58] Married women's formal employment outside the home grew from only

---

[50] Riley, 'War in the Nursery', above n 45, 84.

[51] ibid, 84.

[52] ibid, 83.

[53] ibid, 83.

[54] Ministry of Health (1945) *Deputation on Nursery Provisions to the Ministers of Health and Education Public Records*, MH45.

[55] Riley, 'War in the Nursery', above n 45, 89.

[56] D Riley, *War in the Nursery: Theories of the Child and Mother* (London, Virago, 1983), 11.

[57] ibid. For a fuller discussion of the post-war state's provision of nursery care and its relationship with maternalistic ideals, see ch 3, this volume.

[58] C Grant, *Homecoming: Voices of the Windrush Generation* (London, Vintage, 2019).

10 per cent between the wars to more than double that by 1951.[59] As a proportion of the female workforce, married women's share grew from 16 per cent in 1931 to nearly 45 per cent at the beginning of the 1950s, passing the 50 per cent mark in 1957.[60] The post-war reconstruction saw the creation of jobs for women within the expanding welfare state in areas such as nursing, cleaning and clerical work. Job creation was also evident in the banking, textile and light industries where routine and repetitive secretarial and assembly work was largely performed by women. As well as being highly segregated along gender lines, such private-sector employment shared certain common characteristics with the newly created public-sector jobs in that it was labelled as 'women's work' and, accordingly, paid at a lower rate than work performed predominantly by men.[61] Furthermore, the increased employment opportunities for women were subject to certain ideologically driven constraints as married women, particularly those with children, were discouraged and, in some cases, prohibited from taking up paid employment. Well into the 1950s the public sector operated marriage bars, which prevented married women from entering certain occupations – notably higher paid teaching and clerical jobs – and enabled women's dismissal upon marriage.[62]

C. Change or Continuity?

The apparent conflict between, on the one hand, the state's need to encourage women to participate and remain in waged work in order to fill labour shortages and, on the other, the preservation of social stability through maintenance of the gender order appeared to pose no particular difficulty for policymakers so long as women's waged work was classified as secondary to that of men and also to their responsibilities as homemakers and carers. Although increasingly conscious of the need to attract women's votes, the leading political parties adopted contrasting strategies. The Conservative Party's charter for women, 'A True Balance: In the Home, in Employment and as Citizens',[63] appealed to the growing women's movement by calling for equal pay in the public sector and equal citizenship, policies which made their way into the party's 1950 manifesto.[64] Labour Party propaganda

---

[59] J Lewis, *Women in Britain since 1945* (Oxford, Blackwell, 1992) 65. As McCarthy points out (citing V Klein, *Britain's Married Women Workers* (London, Routledge, 1965) 25): 'The true post-war figures were probably even higher, as census data continued to under-report women's part-time employment.' H McCarthy, 'Social Science and Married Women's Employment in Post-War Britain' (2016) 233 *Past and Present* 1, 269, 269.

[60] McCarthy 'Social Science and Married Women's Employment in Post-War Britain', above n 59.

[61] S Dex, *The Sexual Division of Work: Conceptual Revolutions in the Social Sciences* (New York, St Martin's Press, 1985).

[62] Fredman, *Women and the Law*, above n 15.

[63] Conservative and Unionist Central Office (1949).

[64] I Zweiniger-Bargielowska, *Austerity in Britain: Rationing, Controls, and Consumption, 1939–1955* (Oxford, Oxford University Press, 2000) 232.

aimed at women focused on their roles as wives and mothers,[65] with the Labour government considering equal pay to be inflationary as illustrated by its claims in a 1946 constituency discussion pamphlet that pay inequalities were necessary in order to promote motherhood as an attractive alternative to paid employment.[66]

As Lewis has noted, the provision of childcare in the establishment of the Keynesian welfare state was subject to a post-war preoccupation with improving economic standards. This was translated by the political Right into a concern with 'combating poverty and disadvantage' and by the political Left into a desire 'to confine provision to the poor and disadvantaged', with neither position likely to result in universal childcare provision.[67] The separate systems of nursery education and day care which had emerged in the inter-war years were thus further entrenched.

This view of state-provided childcare as an undesirable alternative to maternal care, only to be resorted to in specific and unfortunate circumstances related to the mother's failings, contributed to the polarisation of the working mother and her stay-at-home counterpart and the problematisation of the former. This characterisation is illustrated by documentation related to the training and practice of medical and social workers in the 1940s. As Starkey's examination of such literature reveals, the construct of the 'problem mother' which emerges,

> demonstrates the influence of class as much as gender. For example, both the case notes and the professional literature fail to take into account the employment patterns of working-class women, both formal and informal, and are quick to condemn those that deviate from the middle-class ideal of a home-based wife. The values to be inculcated in the task of rehabilitating 'problem mothers' are middle-class, suburban values and reveal, if not a distaste for inner-city life, a preference for suburban and rural surroundings.[68]

As such insights show, in the successful reconstruction of a post-war economy and despite the emergence of the welfare state, the preservation of a stable and enduring gender order built around the male breadwinner/female homemaker model was paramount. The state's apparently duplicitous encouragement and abhorrence of working mothers did not present a paradox as long as men remained the primary earners with the male wage protected. Consequently, women's work outside of the home was considered as secondary, only to be undertaken by those able to balance it with their home-making and care responsibilities for pin money in order to supplement the 'family wage'.[69] The provision of unpaid care remained

[65] ibid.

[66] Labour Party, 'Is Woman's Place in the Home?' *Discussion Series No 9*, London, 1946.

[67] J Lewis, 'The Failure to Expand Childcare Provision and to Develop a Comprehensive Childcare Policy in Britain during the 1960s and 1970s' (2013) 24 *Twentieth Century British History* 2, 249, 251.

[68] P Starkey, 'The Feckless Mother: Women, Poverty and Social Workers in Wartime and Post-war England', (2000) 9 *Women's History Review* 3, 539, 550.

[69] See Harkness, Machin and Waldfogel, 'Evaluating the Pin Money Hypothesis: The Relationship between Women's Labour Market Activity, Family Income and Poverty in Britain', above n 35.

an exclusively female activity that took place within the private and unregulated confines of the family home and was prioritised over any other activity – be it waged work or leisure – that might be performed alongside it. State interference in household arrangements, although seemingly innocuous and laissez-faire, was distinctly coercive as far as protecting and maintaining the gender order was concerned. As Fudge puts it,

> In developed economies after World War II, employment and the family were sharply separated and regulated by their own distinctive technologies. The boundaries between home/market and public/private became deeply inscribed in contemporary legal doctrines, discourses, and institutions such that the initial jurisdictional classification appeared natural and inevitable and not political and ideological.[70]

At this time, employment equality was simply not part of the policy discourse, but that would begin to change over the next decade as various social groupings and organised political forces fuelled by the continuing growth in women's employment started to demand change.

IV. The 1960s and 1970s: The Fight for Equality

Women's labour market participation continued to increase in the decades following the war so that, between 1955 and 1965, the number of women in the labour force as a percentage of all women of working age (15–64) rose from 45.9 per cent to 51 per cent. However, of particular note in the 1950s and 1960s was the growth of employment among married women, largely in part-time jobs. In 1951, 38 per cent of the female workforce was composed of married women and by 1971 this proportion had increased to 63 per cent. Despite this change in women's labour market behaviour, the practice of dismissing women when they became pregnant continued[71] and it remained legal to pay women less than men even when undertaking the same work. The lack of protection for pregnancy- and maternity-related discrimination and the dearth of affordable good-quality childcare contributed to an M-shaped or bimodal aggregate pattern of women's employment when plotted over the life course, with peaks occurring in the early 20s prior to childbirth and beyond the age of 45.[72] Rather than stopping work at marriage, women

---

[70] Fudge, 'A New Vocabulary and Imaginary for Labour Law: Taking Legal Constitution, Gender and Social Reproduction Seriously', above n 17, 14–15.

[71] Although the Employment Protection Act 1975 made it illegal to sack a woman due to pregnancy and introduced statutory maternity provision (see further ch 3, this volume), it would be 20 years before more comprehensive protection of pregnancy was introduced by way of a positive maternity rights regime with the implementation of Directive 92/85/EEC. The necessary cultural shift within workplaces has been particularly slow, so that women in the UK labour market still experience high levels of pregnancy discrimination.

[72] Dex, *The Sexual Division of Work: Conceptual Revolutions in the Social Sciences*, above n 61, 4.

continued in paid employment up until childbirth, often returning following the years of family formation with much of the expansion in women's jobs in part-time work.

Alongside these changes to women's employment patterns, claims for improved social rights including equal pay for women and men began to feature in civil rights campaigns in both the USA and across mainland Europe. The UK's campaign for equal pay, which had its origins in the 1950s, continued to gain momentum throughout the decade. Such developments were the result of a perfect storm of social and economic change within the UK and other post-war economies. The growth of capitalism as the dominant economic model saw an increased preoccupation with 'the market' as the centrifugal force of all economic activity which brought with it a liberal focus on individualism and the marketised identity which 'penetrated ever deeper into the social fabric'.[73] The rise of capitalism was accompanied by challenges to the stability of the traditional nuclear family model as divorce rates and lone parenthood rose and fertility rates across Europe declined.[74]

Technological advances and the mass production of household appliances reduced the burden of household chores, freeing up women's time. Perhaps more importantly, medical and legal advances in the 1960s gave women access to contraception and abortion, enabling them to control their fertility.[75] As these shifts in social arrangements illustrate, capitalism's focus on waged work and indifference to 'private' family arrangements, including the provision of care, created an interesting paradox whereby its assumption regarding the endurance of the gendered division of labour within families on which it is so reliant was in conflict with its unswerving promotion of the unencumbered 'standard worker' as the model to which all productive workers should aspire. As Crompton has noted, the advocacy of economic liberalism or 'marketisation' is somewhat undermined by its facilitation of 'changes in both employment and the family that are widely regarded in a negative light'.[76] Such changes were led and supported by women's enhanced freedom over their own bodies and fertility. Contrasting the changing lives of women with the social *mores* of the time, Sheila Rowbotham noted,

> It was ignored that it was rather naïve to expect women to fulfil some abstracted 'natural' function in a most unnatural society particularly when contraceptives were reducing the time women were spending in childbirth.[77]

Such naivety was soon countered by a growing awareness that challenges to state-sanctioned oppression and discrimination and new claims to equality were on the

---

[73] R Crompton, 'Employment, Flexible Working and the Family' (2002) 53 *British Journal of Sociology* 4, 537, 538.

[74] D Sporton, 'Fertility: The Lowest Level in the World' in D Noin and R Woods (eds), *The Changing Population of Europe* (Oxford, Blackwell, 1993).

[75] The contraceptive pill became available to married women in 1961 and to all women in 1967. Abortion was legalised under the Abortion Act 1967.

[76] Crompton, 'Employment, Flexible Working and the Family', above n 73, 538.

[77] S Rowbotham, *Woman's Consciousness, Man's World* (London, Verso, 1973) 6.

ascendency within and beyond the UK. Racial segregation, a long-time cultural mainstay of the USA's southern states, became the focus of a high-profile political campaign attracting wide public support which was soon adopted by mainstream political parties. The intensification of calls for sex equality provided some much-needed impetus to the campaign for equal pay within the UK which was further bolstered by the political objective of gaining membership of the European Economic Community[78] and the corresponding need to comply with international standards.[79] Solidarity through trade union membership and activism, traditionally the preserve of the male working class, was steadily, if slowly, growing among the increasing numbers of women public sector workers whose union membership rose from 24 per cent of all women workers in 1946 to 29 per cent in 1969.[80] However, despite its increasingly female workforce, the public sector was still dominated by high degrees of gender segregation with large numbers of women employed as cleaners, secretaries and typists while the private sector remained largely non-unionised. Furthermore, the leadership of trade unions remained predominantly male, with priorities which were often not reflective of women's demands.

In 1968, women sewing machinists employed at Dagenham's Ford plant went on strike demanding that their pay be more closely equated to that of male assembly workers. They succeeded in reaching a negotiated agreement for 92 per cent of the men's pay. Detailed accounts show that, far from taking a supportive and proactive approach, the trade unions involved 'ambivalently decided to pursue the dispute as an equal pay issue, particularly when the new Secretary for Employment and Productivity, Barbara Castle, took a personal interest in settling the dispute'.[81] Castle tabled draft equal pay legislation and, in 1970, the Equal Pay Act was passed providing a right to equal pay for women and men in the public and private sectors for performing the same or broadly similar work.[82] Despite the linkage of the Act to the Dagenham strike in the public's consciousness, the Equal Pay Act was not of any practical use to the Ford workers' claim, which was based on the equal value of the women's jobs with those of their male colleagues. The Act initially did nothing to address the gendered occupational segregation that characterised the UK's labour force and also failed to offer any route to litigation for those women employed in workplaces which did not have job evaluation. Ultimately the UK

---

[78] The Treaty of Rome 1957 (then Art 119, ex Art 141), contained a provision for 'equal pay for equal work', now extended and contained in Art 157 TFEU.

[79] The ILO's Equal Remuneration Convention 1951 (Convention 100) provided for equal pay of work of equal value, and the Discrimination (Employment and Occupation) Convention 1958 (Convention 111), Art 5, allows for special measures to meet the needs of 'persons who for reasons such as sex, age, disablement, family responsibilities or social or cultural status are generally recognized to require special protection or assistance'.

[80] R Undy, Trade Union Organisation 1945–1995 (2012) Union Makes Us Strong website, available at www.unionhistory.info/britainatwork/narrativedisplay.php?type=tradeunionorganisation.

[81] See H Conley, 'Trade unions, equal pay and the law in the UK' (2014) 35 *Economic and Industrial Democracy* 2, 309, 314.

[82] Although the Act did not come into force until 1975 alongside the Sex Discrimination Act.

government's hand was forced, through its EC membership, to enact amending legislation allowing for equal value claims to be brought in the UK.[83]

A. The Limits of Formal Equality

The Equal Pay Act received Royal Assent in 1970 but was not implemented in the UK until 1975, accompanied by the Sex Discrimination Act 1975 (SDA), so as to give employers an opportunity to prepare for the changes required. The SDA's scope was wider than employment and extended to education and housing. The term 'sex discrimination' included discrimination on the grounds of marital status,[84] which did not cover single persons.[85] In the employment context, the Act was primarily concerned with ensuring equal (the same) treatment between men and women in the terms and conditions of employment beyond pay. In cases of individual discrimination, it operated by imposing a negative duty on employ-ers not to subject a woman to 'less favourable' treatment than that received by a comparable man.[86] This 'formal equality' approach has sustained and is replicated in the current protection against direct discrimination in the Equality Act 2010.[87] Many of the early cases brought under the SDA were concerned with stereotypi-cal ideas relating to women's suitability to particular types of work and working arrangements[88] and the courts and tribunals did not always find the transition from difference to equality easy.[89]

Early assessments of the legislation's impact were mixed: research conducted by the London School of Economics Equal Pay and Opportunity Project in the three years following the implementation of the Equal Pay and Sex Discrimination Acts found that the introduction of equal pay had resulted in considerable and sometimes dramatic narrowing of differentials between the basic rates of the main groups of manual and white collar women workers, and those of men.[90] In rela-tion to the sex discrimination provisions, whose full implementation was reliant on amendments to organisational practices, changes had been few and largely superficial with most employers assuming that their policies and practices met the requirements of the law without systematically examining them to ensure that they did so.[91] By 1980, the case law was beginning to expose gaps in the protection

---

[83] By way of the Equal Pay (Amendment) Regulations 1983, SI 1983/1794. See *EC Commission v UK* [1983] ECR 3431, in which the ECJ ruled that the UK's failure to provide a means of ensuring compul-sory job evaluation was contrary to EU law.

[84] SDA 1975, s 3.

[85] *Bick v Royal West of England School for the Deaf* [197] IRLR 326.

[86] SDA 1975, s 1(1)(a).

[87] s 13.

[88] See, eg, *Ministry of Defence v Jeremiah* [1980] ICR 13 (CA); *Hurley v Mustoe* [1981] IRLR 208 (CA).

[89] Fredman, *Women and the Law*, above n 15, 302–03.

[90] M Snell, 'The Equal Pay and Sex Discrimination Acts: Their Impact in the Workplace' (1979) 1 *Feminist Review* 37, 39.

[91] ibid, 48.

offered by the legislation including a lack of specific protection for discrimination on the grounds of pregnancy or maternity or for sexual harassment[92] within workplaces, as well as the Act's explicit exclusion of the retirement age, which was different for men and women.[93]

B. Same or Different?

The development of the UK's sex discrimination legislation has been heavily influenced by EU law with the European Court of Justice[94] being particularly active in providing some much-needed interpretation through the preliminary reference procedure by which tribunals and courts are able to refer cases where the provisions of EU law require interpretation.[95] With regard to pregnancy, the need for a comparator in order to succeed in a claim for direct discrimination highlighted the Act's lack of recognition that women, although 'the same' as men in most normative respects, were different in one fundamental way. In *Turley v Allders Department Stores Ltd*,[96] the SDA was held not to apply in circumstances where a woman was dismissed because of pregnancy on the grounds that there was 'no equivalent male'. Subsequently, in *Hayes v Malleable Working Men's Club*,[97] the Act was held to apply only where a comparison could be made with a sick man who would need equivalent time off to that required by a woman who was pregnant or who had recently given birth. In 1991 the European Court of Justice established that pregnancy discrimination *is* direct sex discrimination with the fact that only women can be pregnant obviating the need to compare the treatment received by a woman on the grounds of her pregnancy with that received by any man, sick or not.[98] Nonetheless, and despite the introduction of a raft of specific statutory provisions intended to provide protection in employment to women on the grounds of pregnancy and maternity (see chapter three), such discrimination persists.[99]

The classification of pregnancy as an exception to the equal treatment approach illustrates the UK legislation's reliance on formal equality which prioritises process

---

[92] Related claims could only succeed where the facts constituting harassment could be made to fit the framework of direct discrimination, see *Strathclyde Regional Council v Porcelli* [1986] IRLR 134.

[93] The House of Lords' judgment in *Marshall v Southampton & SW Hampshire Area Health Authority* [1986] IRLR 140 resulted in amendments introduced by Sex Discrimination Act 1986 ss 2 and 3, which provided for equal retirement ages for men and women.

[94] Now the Court of Justice of the European Union.

[95] Ex Art 234 EC, now Art 267 TFEU.

[96] [1980] ICR 66.

[97] [1985] ICR 703.

[98] *Handels-og Kontorfunktionaerernes Forbund i Danmark (Hertz)* [1991] IRLR 3; *Dekker v Stichting Vormingscentrum Voor Jong Volvassen (VJV Centrum) Plus* [1991] IRLR 27; see also *Webb v EMO Air Cargo UK Ltd* [1993] IRLR 27 (HL) [1994] IRLR 382 (ECJ).

[99] See EHRC, *Pregnancy and Maternity-Related Discrimination and Disadvantage* (Manchester, Equality and Human Rights Commission, 2018).

over outcome. Based on the Aristotelian formula that 'likes should be treated alike'[100] as a means of achieving social and economic parity for women and men, this approach is severely limited as it fails to take account of the legacy of historical inequality and its effect on current institutional arrangements, perceptions and belief, practices and behaviours. Through its symmetrical application, the UK's legislative concept of direct discrimination is rendered incapable of making any adjustment to employment processes or practices as a means of accounting for the fact that women, despite their normative similarities to men, are situated differently due to the unequal division of labour within households. By simply accommodating such difference through the provision of equal (the same) treatment with no specific adjustment, the law is incapable of producing the redistributive effect necessary to counter existing inequalities. Furthermore, rather than exposing corresponding cultural and institutional inequality, the formal equality approach embeds it in social and economic structures enabling its reaffirmation and perpetuation at state and organisational levels. Challenges to such, often hidden, causes of gender inequality have been largely driven by the indirect discrimination provisions of the SDA.

C. Indirect Discrimination

Like equal value, its conceptual counterpart in the Equal Pay Act, indirect sex discrimination recognises that women's lived experiences may result in differences in their engagement with paid work. Such differences are likely to deviate from the normative model of the standard worker and should not result in value judgements related to status or commitment. The inclusion of the concept of indirect discrimination in the SDA was heavily influenced by the US concept of 'disparate impact'.[101] By introducing a group dimension to law's construction of discrimination, indirect discrimination has the potential to challenge the formal equality approach by recognising that women and men are differently situated so that the same (equal) treatment may lead to different and unjust outcomes. In the original wording of the Act, it was to apply in circumstances where, with or without intention to discriminate, a condition or requirement was applied or a practice established[102] which it was in practical terms more difficult for a particular group to fulfil or comply with than others who did not belong to the group.[103] Unlike direct discrimination, a finding of indirect discrimination does not rely on there being less favourable treatment: there is the same (neutral) treatment, but the impact of the treatment on the group, and hence the individual, results in

---

[100] Aristotle, Nicomachean Ethics, V.3. 1131a10-b15; Politics, III.9.1280 a8-15, III. 12. 1282b18-23.
[101] See *Griggs v Duke Power Co* [1971] 401 US 424.
[102] Now 'provision, criterion or practice' – see Equality Act 2010 s 26.
[103] Such groups are now defined by reference to the 'protected characteristics' identified in Equality Act 2010 s 14.

disadvantage. In contrast with direct discrimination it is possible to justify indirect discrimination, so long as the act or omission complained of can be shown to be a proportionate means of achieving a legitimate aim.[104]

The concept of indirect discrimination has been a cornerstone of sex discrimination law since the early days of the SDA and continues to be the main catalyst for the progressive development of the law.[105] However, like its direct discrimination stablemate, the concept as enacted in UK law does contain certain conceptual weaknesses. Justification of indirect discrimination has perpetuated the *de facto* differentiation of 'men's' and 'women's' work with reference to other common features beyond the sex of the workers. Moreover, the provision's potential to address historical disadvantage is severely hindered by the absence in UK law of any mechanism for bringing group actions and by the lack of capacity to argue historical disadvantage in relation to individual experience. The absence of group action has prevented the effective mobilisation of social justice arguments in the discrimination and equal pay contexts, whereas the exclusion of historical disadvantage as a specific cause of action prevents the law's symmetrical application in a potentially important context: the extension of discrimination law to men who wish to claim rights related to their family and care responsibilities.[106] Rather than being gendered in an essentialist sense, caring is gender coded[107] so that men who are primary caregivers will also face workplace discrimination. However, unlike women, who are, ostensibly at least, able to bring an indirect discrimination claim in such circumstances,[108] men lack the necessary disparate group impact. The formal equality approach enshrined in the legislation, although of crucial importance to individual women seeking to take action against their employers for discriminatory treatment, has always lacked the capacity to address the structural and institutional causes of inequality.

D. The Rise of the Lone Parent Household

Despite the state's reluctance to expand its provision of childcare in the post-war era, women's continued presence in the labour market during the 1980s was seen as desirable on economic grounds. First, a largely female workforce was used to fill the growing number of jobs linked to the provision of personal care, secretarial and clerical support created by the expansion of the service sector and, second, paid work for women provided an alternative to welfare state provision for the

---

[104] C 170/84 *Bilka-Kaufhaus GmbH v Weber Von Hartz* [1986] IRLR 317.

[105] Busby, *A Right to Care? Unpaid Care Work in European Employment Law*, above n 5.

[106] S Fredman, 'Reversing Roles: Bringing Men into the Frame' (2014) 10 *International Journal of Law in Context* 4, 442.

[107] Crompton, 'Employment, Flexible Working and the Family', above n 73, 549.

[108] *London Underground Limited v Edwards (No 2)* [1998] IRLR 364.

growing numbers of lone parent households which were predominantly headed by women.[109]

Policymakers' interest in lone parent families in the UK grew during the 1980s, partly as a result of their increased visibility but also because of their association with non-traditional family behaviours including rises in the divorce rate and in childbearing outside marriage.[110] Interpreted as a sign of the decline in traditional family values, the rise of the single parent family was increasingly constructed as a social problem with, from some quarters, blame attributed to the female heads of such households.[111] Lone parent families are on average more likely to be headed by women from poorer socio-economic backgrounds[112] so that children living in lone parent households are at a significantly higher risk of poverty.[113] However, the heterogeneity of lone parent households in terms of class, race and age[114] can make it difficult to attribute specific shared characteristics as a means of developing targeted policy. One common and enduring feature among lone parent households in the UK in comparison to their European counterparts has been a low parental employment rate.[115]

Estimates of the numbers of lone parent households living in the UK over time vary depending on the source used.[116] According to Berrington's consolidation of a range of sources, the proportion of families with dependent children which were lone parent families grew from 8 to 19 per cent between 1971 and 1991.[117] The increase up until 1985 can be attributed to rising divorce rates[118] and, thereafter, a marked rise in never married lone mothers.[119] The concerns of policymakers

[109] Over 90 per cent of lone-parent households are headed by a mother. The proportion of lone-parent families headed by a father between 1971 and 1991 remained fairly constant at approximately 9 per cent of the total: see A Berrington, *The Changing Demography of Lone Parenthood in Britain* (ESRC Centre for Population Change, Working Paper 48, 5, 2014).

[110] ibid, 2; L Burghes and M Brown, *Single Lone Mothers: Problems, Prospects and Policies* (London, Family Policy Studies Centre, 1995).

[111] J Lewis, 'Lone Mothers: The British Case' in J Lewis (ed), *Lone Mothers in European Welfare Regimes: Shifting Policy Logics* (London, Jessica Kingsley Publishers, 1997). For a consideration of the negative representations of lone mothers in the popular press and political rhetoric of the 1990s, see K Atkinson, S Oerton and D Burns. '"Happy Families?": Single Mothers, the Press and the Politicians' (1998) 22 *Capital and Class* 1, 1.

[112] J Ermisch, *Lone Parenthood: An Economic Analysis* (Cambridge, Cambridge University Press, 1991).

[113] S Harkness, P Gregg and L MacMillan, *Poverty: The Role of Institutions, Behaviours and Culture* (York, The Joseph Rowntree Foundation, 2012).

[114] A Phoenix, 'Social Constructions of Lone Motherhood: A Case of Competing Discourses' in EB Silva (ed), *Good Enough Mothering? Feminist Perspectives on Lone Motherhood* (London, Routledge, 1996).

[115] J Bradshaw and J Millar (1991), 'Lone Parent Families in the UK: Research Findings and Policy Issues' (1991) *Benefits* 7.

[116] J Haskey, 'Trends in the Numbers of One-Parent Families in Great Britain' (1993) 71 *Population Trends* 26; Berrington, *The Changing Demography of Lone Parenthood in Britain*, above n 109, 4.

[117] Berrington, *The Changing Demography of Lone Parenthood in Britain*, above n 109, 5.

[118] Following the enactment of the Divorce Law Reform Act in 1971, see Haskey, 'Trends in the Numbers of One-Parent Families in Great Britain', above n 116.

[119] Berrington, *The Changing Demography of Lone Parenthood in Britain*, above n 109, 5.

about the rising numbers of lone parent families can be summed up by the authors of an empirical study funded by the Department of Social Security and published in 1991:

> Very many of these families are dependent on Income Support for all or most of their incomes, and this reliance on Income Support has been increasing rapidly in recent years. Nearly three-quarters of all lone parents are in receipt of Income Support, up from about 37 per cent in 1971. This has consequences both for the families and for the state.[120]

The high rates of poverty among such households were noted, with a particular focus on the effects on children. Interestingly, the impacts of bringing up children in conditions of acute poverty on the women themselves was not explicitly referred to. Consequences for the state were set out in terms of the costs of supporting lone-parent families on Income Support which, it was estimated, had risen from £1.4bn in 1981/82 to £3.2bn in 1988/89 with less money being recouped from the '"liable relatives" (in general the fathers of these children)'.[121] The report noted the need for sensitivity in policymaking in this area which was linked to 'personal behaviour, human relationships at their most intimate, and the needs and interests of children'[122] so that policymakers were faced with trying to reconcile a number of competing objectives. These included

> maintaining the living standards of children on relationship breakdown; enabling parents to support vulnerable children; and recognising the special needs and extra costs of families with only one parent – but at the same time not encouraging marital breakdown nor putting barriers in the way of re-marriage. In addition there are very difficult questions concerning the extent to which lone mothers should be expected (or compelled) to support themselves through employment; and concerning the extent to which the absent fathers should be expected (or compelled) to financially support their 'ex-families'.[123]

In their assessment of the employment experiences of the lone parents surveyed, the authors found that, of the 42 per cent who were engaged in paid work, 24 per cent worked full-time (24 or more hours), 17 per cent worked part-time and one per cent were self-employed. The jobs undertaken were classified as 'typical "women's jobs" – in clerical, secretarial, retail, catering, and domestic work'. Wages were far lower than the national average for full and part-time workers.[124] Despite their low pay, those in work had higher incomes than those who were reliant on benefits. Although not all of those on income support expressed a desire to

---

[120] Bradshaw and Millar, 'Lone Parent Families in the UK: Research Findings and Policy Issues', above n 115, 7.

[121] ibid.

[122] ibid.

[123] ibid.

[124] 65 per cent of the full-timers and 93 per cent of the part-timers earned less than two-thirds of the median full-time male wage: Bradshaw and Millar, 'Lone Parent Families in the UK: Research Findings and Policy Issues', above n 115, 9.

go out to work, citing the young ages of their children and the need to be available to compensate for the trauma of family breakdown, a quarter did want to work but were prevented from doing so due to the lack of available and affordable childcare.[125]

V. The 1980s and 1990s: The Flexible Workforce

The conundrum of how to combine paid work with unpaid care was already being answered for some by the exponential growth in part-time work which had been taking place since the 1970s. Despite the growth of women's participation in the paid labour force and new legal rights to equal pay and protection from sex discrimination, the division of labour within two-parent households remained static with women continuing to perform the majority of unpaid domestic work.[126] One way in which women's 'double burden' could be lessened whilst preserving the normative 'standard worker' model was through the development of 'atypical' jobs which, with their deviation from the standard 40 hours plus per week, were classified as 'part-time'. The expansion in jobs filled by women during the 1970s and 1980s was predominantly in part-time work within the service industries and public sector.[127] In 1971, the first year for which reliable statistics on part-time work are available, 34 per cent of women worked in part-time jobs compared with 42 per cent a decade later.[128] In subsequent decades this number has fluctuated at around the 39–45 per cent mark.[129]

The growth in part-time jobs has been attributed to the combined forces of increased demand by women workers and organisational and sectoral changes, including the shift away from the manufacturing and towards the service sector.[130]

---

[125] ibid, 9.

[126] Time series data from 1965, 1975 and 1985 showed that women's hours of household labour declined substantially, while men's hours increased marginally; see J Gershuny and JP Robinson, 'Historical Shifts in the Household Division of Labor' (1988) 25 *Demography* 537.

[127] As data on part-time work were not officially collected until 1971, it is difficult to pin down the rate and specific period of expansion in the post-war labour market. It is likely that the expansion actually took place over a long period with the 1960s being the decade of most growth in the ratio of part-time to total employment; see I Bruegel and D Perrons (1998), 'Deregulation and Women's Employment: The Diverse Experiences of Women in Britain' (1998) 4 *Feminist Economics* 1, 103, 111.

[128] S Dex and S Perry, 'Women's Employment Changes in the 1970s' (1984) 92 *Employment Gazette* 4, 151.

[129] In 2010 39 per cent of all employed women in the UK worked part-time (fewer than 30 hours per week) compared with an OECD average of 24 per cent; see J Plunkett, *The Missing Million: The Potential for Female Employment to Raise Living Standards in Low to Middle Income Britain* (London, Resolution Foundation, 2011).

[130] Bruegel and Perrons have characterised the growth of part-time work among women as a 'self-reinforcing process' by which the need for new labour reserves and prevailing stereotypes 'meant that part-time jobs were offered in typically female areas', thus 'locking part-time workers and "women's work" tightly together' ('Deregulation and Women's Employment: The Diverse Experiences of Women in Britain', above n 127, 112).

An accurate assessment of the extent to which these factors led and followed each other is difficult to determine due to the lack of a statutory definition of part-time work in the UK in contrast to some other European countries. In France, for example, four-fifths or less of the working week amounts to part-time and in the Netherlands it is defined as less than 35 hours.[131] In the UK the two most commonly used methods of defining part-time work are self-assessment, which is how such work is defined in the Labour Force Survey, and a working week of less than 30 hours, which is the method used by the Office for National Statistics (ONS) in employer surveys. Those part-time workers paid below the Lower Earnings Limit, which triggers National Insurance contributions, are not included in the New Earnings Survey and are thus excluded from official statistics. In 1996 it was estimated that between a fifth and a third of part-time workers were not counted for this reason.[132]

A. Part-time Work and Legal Protections

There has been some levelling-out of the legal protection provided on the basis of hours of work in recent years but until the mid-1990s full and part-time work were clearly distinguished by the eligibility requirements for substantive rights. Corresponding entitlements to social security and other employment-related benefits were also impacted by such distinctions. Access to the main statutory employment protection rights were restricted to those working under a contract of employment for 16 hours a week or more with two years' continuous service or, for those working between 8 and 15 hours a week, five years of continuous service. Many occupational benefits were available only to those working more than 16 hours, including holiday, sick pay and company pension schemes. Such restrictions had a clearly disproportionate impact on the high numbers of part-time women workers. In 1993, the House of Lords, interpreting European equal treatment provisions, ruled that the UK's restrictive approach to eligibility to unfair dismissal and redundancy payments based on hours of work amounted to indirect sex discrimination on the grounds that women were more likely to work part-time.[133] New regulations were introduced which provided a one-year qualification period for all employees regardless of hours of work.[134] Nevertheless, the contractual and continuous service requirements continued to present substantial barriers for those working under temporary and casual arrangements.

---

[131] A Hegewisch, 'Part-time Working in Europe' (1996) *Flexible Working* May, 14.
[132] ibid.
[133] *R v Secretary of State for Employment ex parte Equal Opportunities Commission* [1994] IRLR 176.
[134] The Employment Protection (Part Time Employees) Regulations 1995 implemented by Employment Rights Act 1996 s 108. This was later increased to a two-year qualification period by the Unfair Dismissal and Statement of Reasons for Dismissal (Variation of Qualifying Period) Order 2012 (SI 2012/989).

The growth of part-time working arrangements continued well into the 1990s driven by its appeal to employing organisations with flexibility seen as a necessary response to increased globalisation.[135] Reduced levels of employment protection gave rise to lower employment costs and a flexible, often unskilled, labour force which could be laid off in times of recession with relative ease and re-employed when needed. The effects of increased precariousness were felt by individual workers whose transient employment patterns had negative impacts on their financial independence and security as well as on their career aspirations.[136] The locking together of part-time work and 'women's work'[137] meant that these effects were profoundly gendered. An analysis of the case law relating to female part-time workers' non-discrimination and equal pay claims between the 1970s and early 2000s revealed that state and employer assumptions concerning part-time workers' organisational integration and commitment to paid work were commonly used to justify lower pay rates and the denial of workplace benefits.[138] The state's tacit endorsement of such assumptions was evidenced by its lack of activity in equalising the legal rights of part- and full-time workers.[139] Through its non-interventionist stance, the state continued to exploit women's care commitments as a means of marginalising their paid work and reducing employers' costs, thus reaffirming the established gender order and further entrenching the standard worker model.

VI. New Labour: The Birth of 'Family-Friendly' Employment Policy

In 1997 the election of a Labour government heralded a change in the state's approach to employment policy. New Labour had come to power on a commitment to a 'family-friendly' agenda in its manifesto. In one of its first acts, the new government halted the UK's opt-out from the European Social Chapter of the Maastricht Treaty, which had been negotiated by the previous Conservative administration, so that the Parental Leave Directive[140] (discussed in chapter three)

---

[135] Fudge and Owens (eds), *Precarious Work, Women, and the New Economy: The Challenges to Legal Norms*, above n 3, ch 1.

[136] ibid.

[137] Bruegel and Perrons, 'Deregulation and Women's Employment: The Diverse Experiences of Women in Britain', above n 127.

[138] See Busby, *A Right to Care? Unpaid Care Work in European Employment Law*, above n 5, ch 5. Although the analysis presented focused on cases heard by the ECJ, many of the cases originated in the UK.

[139] Equalisation of the treatment and pay of part-time employees and temporary workers with their full-time and permanent counterparts was not attempted until the implementation of the Part-time Workers Directive 97/81/EC, implemented by the Part-time Workers (Prevention of Less Favourable Treatment) Regulations 2000, and the Fixed-Term Workers Directive 99/70/EC, implemented by the Fixed-Term Employees (Prevention of Less Favourable Treatment) Regulations 2002.

[140] Parental Leave Directive 96/34/EC (now replaced by Parental Leave Directive 2010/18/EC), implemented by Parental Leave (EU Directive) Regulations 2013.

was implemented in the UK.[141] New Labour's family-friendly[142] strategy was introduced in its 1998 White Paper 'Fairness at Work',[143] which had the stated aim of building a society 'where to be a good parent is not in conflict with being a good employee'.[144] This heralded the introduction of a range of policies which emphasised the use of flexible working arrangements as a means of enabling working parents to reconcile their paid work and unpaid care responsibilities (see chapter three). Alongside its employment policy, the government introduced its National Childcare Strategy,[145] which sought to make good-quality childcare more affordable and to increase the provision of nursery places.[146] This defamilisation of childcare was aimed at reversing the UK's poor record in this respect. Within the EU, the UK had always been somewhat unusual in its largely privatised provision of childcare. The Conservative governments of the 1980s and 1990s had done little to improve this, despite the Equal Opportunities Commission's recommendation that a national childcare strategy should be introduced.[147] Under the Conservatives, state nursery provision, which had never been particularly prevalent, had been reduced by nearly a half[148] so that, by the mid-1990s, only 2 per cent of childcare for under-3s was publicly funded.[149] For children aged 4–6, public provision was at 60 per cent, largely due to the fact that the majority of children in this age range were in primary school education.[150]

A. The Place of Care

New Labour's centrist 'third way'[151] approach towards social citizenship marked a transition away from a familistic policy regime and towards a more individualistic approach characterised by the promotion of universal employment in recognition of women's permanence in the labour market and the need for women and men to be able to form and maintain autonomous households. This approach was bolstered

---

[141] Employment Act 1999.

[142] Later renamed 'work–life balance' (WLB).

[143] Cm 3968.

[144] ibid, Foreword by Tony Blair.

[145] Outlined in Department for Education and Employment, *Meeting the Childcare Challenge*, Cm 3959 (London, The Stationery Office, 1998).

[146] A Mooney, A Knight, P Moss and C Owen, *Who Cares? Childminding in the 1990s* (London, Family Policy Studies Centre for the Joseph Rowntree Foundation, 2001).

[147] B Bagilhole and P Byrne (2000), 'From Hard to Soft Law and from Equality to Reconciliation in the United Kingdom' in L Hantrais (ed), *Gendered Policies in Europe: Reconciling Employment and Family Life*, (London, Macmillan, 2000).

[148] L Harker, 'The Provision of Childcare: The Shifting Public/Private Boundaries' (2000) 7 *New Economy* 3, 172.

[149] C Skinner, 'Childcare Provision' in J Bradshaw (ed), *The Well-being of Children in the UK* (London, Save the Children Fund, 2002).

[150] European Commission Network on Childcare, *Quality Targets in Services for Young Children* (Brussels, European Equal Opportunities Unit, 1996).

[151] A Giddens, *The Third Way: The Renewal of Social Democracy* (Cambridge, Polity Press, 1998).

by the government's recognition of children's economic status[152] when, in March 1999, it made an historic commitment to end child poverty within 20 years (which is further explored in chapter four of this volume). Related policies included the introduction in 2003 of a Minister of State for Children in the Department for Education and Skills, with responsibility for children's and family services,[153] and a new child tax credit.[154] Child tax credit, payable to parents whether they undertook paid work or not, would operate alongside working tax credit, a means-tested supplement to low wages regardless of the presence of children. In 2004, the government published a 10-year strategy, 'Choice for Parents, the Best Start for Children', in which it set out its long-term vision and identified several key targets: first, that every child would get the best start in life, second, that parents would be given more choices regarding how to balance work and family life, and third, that the equal participation of both mothers and fathers in bringing up their children would be facilitated.[155]

As McColgan has argued, New Labour's approach to embedding care commitments within the employment law framework was clearly representative of a commitment to supporting working families.[156] However, that the underlying rationale was rooted in a neoliberal agenda which conceptualised the family as first and foremost an economic unit is evidenced by the lack of clear policy aimed at improving women's equality within workplaces or facilitating fathers' engagement in unpaid care within the family.[157] As Fredman highlights, the driving force for the reforms was undoubtedly the view that the provision of employment rights facilitates productive and committed workers by alleviating, rather than creating, burdens for businesses.[158]

Success in achieving the interrelated goals of gender equality and the elimination of child poverty will depend on improving the quality of women's paid

---

[152] See the United Nations Convention on the Rights of the Child, ratified by the UK in 1992: Art 27 places an obligation on government to guarantee a child an adequate standard of living, and Art 4 places a duty upon the government to ensure a child's economic rights.

[153] Responsibility for children's social services was transferred from the Department of Health to the Department for Education and Skills (DfES) along with the Family Policy Unit, which was previously under the control of the Home Office. The DfES was also given responsibility for family law policy, previously the domain of the Lord Chancellor's Department.

[154] Which consolidated different sources of welfare support for children, previously provided through income support, jobseeker's allowance, working families' tax credit; disabled person's tax credit and the children's tax credit.

[155] For a critique of New Labour's WFB policy, see ch 3, this volume.

[156] A McColgan, 'Family Friendly Frolics? The Maternity and Parental Leave etc Regulations 1999' (2000) 29 *Industrial Law Journal* 2, 125.

[157] The same argument can be applied to the law and policy trajectory of the EU over the past 30 years – see N Busby and G James, 'Regulating Working Families in the European Union: A History of Disjointed Strategies' (2015) 37 *Journal of Social Welfare and Family Law* 3, 295; N Busby, 'The Evolution of Gender Equality and Related Employment Policies: The Case of Work–Family Reconciliation' (2018) 18 *International Journal of Discrimination and the Law* 2-3, 104.

[158] S Fredman, 'Women at Work: The Broken Promise of Flexicurity' (2004) 33 *Industrial Law Journal*, 299.

work and increased state provision of childcare and other services that enable the balancing of care and paid work. Both of these objectives were placed firmly on the political agenda by the New Labour government, albeit with varying degrees of commitment and success. Through a dual process of 'defamilisation' and 'refamilisation' of care, state policies were proffered as a means of increasing women's labour market participation by, on the one hand, moving care away from families to facilitate maternal employment and, on the other, by providing parental leave schemes and other family-based employment rights aimed at enhancing the ability of working parents to provide care for their children. However, the effective consolidation of these two policy strands relies to a large extent on the de-gendering of care so that it is not seen as the exclusive preserve of women but as an ineluctable consequence of the human condition for which everyone is responsible. Beyond the promotion of largely rhetorical ideals such as 'new fatherhood' and the utilisation of gender-neutral language, this crucial element was not identified as a specific policy goal and so was largely absent from the overall framework (see further chapter three).

The individualised nature of New Labour's WFB policies and their operation through rights-based litigation[159] appear somewhat incongruous if care is placed in its wider context as an activity whose successful exercise is largely dependent on notions of solidarity and collectivism. In its reliance on the individualised approach, the framework is rationalised, not by the need to recognise and value caregiving in its own right, but rather by the right of an individual woman to have the same labour market experience as a man regardless of her care responsibilities. Whilst New Labour policy's recognition that care responsibilities should be acknowledged within the employment law framework represented an important step forward, the impact was limited due to its failure to challenge the gender coding of care. A further limiting factor, which has endured up until the present day, is the framework's acquiescence to deregulation through its alignment with the narrow concept of employment. By confining the relevant protections to those engaged under employment contracts, the framework excludes those most in need.

VII. Post-2010: Work–Family Balance in an Age of Austerity

Despite changes of government in 2010 and 2015, New Labour's policy trajectory in the current context has sustained up to the present day. Referring to the coalition government of 2010–2015, Hepple observed that, despite a distinctly deregulatory approach to some areas of labour law, there was continuity in 'New Labour's "Third Way"' of regulating for competitiveness and social inclusion, including in the area

---

[159] E Barmes, *Bullying and Behavioural Conflict at Work: The Duality of Individual Rights* (Oxford, Oxford University Press, 2015).

of WFB legislation with a continuation, not just of the previous administration's policy aims, but also of their underpinning ideology.[160] The WFB reforms introduced by New Labour and those of the succeeding Coalition and Conservative governments were thus based on a consistent dual aim to accommodate the (often competing) interests of 'all actors in the employment relationship itself and in the wider social and economic contexts'.[161]

Although the policy rhetoric may have remained broadly the same since the New Labour government of the late 1990s, the political context within which more recent developments have taken shape has changed profoundly since 2010. The programme of swingeing cuts to public services, public sector employment and social security implemented by the Coalition government and continued by subsequent Conservative administrations has been rationalised on the basis of the global economic crisis and national budget deficit but has a deeper ideological grounding in neo-liberal economic theory.[162] The impact was and continues to be keenly felt by women in their role as the primary providers of unpaid care[163] which has been marginalised by policymakers' attempts to rebalance the relationship between paid work and welfare. The public sector equality duty (PSED),[164] by which public authorities are required to assess and monitor the equality impacts of all policies, has failed to deliver on its promise of a proactive approach to the elimination of inequalities.

Spending decisions and related policies enacted over the last decade as part of the drive for austerity have further entrenched gender roles and led to regression in the attainment of substantive equality. Welfare cuts have disproportionately affected women[165] with employment policy and related labour market developments also impacting more directly on women than men.[166] A key focus, not just in the UK but in the wider EU, has been on the push to increase women's labour market participation rates with the prioritisation of paid work over reproductive labour and unpaid care obligations.[167] The introduction of a cap on the maximum amount of benefits (including child tax credit and child benefit) that working age

---

[160] B Hepple, 'Back to the Future: Employment Law under the Coalition Government' (2013) 42 *Industrial Law Journal* 3, 203, 205.

[161] O Golynker (2015), 'Family-friendly Reform of Employment Law in the UK: An Overstretched Flexibility' (2015) 37 *Journal of Social Welfare and Family Law* 3, 378, 382.

[162] Hepple, 'Back to the Future: Employment Law under the Coalition Government', above n 160.

[163] Women's Budget Group (2018), The Impact of Austerity on Women in the UK, https://wbg.org.uk/resources/the-impact-of-austerity-on-women/.

[164] Equality Act 2010, s 149.

[165] J MacLeavy, 'A "New Politics" of Austerity, Workfare and Gender? The UK Coalition Government's Welfare Reform Proposals' (2011) 4 *Cambridge Journal of Regions Economy and Society* 3, 355.

[166] J Rubery and AL Rafferty, 'Women and Recession Revisited' (2013) 27 *Work, Employment and Society* 3, 414.

[167] MacLeavy, 'A "New Politics" of Austerity, Workfare and Gender? The UK Coalition Government's Welfare Reform Proposals', above n 165, 11.

people who are not employed for 16 hours or more a week can receive,[168] and the limit on claims to two children per family has, according to the Department of Work and Pensions' data, led to capping for 120,297 single-claimant women compared with just 13,743 men, the vast majority being mothers of dependent children.[169] The cap and freeze on working age benefits[170] have resulted in an increase in child poverty.[171] The shift away from public-sector employment through increased privatisation[172] and reductions to public services have increased the precariousness of much of the work already being undertaken by those with care responsibilities.[173] Although the increase in the employment rates of mothers has sustained,[174] the precariousness of much of the work undertaken by women is likely to have impacted negatively on fathers' enhanced participation in family care. In 2016 the UK voted marginally in favour of leaving the EU. Its departure in January 2020 is likely to exacerbate this retrenchment of gender roles at the household level: EU law has traditionally prevented deregulation in work–family reconciliation policies and the UK is unlikely to keep pace with improvements to the European framework after the transition period, which ends on 31 December 2020.[175]

VIII. Imagining the Future: Vulnerability Theory and Women's Work

As this chapter has shown, despite half a century of anti-discrimination legislation, the attainment of gender equality through the regulation of work and family

---

[168] Introduced in the October 2010 Spending Review by the coalition government at a rate of £26,000 per year and reduced in 2016 to £20,000 (£23,000 in Greater London); see the Welfare Reform Act 2012, s 96 and the Benefit Cap (Housing Benefit) Regulations 2012.

[169] See www.theguardian.com/society/2019/jan/04/benefit-cap-single-mothers-make-up85percent-of-those-affected-data-shows.

[170] The policy, which was introduced by the Conservative government in 2015, saw a range of benefits frozen for a five-year period due to end in April 2020. Analysis by the Resolution Foundation found that, even after the end of the freeze, its impacts on lower income families will continue, and the social security safety net for working-age families will continue to be eroded relative to earnings and pensions; see www.resolutionfoundation.org/app/uploads/2019/10/Benefits-erosion-spotlight-1.pdf.

[171] The Institute for Fiscal Studies has estimated that 5.1 million children will be living in poverty by 2021/22. See *Living Standards, Poverty and Inequality in the UK: 2016–17 to 2021–2022* (London, IFS, 2017).

[172] For an analysis of the effects of privatisation on equal pay see LJB Hayes, *Stories of Care: A Labour of Law, Gender and Class at Work* (London, Palgrave Macmillan, 2017) 57–64.

[173] Fudge and Owens (eds), *Precarious Work, Women, and the New Economy: The Challenges to Legal Norms*, above n 3.

[174] Reaching an all-time high of 75.1 per cent in June 2019: Office for National Statistics, *Families and the Labour Market, UK* (2019), available at www.ons.gov.uk/employmentandlabourmarket/peopleinwork/employmentandemployeetypes/articles/familiesandthelabourmarketengland/2019.

[175] See N Busby, 'The Evolution of Gender Equality and Related Employment Policies: The Case of Work–Family Reconciliation', above n 157.

reconciliation has never been a policy priority per se. On the contrary, social and economic policy has continued to be premised on often-outdated notions of 'the family' rather than the lived experiences and aspirations of households and their individual members. The law and policy framework's reliance on the stereotypical standard worker model has resulted in the othering of those who are unable to comply with the, often unattainable, 'norms' that the model represents. Although much of the rhetoric surrounding the framework's development appears to recognise that the male breadwinner/female carer model is no longer an appropriate target, the practice and operation of the provisions themselves and their collective impact too often re-entrench such gendered divisions and thus reaffirm the valorisation of productive labour and the undervaluing of reproductive labour. As a result, the institutions which regulate the world of paid work and the relationships on which that regulation is based replicate and reproduce existing inequalities rather than challenging and overcoming them. As an historical analysis demonstrates, women's necessary engagement in both paid work and unpaid care has in different contexts and at different times resulted in the exercise of state control and coercion, limiting individual choice and restricting personal freedom.

Fineman's vulnerability approach with its focus on the universality of vulnerability as 'the characteristic that positions us in relation to each other as human beings'[176] has much to offer in the current context. Its recognition that, although all humans 'stand in a position of constant vulnerability, we are individually positioned differently' underpins the importance of maintaining and improving the current protections offered by sex equality laws which provide the 'means to address and confront misfortune' enabling individual women and the relevant institutions associated with work to build the resilience necessary to overcome disadvantage. However, vulnerability theory also offers a radical challenge to the status quo. Given the continued gender coding of care within legal and policy frameworks and the negative effects of this on women's paid work experiences with no compensatory or mitigating impact on the disproportionate burden borne in relation to unpaid care, this alternative has an undoubtedly transformative capacity.

Replacement of the 'liberal subject', autonomous, independent and represented in the current context as the standard worker, with the 'vulnerable subject'[177] as the focus and target of law and policy has the potential to open up the regulatory space, enabling the inclusion of all forms of labour, productive and reproductive. Turning her attention to vulnerability theory's application to labour market

---

[176] MA Fineman, 'Equality, Autonomy, and the Vulnerable Subject in Law and Politics' in MA Fineman and A Grear (eds), *Vulnerability: Reflections on a New Ethical Foundation for Law and Politics* (London, Routledge, 2014) 9.

[177] MA Fineman, 'The Vulnerable Subject: Anchoring Equality in the Human Condition', above n 7.

regulation,[178] Fineman rejects the notion of a 'free market' as a naturally occurring phenomena and argues that the necessity of law's involvement,

> substantially undermines the prevalent notion that conditions of work and the nature of the employment relationship are predominantly private matters to be negotiated and bargained for by relatively unfettered individuals within an open and free labor market.[179]

In absorbing societal rules and values, 'law typically enfolds social and legal power and privilege within the identities [of employer and employee], affecting not only the options and aspirations of each individual, but the wellbeing of society as a whole'.[180] The atomisation of a negotiated transaction culminating in the employment contract detracts from law's important contribution in this context, obscuring the role of the state and minimising society's interest in the terms and conditions under which all work is performed, and in their consequences. As an alternative, Fineman posits that such arrangements should form 'an integral part' of a broader social contract with its regulation taking place 'within the confines of the assumptions, beliefs, norms, and values governing society as a whole'.[181] As well as positioning the labour for wages exchange in its wider socio-economic context, this approach recognises law's social value and reconstitutes its important public interest function as a means of achieving democratic accountability.

Jonathan Fineman cites vulnerability theory's use in exploring the inherent power imbalance in the employment relationship. By contextualising the individual within a network of institutional arrangements,[182] consideration can be given to the 'the ways in which privilege or advantage can be conferred through institutional operation and law'[183] exposing the need for more than individualised claims of discrimination. This is not to say that established identities or 'protected characteristics' and the targeting of antidiscrimination provisions should or would be replaced by the alternative offered by the vulnerability approach. Rather, that impermissible bias and discrimination based on an individual's difference from a standard normative model would continue to be addressed by law and policy supplemented or complemented by what vulnerability theory has to offer.[184] The recognition of personal difference, and the effect that this has on an individual's ability to build resilience, is in fact critical to a vulnerability approach. Solidarity,

---

[178] MA Fineman, 'Introducing Vulnerability' in MA Fineman and J Fineman (eds), *Vulnerability and the Legal Organization of Work* (London, Routledge, 2017), 1.

[179] ibid, 1.

[180] ibid, 1.

[181] ibid, 2.

[182] J Fineman, 'The Vulnerable Subject at Work: A New Perspective on the Employment At-Will Debate' (2013) 43 *Southwestern Law Review* 275.

[183] ibid, 303.

[184] MA Fineman, 'Equality and Difference – The Restrained State' (2015) 66 *Alabama Law Review* 3, 609, 618.

inspired and catalysed by exclusion on the grounds of individual difference, can in and of itself be a source of resilience through 'community building and political action'.[185] However, unlike traditional anti-discrimination approaches which rely on comparisons between a standard subject and by definition a non-standard other, a vulnerability approach has the capacity to recognise that difference can occur not just on the grounds of personal characteristic but also by the mere fact of being differently situated. This is recognised in the distinction between those differences that arise 'because we are embodied beings and those that arise because we are social beings embedded in social relationships'.[186]

Embodied differences include the obvious biological distinctions between women and men, those that arise through development stages or events such as infancy and ageing as well as differences that are produced through social relations and conventions and which remain socially or politically significant, including gender.[187] Discrimination arising through such embodied difference has tradition-ally taken the form of subordination or exclusion with the relevant characteristic seen as a sign of 'inadequacy, inferiority, or weakness'[188] or, in the case of infancy and old age, 'the imposition of a form of "paternalistic" discrimination based on a lack of capacity and capability'.[189] If the story of women's relationship with work – both paid and unpaid – is considered in its historical context, it is easy to recognise the categorisation or othering that has occurred and which has conspired to keep women out of, or to marginalise women's presence in, traditional male domains. However, not all existing inequality can be attributed to conscious discriminatory behaviour which has its roots in biological difference or associated social relations and practices. Alongside such differences are those related to specific charac-teristics or capabilities, equally embodied, but which have become the bases for social categories with institutional and political significance. Rather than being associated with biological or developmental distinctions and thus universal in nature, these differences are socially imposed.[190] Fineman's notion of 'deriva-tive dependency' is used to describe the privatisation of inevitable dependency within the family which occurs on the part of those who provide care.[191] Derivative dependency has taken a specifically gendered form through its assignation to women in their roles as wives, mothers and daughters. It is this area that requires further exploration in the quest to identify a potential solution to the unsolved conflict between paid work and unpaid care and which will provide the focus for chapter three.

---

[185] ibid.
[186] ibid.
[187] ibid, 619.
[188] ibid, 619.
[189] ibid.
[190] ibid.
[191] MA Fineman, 'The Neutered Mother' (1992) 46 *University of Miami Law Review* 653, 661; MA Fineman, *The Autonomy Myth: A Theory of Dependency* (New York, New Press, 2004) 34–37.

IX. Conclusions

As this chapter has demonstrated, women's relationship with paid work is deeply intertwined with their performance of care. Although many women continue to engage in both activities throughout the life course, the economic independence of such worker-carers is deeply compromised through the interaction of a range of social institutions and practices. Their need for state resources where a supportive family structure is absent or unable to provide adequate support is highly likely, yet such reliance continues to be discouraged and, at times, actively vilified. This form of dependence is, thus, a cause of inequality which is grounded in stereotypes and discriminatory beliefs. Thus, although the performance of care alongside paid work certainly does result in discrimination, the reasons for the unfavourable treatment are no longer based on the sex of the carer but on the function and performance of care itself. Such treatment cannot be satisfactorily addressed using existing anti-discrimination laws.[192]

A vulnerability analysis shows how the disadvantages caused by participation in care have become detached from the personal characteristics of the individual performing it, largely through the operation of anti-discrimination law itself and its blindness to how groups, and their members, may be differently situated as well as differently constituted. The performance of care is gender-neutral so that men who perform it will also be subject to the economic and professional disadvantages suffered by women, and yet its continuing gender coding means that it is predominantly women who undertake it and who thus suffer such disadvantage. The social processes in which we all engage throughout our lives position us differently 'within webs of economic, social, cultural, and institutional relationships that profoundly affect our individual destinies and fortunes'.[193] Vulnerability theory's focus on such 'embedded differences'[194] enables consideration of how, as the analysis in this chapter has shown, those institutions and relationships are profoundly gendered. This highlights how, rather than being outside of the norms of social and economic behaviour, dependency and caregiving are inevitable constituents of the human experience. In the next chapter the gendering of care is further explored through an historical analysis of how the law and policy framework has shaped women's and men's respective roles as mothers and fathers.

---

[192] Fineman, 'Equality and Difference – The Restrained State', above n 184, 621.
[193] ibid, 622.
[194] ibid.

3

Mothers and Fathers

I. Introduction

As chapter two has shown, women have always engaged in paid work within and outside of the home, often alongside care responsibilities. Public policy has, at times, encouraged and facilitated women's labour market engagement and, at other times, constrained it depending on wider economic and social conditions. Women's paid work and unpaid care are inextricably linked to such an extent that, whether a woman is a mother or not, her career path may well have been shaped by perceptions of maternalism and motherhood.[1] In the case of an individual woman, such perceptions may be linked to assumptions about the likelihood that she might have children at some stage, or they may result from more general stereotypical ideas about women's apparent propensity to provide care and to engage in related domestic work which shape and influence the type of paid work that large numbers of women undertake. The story of how law and policy have shaped and influenced fathers' ability to undertake the care of their children alongside paid work is very different, with little state involvement beyond a relatively recent and largely rhetorical turn to notions of 'shared parenting'. However, like mothers' paid work experiences, fathers' engagement with unpaid care is deeply entrenched in gendered expectations – both personal and societal.[2] State influence on the normative expectations surrounding working families may not appear to encroach on the personal choices that men make regarding how to fulfil their role as fathers. However, it is this non-engagement alongside the inherent instrumentalisation of women's work and family lives through public policy which, combined, have had and continue to have a profound effect on the lived experiences of both women and men at the household and workplace levels.[3]

This chapter will explore the development and provision of law and policies which are intended to enable mothers and fathers to combine care responsibilities

---

[1] S Fredman, *Women and The Law* (Oxford, Oxford University Press, 1997) chs 3 and 4.

[2] T Miller, 'Falling Back into Gender? Men's Narratives and Practices around First-time Fatherhood (2011) 45 *Sociology* 6, 1094; T Miller, *Making Sense of Fatherhood: Gender, Caring and Work* (Cambridge, Cambridge University Press, 2011).

[3] G James, 'Mothers and Fathers as Parents and Workers: Family Friendly Employment Policies in an Era of Shifting Identities' (2009) 31 *Journal of Social Welfare and Family Law* 3, 271.

with paid work, including maternity, paternity and parental workplace and ancillary rights, such as the right to request flexible working. The resulting work–family balance (WFB) framework, often referred to by policymakers as 'reconciliation' or 'work–life balance' policy, is complex and this chapter is not intended to provide an authoritative statement of the current law but rather to explore its development and the nature and extent of its protection and, in doing so, to identify its rationale and underlying ideology. The overall purpose is to interrogate how the resulting UK law and policy framework has shaped, or been shaped by, the lived experiences of mothers and fathers. As chapter two has shown, the division of labour at the household or family level is profoundly gendered and the allocation of responsibility for care has multiple discernible impacts on the workplace experiences of women. However, men in their capacity as social beings are also affected if they are not able to participate in caregiving either because of institutional barriers or social and personal perceptions of masculinity and of what it means to be a good father.[4] As chapter two has shown, the anti-discrimination approach will not necessarily offer the same opportunities for legal redress to men as it does to women in respect of their care responsibilities.[5] The allocation of caregiving to women, beyond the very early stages of a child's life, is not biologically determined but arises through the gender-coding of social activity. As this chapter demonstrates, this coding is reaffirmed and further entrenched by and within the WFB framework itself. The chapter's central argument is that the shifting identities of mothers and fathers, as evidenced by empirical accounts of lived experience within households and workplaces, and the dominant ideologies on which WFB policy is premised and the way in which its provisions operate and interact, are not compatible. Men's greater engagement with unpaid care will not happen without policy intervention which is required to go beyond the rhetorical if it is to be truly effective.

The chapter is structured as follows. In section II, the context within which the UK's reconciliation policy has developed is explored through its historical roots and the origins of state intervention. This can be tracked through the state's withdrawal of nursery provision in the post-war era (see also chapter two) and its promotion of the role of the housewife during the 1950s. As this analysis shows, despite the ideological assumptions underpinning state policy during the post-war reconstruction which located women's place firmly in the home, mothers' employment rates continued to rise heeding the impending challenges to the gender order that would emerge in the 1960s. Nonetheless, men's contribution to their families remained firmly entrenched in their role as breadwinner, a position that

---

[4] R Collier, "'Feminising" the Workplace? Law, the "Good Parent" and the "Problem of Men"' in A Morris and T O'Donnell (eds), *Feminist Perspectives on Employment Law* (London, Cavendish Publishing, 1999) 187; R Collier, 'A Hard Time to be a Father?: Reassessing the Relationship between Law, Policy, and Family (Practices)' (2001) 28 *Journal of Law and Society* 4, 520.

[5] See S Fredman, 'Reversing Roles: Bringing Men into the Frame (2014) 10 *International Journal of Law in Context* 4, 442, 451–53.

was reaffirmed by and reflected in the pervasive industrial relations system of the day. In section III, the emergence of a reconciliation framework is considered from its early beginnings within the employment protection provisions introduced in the 1970s, through to the EU's intervention by way of the Pregnant Workers Directive in 1992. Recognition of the need to accommodate parental responsibility within workplaces was further developed under the New Labour government in the late 1990s as explored in section IV. As this analysis reveals, despite the language of shared parenting within the policy rhetoric surrounding the move towards 'family-friendly' policy, this shift did not result in any significant change in care arrangements at the household level. In section V, our consideration of the current framework reveals a range of substantial flaws and weaknesses which are both caused and reaffirmed by the dominant and outdated ideologies relating to motherhood and fatherhood which continue to underscore policy provision and development in this area. Section VI comprises our call for change consisting of an alternative approach to dependency and care. The chapter concludes by reiterating the suitability of a vulnerability approach in this area, specifically through its ability to assist in the disengagement of care from gender as a means of deconstructing the relevant relationships and institutions and advancing social justice. This would require a new framework which places caregiving at the centre of a range of related social and economic policies incorporating social security and taxation as well as family and labour law.[6] The silos and demarcations that characterise the law's current operation mitigate against such a care-centred approach so that, without radical change, progress is unlikely.

II. Contextualising Reconciliation Policy

Policies aimed at reconciling the demands of home/personal and work/professional life are a relatively new addition to the labour law framework. UK law's intervention in this area has its roots in the expansion of maternity rights in the 1990s which came about through its implementation of the EU's Pregnant Workers Directive,[7] discussed further below. The European approach to family formation and the related needs of workers[8] differs substantially from UK law's traditional approach to such matters, which was that pregnancy and maternity,

---

[6] See N Busby, 'Labour Law, Family Law and Care: A Plea for Convergence' in J Herring and J Wallbank (eds), *Vulnerabilities, Care and Family Law* (Oxford, Routledge, 2014) 181.

[7] Directive 92/85/EEC on the introduction of measures to encourage improvements in the safety and health at work of pregnant workers and workers who have recently given birth or are breastfeeding.

[8] Which forms part of a broader and long-standing conception of the working environment and the need to protect the health and safety of workers as exemplified by Art 3 of the 1961 version of the European Social Charter, which set out a right to safe and healthy working conditions and, more recently, Art 31(1) of the EU Charter of Fundamental Rights, which provides that 'Every worker has the right to working conditions which respect his or her health, safety and dignity'.

never mind the longer-term provision of care, were simply 'incompatible with continued participation in the formal, paid workforce'.[9]

The Factory and Workshop Act 1891, the first UK labour law statute to acknowledge childbirth, prohibited the employment of women in factories and workshops within four weeks of giving birth.[10] Marriage bars, which operated during the inter-war period to automatically dismiss women from some public sector jobs upon marriage, were upheld by the courts long after their legality was statutorily supported.[11] Even the advent of the Welfare State did not herald a new dawn of work-related rights for carers which were clearly not part of Beveridge's vision. On the contrary, he 'envisaged welfare rights as playing a central role in encouraging women to remain at home as full-time mothers'.[12] This view was reflected in the National Insurance Act 1946 which, whilst providing a maternity grant intended for non-medical expenses, also provided that women could be ineligible if they undertook paid work during the period of maternity payment or if they failed 'without good cause to observe any prescribed rules of behaviour'.[13]

A. Class Divisions in 1940s Nursery Provision

As chapter two has shown, most mothers' ability to work outside of the home during and following the Second World War was wholly dependent on the state's provision of childcare which had expanded in the war years only to be swiftly reduced at the advent of peace. In her consideration of the approach taken to publicly provided childcare by key policy actors, Riley shows how such decision making was shaped by contemporary ideology regarding women's position in society as well as by paternalistic notions of what was best for children.[14] Nonetheless, the state's attitude to day nurseries was somewhat contradictory: whilst the Ministry of Health recognised their positive benefits for mothers and children, in those areas where industry no longer needed women workers, the nurseries were deemed to constitute an unjustifiable expense. The government was thus compelled to blame the post-war closures on a lack of demand, which really referred to industrial contingencies, implicitly confirming the nurseries' beneficial effects.[15] Most importantly, however, the closure of the nurseries and the focus on maternalism which followed was supported almost unanimously by groups and

---

[9] Fredman, *Women and The Law*, above n 1, 181.

[10] Factory and Workshops Act 1891, s 17.

[11] See *Price v Rhondda UDC* [1923] 2 Ch 372, in which women teachers whose employment had been terminated on the grounds of the marriage bar sued Rhondda Urban District Council, arguing that the Sex Disqualification (Removal) Act made such dismissals illegal. The court upheld the dismissals, ruling that the Act merely provided that marriage did not disqualify women from employment, but did not mean that married women were necessarily entitled to employment.

[12] Fredman, *Women and The Law*, above n 1, 182.

[13] National Insurance Act 1946, s 14(3); see further Fredman, *Women and The Law*, above n 1, 182.

[14] D Riley, *War in the Nursery: Theories of the Child and Mother* (London, Virago, 1983).

[15] ibid, 119.

politicians from across the political spectrum. Women's groups shared the enthusiasm for the new ideology of motherhood which emerged in the context of a nationwide concern for social stability and restoration of the birth rate.

In the Commons adjournment motion on nurseries in March 1945[16] pro-nursery MPs argued that continued provision would, inter alia, provide educational value for the mothers of the future through the teaching of 'mothercraft' to schoolgirls in the nursery setting. Labour members stressed the importance of achieving class parity in access to childcare. MPs from both the Conservative and Labour parties argued that nursery provision would broaden the appeal of parenthood and thus assist in halting the declining birth rate.[17] Furthermore, it was argued that marital disharmony and divorce might be avoided through the use of nursery provision to alleviate the post-war housing emergency. As Hector McNeil (Labour Party MP for Greenock) explained,

> Take the case of a young couple who dance together and go to the pictures together … They live in a room in a sub-let house, and then, most properly, along comes an infant, and the girl is tied there night and day. The husband will not, and cannot, sit with her all the time and their companionship is destroyed. He goes off to pubs or politics – one is as bad as the other if it splits the home. The provision of day nurseries to meet that kind of condition is, I am inclined to argue, essential until such time as we have reasonable homes, with the development of trained homeminders.[18]

The government's response was given by Florence Horsbrugh, Parliamentary Under-Secretary for the Ministry of Health, who argued that the proposal to shut half of the wartime nurseries was motivated purely by a lack of demand, offering 'facts and figures about several war-time nurseries where there is the staff, but where there are very few clients, if one might use that term',[19] and where numbers had dwindled in some cases to 'two, three, four or five children only, and where in a great many cases, the mothers of those children are not on war work'.[20] In concluding her remarks, Ms Horsbrugh noted that ''no local authority which has asked to keep a nursery open has been turned down'.[21]

Following the war, the distinction in state provision between nursery education, based on the needs of the child, and day nurseries which provided childcare determined by the needs of the mother, was retained. A 1945 Ministry of Health circular to local authorities provided

> that under normal peace-time conditions, the right policy to pursue would be positively to discourage mothers of children under two from going out to work; to make provision for children between two and five by way of nursery schools and nursery classes;

---

[16] Hansard, HC Deb 9 March 1945, vol 408 cols 2425–50, available at https://hansard.parliament.uk/Commons/1945-03-08/debates/e55d8aec-4839-4985-8912 84aafbbdd7dc/CommonsChamber.

[17] D Riley, 'War in the Nursery' (1979) 2 *Feminist Review* 82, 91.

[18] Hansard, above n 16, 2428.

[19] Hansard, above n 16, 2443.

[20] Hansard, above n 16, 2443.

[21] Hansard, above n 16, 2450.

and to regard day nurseries and daily guardians [childminders] as supplements to meet the special needs ... of children whose mothers are constrained by individual circumstances to go out to work, or whose home conditions are in themselves unsatisfactory from the health point of view; or whose mothers are incapable for some good reasons of undertaking the full care of their children.[22]

Thus a line was clearly drawn between mothers who had to work and those who chose to do so.[23] However, as Lewis has observed, the relevant provision of the Education Act 1944[24] was not clear on what local authorities were expected to provide,[25] and referred merely to them having 'regard to the need for securing that provision is made for pupils who have not attained the age of five years by the provision of nursery schools or ... by the provision of nursery classes in other schools'. Although this fell somewhat short of a 'duty' to provide early years education, 'the archival records make it clear that throughout the 1960s and 1970s civil servants felt that the intention of the 1944 legislation had been to expand nursery education as and when possible'.[26] This resulted in wide diversity across different authorities, with greater provision offered in cities, notably London, than elsewhere.[27] Despite the lack of clarity regarding how best to replace the state-run nurseries that had enabled mothers' wartime employment, a shift in thinking regarding the state's responsibility to provide care for pre-school children had occurred. This development should not be overstated – the indecisiveness and ambivalence that characterised the early days of UK childcare policy remained for several decades. In addition, mothers' engagement in paid work was delineated along class lines and depending on family circumstances: the middle classes were free to choose whether to work while their children (aged two and above) enjoyed the privileges bestowed by a nursery education, whilst those facing more difficult circumstances were compelled to do so by placing their children in non-educational day nurseries whose priority was health and hygiene. The lack of clarity in policy provision thus underscored public opinion concerning the gendered order, reaffirming notions of maternalism and leaving the male breadwinner/female carer model largely undisturbed.

B. Home and Hearth: The 1950s Housewife

Contemporary accounts of social life in late 1940s and early 1950s Britain record a rise in status for women in their role as homemakers or housewives, attributable

---

[22] The National Archives, 'Nursery Provision for Children Under Five', ED 142/56, Circular 221/45, 14 December 1945.

[23] J Lewis, 'The Failure to Expand Childcare Provision and to Develop a Comprehensive Childcare Policy in Britain during the 1960s and 1970s' (2013) 24 *Twentieth Century British History* 2, 249, 253.

[24] s 8(2).

[25] Lewis, 'The Failure to Expand Childcare Provision and to Develop a Comprehensive Childcare Policy in Britain during the 1960s and 1970s', above n 23, 253.

[26] ibid, 253.

[27] ibid.

in part to the significant contribution women had made to the war effort and their ongoing commitment to post-war reconstruction.[28] The Beveridge Report underscored the high regard in which housewives and mothers were now held through their reproductive role in its proclamation that 'in the next thirty years housewives, as mothers, have vital work to do in ensuring the adequate continuance of the British race and of British ideals in the world'.[29] The idea that women's main social contribution was through their role as mothers found support in the highly influential 1951 World Health Organisation report authored by psychoanalyst John Bowlby,[30] in which it was claimed that a child's normal psychological development was dependent on the continuous presence of his or her mother during the early years. Although the report did not directly address the issue of mothers working outside the home, Bowlby's ideas did inform government policy on pre-school childcare and influenced a wider climate of censure towards working mothers with young children.[31] Social norms meant that the government, the general public, and groups representing women's interests including housewives' associations still believed that mothers with children under five should continue to care for them on a full-time basis at home.[32] However, for increasing numbers of married women with older children, combining motherhood and paid work was becoming more popular.[33] The key motivation for mothers taking up paid work was economic. Many working-class women had to work to augment the family income and, for middle-class mothers, paid work provided greater financial independence and enabled the family to achieve a higher standard of living and to purchase newly available consumer durables.[34]

By the end of the 1950s the fact that an increasingly significant proportion of wives and mothers needed and desired to work outside the home led to a growing social acceptance of this trend. The lack of affordable childcare, particularly around school hours, was highlighted in a survey of working mothers conducted by the National Council of Women with the report's authors calling on local authorities

---

[28] C Beaumont, 'What *Do* Women Want? Housewives' Associations, Activism and Changing Representations of Women in the 1950s' (2017) 26 *Women's History Review* 1, 147.

[29] HM Government, *Social Insurance and Allied Services* (The Beveridge Report), Cmd 6404 (London, HMSO, 1942) 53. See further S Spencer, *Gender, Work and Education in Britain in the 1950s* (Basingstoke, Palgrave Macmillan, 2005) 22–48; C Beaumont, *Housewives and Citizens: Domesticity and the Women's Movement in England, 1928–64* (Manchester, Manchester University Press, 2013) 115–29.

[30] J Bowlby, *Child Care and the Growth of Love* (London, Penguin, 1953) later mass-produced in paperback form for a wider audience.

[31] H McCarthy, 'Women, Marriage and Paid Work in Post-war Britain' (2017) 26 *Women's History Review* 1, 46, 50; see ch 2, this volume.

[32] Beaumont, 'What *Do* Women Want? Housewives' Associations, Activism and Changing Representations of Women in the 1950s', above n 28, 157.

[33] D Smith Wilson, 'A New Look at the Affluent Worker: The Good Working Mother in Post-War Britain' (2006) 17 *Twentieth Century British History* 2, 206.

[34] Beaumont, 'What *Do* Women Want? Housewives' Associations, Activism and Changing Representations of Women in the 1950s', above n 28, 157; Smith Wilson, 'A New Look at the Affluent Worker: The Good Working Mother in Post-War Britain', above n 33.

and employers to do more to help by providing subsidised childcare and allowing mothers to work flexible hours.[35] Whether, and to what extent, this shift in the aspirations and experiences of women and its wider social acceptance influenced a change in gender roles within households is difficult to discern.

McCarthy has shown how changing social and economic circumstances in the post-war era and the resulting changes to women's lives and in the norms and expectations governing relations between husbands and wives gave rise to a dominant academic narrative that '1950s Britain was witnessing a gradual but unmistakable shift away from rigidly segregated and unequal conjugal roles and towards a more egalitarian model in which spouses pulled together as partners making joint decisions and sharing increasingly home-centred lives'.[36] In challenging this vision, McCarthy argues that much of the evidence drawn on by sociologists, psychologists and marriage guidance experts of the day, when read alongside contemporaneous media reports, indicate a far more complex picture.

> Working wives could imperil marital harmony because of the challenge they posed to men's 'traditional' identity as providers and to the legitimacy and modernity of the full-time housewife-worker in the home, a model of more recent vintage rooted in the social-democratic and pro-natalist politics of the 1940s.[37]

Furthermore, women's wages did make a difference: although they may not have provided complete freedom from economic dependency, they did offer 'a small slice of financial autonomy' and, importantly, they increased women's power within marriage.[38]

The idea that married women's renewed relationship with paid employment led to a shift in established gender identities is central to any understanding of law's (non) engagement with household arrangements. Rather than grasping the opportunity presented to reimagine policy provision as a means of enabling carers to manage their 'dual role',[39] supporting women as paid workers and encouraging men to participate in family care, the state maintained a largely non-interventionist stance. Throughout the 1970s, women's needs as earners and carers continued to be subjugated to other policy concerns through a combination of patriarchal dominance and the growing influence of the market. It would be three decades before work and family reconciliation began to emerge as a distinct policy domain. Even at that late juncture, rather than viewed as central in the prioritisation of social policy concerns, the requirements of combining paid work with high levels of care were accommodated through a series of incremental policies that entrenched gendered expectations and preserved the status quo within households and workplaces.

---

[35] Smith Wilson, 'A New Look at the Affluent Worker: The Good Working Mother in Post-War Britain', above n 33, 206–29.

[36] H McCarthy, 'Women, Marriage and Paid Work in Post-war Britain' above n 31, 47.

[37] ibid, 48.

[38] ibid, 48.

[39] ibid, 47.

C. Industrial Relations and Legal Abstentionism

In the regulatory context, alongside the continuing emphasis on contractual relations within workplaces (see chapter two), the dominance of collective laissez-faire[40] also provided a means of obscuring the relationship between unpaid care and paid work. This particular form of collective bargaining, characterised by an absence of state interference, emerged in the aftermath of the Second World War as the centrepiece of the UK's system of industrial relations and also provided the main conceptual lens through which labour law was viewed and analysed. However, the central tenets underpinning the model are problematic if labour law's aim is to ensure an inclusive approach capable of providing protection for all its subjects. The assumptions on which collective laissez-faire are based, including its central premise that voluntary collective bargaining is the best way of safeguarding workers' interests, imply certain presumptions, specifically that collective bargaining is an effective method of representing the interests of all workers which largely coincide.[41] The trade union movement has been shown historically to have overlooked certain types and categories of work and to have failed to advance the interests of those performing and populating it, most notably women.[42] The lack of union coverage and the resulting exclusion of large groups of women workers from collective bargaining, coupled with a lack of legal intervention due to the emphasis placed on voluntarism, was not conducive to improving the prospects and workplace experiences of all workers or, by extension, to exerting any influence over gender relations within households. The assumption that collectivism would provide a 'countervailing force' in the imbalance of power between employer and worker cast the employment protection provisions introduced in the 1970s and 1980s[43] as a 'floor of rights'[44] when, in reality, for many non-unionised (women) workers they represented a ceiling.[45] In the case of male workers, although collective bargaining may have provided a suitable process for determining the nature of their relationships with their employers, it had no role in influencing their

---

[40] In 1954, Otto Kahn-Freund observed that 'there is, perhaps, no major country in the world in which the law has played a less significant role in the shaping of these relations than in Great Britain and in which today the law and the legal profession have less to do with labour relations'. Kahn-Freund, 'Legal Framework' in A Flanders and H Clegg (eds), *The System of Industrial Relations in Great Britain: Its History, Law, and Institutions* (Oxford, Blackwell, 1954) 42, 44.

[41] J Conaghan, 'Feminism and Labour Law: Contesting the Terrain' in A Morris and T O'Donnell (eds), *Feminist Perspectives on Employment Law* (London, Cavendish Publishing, 1999) 13–41, 24.

[42] See S Boston, *Women Workers and the Trade Union Movement* (London, Davis Poynter, 1980); J Wajcman, 'Feminism Facing Industrial Relations in Britain' (2000) 38 *British Journal of Industrial Relations* 2, 183. For an empirical account of low-paid women workers' relationship with the trade union movement in the 1970s, see A Pollert, *Girls, Wives, Factory Lives* (London, Macmillan Press, 1981), especially ch 9. For a contemporary exploration of the relevant issues, see LJB Hayes, *Stories of Care: A Labour of Law, Gender and Class at Work* (London, Palgrave Macmillan, 2017).

[43] Which included, inter alia, the right not to be unfairly dismissed but not the right to return following a period of maternity leave.

[44] L Wedderburn, *The Worker and the Law* (London, Sweet & Maxwell, 1986).

[45] Conaghan, 'Feminism and Labour Law: Contesting the Terrain', above n 41.

presence or engagement in the home. In fact, the model promoted by unions and affirmed by the bargaining process was that of the male breadwinner predicated on the need to protect the family wage,[46] which reinforced the public/private divide and the established gender order.

In its assumptions regarding the household and workplace as discrete autonomous locales independent of each other, collective laissez-faire entrenched the separation of work and family life within the industrial relations system, belying the interconstitutive nature of the relationship between them.[47] As Conaghan notes,

> [t]he spheres of production and reproduction are neither fixed nor separate but constantly changing and interacting. The fundamental dynamics of the workplace – who occupies it and on what terms – are shaped to a large extent by the allocation of power and responsibility within the family. Similarly, the allocation of power at and over work contributes to the maintenance of particular relational structures within the family.[48]

The development and arrival of sex discrimination and equal pay legislation during the 1970s (charted in chapter two), although undeniably important in improving the workplace experiences of women, was limited both in its approach and by the wider labour law context in which it was placed. The decline of collective bargaining and rise of individualised employment rights during the 1980s and 1990s may have changed the nature of industrial relations, but the influence of collective laissez-faire lingers on. Its dominance throughout the second half of the twentieth century through non-intervention in the relevant structural and institutional contexts, non-prioritisation of the specific concerns of women workers and the continuation of an industrial model based on notions of the family wage has led to a lack of recognition among policymakers that targeted, concerted effort would be required to realise the reconciliation of paid work and unpaid care within a labour law framework. Developments, where they did occur, were focused on the need to promote equality of opportunity between the sexes: if women were present in the workplace, then they were entitled to act and be treated in the same way as their male colleagues without discrimination.

Chapter two has highlighted the deficiencies of the UK's anti-discrimination legislation as an effective antidote to the systemic and institutionalised inequality experienced by those required to provide high levels of care alongside paid employment. In its requirement of comparison against a paradigm standard worker model, this approach has the effect of othering those who are unable to comply with it, offering compensatory appeasement for any resulting injustice. This has the effect of institutionalising discriminatory behaviour and preserving current

---

[46] For a consideration of the development of the concept of the family wage and the early 20th-century campaigner Eleanor Rathbone's work in calling for its replacement with a system of family allowance, see H Land, 'The Family Wage' (1980) 6 *Feminist Review* 55.

[47] Conaghan, 'Feminism and Labour Law: Contesting the Terrain', above n 41.

[48] ibid.

practice so that working carers continue to be viewed as the exception rather than the norm within workplaces. Had policy been led by a strong framework of self-standing work-based rights for carers and ancillary state services, discrimination and the gender-coding of care may have been more effectively challenged. However, despite the clear need for such a framework in response to the changing patterns of women's lives and as a means of leading the necessary shift in gender relations within homes and workplaces, law's response has been taciturn.

The political commitment necessary to dislodge the employment contract as the regulatory focal point, to proactively replace the standard worker with a more realistic normative model, or to reorient the existing industrial relations machinery so as to ensure greater inclusivity at the institutional level and real flexibility and choice regarding arrangements at the household level, has not been a feature of post-war public policy. The demise of collective bargaining has underscored contract as the centrifugal point of a regulatory system[49] which has its origins in the poor law and that of master and servant overhung with the remnants of patriarchal legal constructs such as coverture. Constructed alongside such obstinately durable features, those measures intended to enable care's reconciliation with paid work form a patchwork of provisions.[50] This is not to say that attempts have not been made by policymakers to reconcile paid work and unpaid care but, in adopting the same approach as the anti-discrimination provisions, such additions to the legal framework have drawn heavily on the notion that care and dependency are to be accommodated as deviations from the norm rather than mainstreamed as inevitable corollaries of the human condition. In its perpetuation of gender inequality within workplaces, this approach has done little to encourage or facilitate fathers' engagement with unpaid care within families. Attention will now be focused on the development of what has become the UK's current WFB framework.

III. The Emergence of a Reconciliation Framework

When it was introduced in the 1970s, employment protection on the grounds of pregnancy and maternity was patchy, with its development incremental, and extremely restrictive so that many women workers were ineligible. It was concentrated on the short period around the birth, taking a narrow view of the needs of mothers which focused on the medicalisation of childbirth and the importance of maternal bonding with no consideration for the father's presence at this stage in a child's life or for the ongoing nature of care requirements. State-provided

---

[49] M Freedland, *The Personal Employment Contract* (Oxford, Oxford University Press, 2003); M Freedland and N Kountouris, *The Legal Construction of Personal Work Relations and Gender* (Oxford, Oxford University Press, 2011).

[50] N Busby and G James (eds), *Families, Care-giving and Paid Work: Challenging Labour Law in the 21st Century* (Cheltenham, Edward Elgar, 2011).

payment of maternity benefit following birth had been part of the UK's framework since 1973[51] and the right to a period of leave from, and return to, work was introduced in 1975 when the Labour government enacted the Employment Protection Act[52] which provided for up to 29 weeks of leave for each pregnancy. Six weeks of the leave was paid at a rate of nine-tenths of the normal weeks' pay, with the remainder unpaid. Maternity pay was originally provided through a Maternity Pay Fund which employers contributed to and from which they were able to claim a full refund.[53] In 1986 the duty to provide maternity pay shifted from the state to the employer and payment was relabelled Statutory Maternity Pay (SMP).[54] The 1975 Act established a right for the mother to return to work with the original employer 'on terms and conditions not less favourable than those which would have been applicable to her if she had not been so absent'.[55] It became automatically unfair to dismiss an employee on the grounds of pregnancy in 1978.[56] Restrictive qualifying conditions meant that many working women were ineligible for these early maternity rights,[57] with the limited right to pay disenabling many of those who did qualify from taking extended leave beyond the six-week period.

A. The Pregnant Workers Directive

The UK's first foray into universal reconciliation legislation was in its implementation of the EU's Pregnant Workers Directive 1992.[58] As reflected in its legal base,[59] the Directive had its roots in the health and safety provisions of European law alongside the need to encourage equal treatment in the workplace. The stated aim of the Directive was to 'encourage improvements in the safety and health of workers'[60] coupled with the 'further harmonisation of conditions in this area'.[61] The Preamble identified pregnant workers and workers who have

---

[51] Social Security Act 1973, s 16 provided for payment at a statutory rate for an 18-week period commencing up to 11 weeks prior to the expected date of birth.

[52] In the same year as the Sex Discrimination Act 1975 and the Equal Pay Act 1970 were enacted.

[53] Fredman, *Women and The Law*, above n 1, 224.

[54] Social Security Act 1986.

[55] Employment Protection Act 1975, s 35.

[56] Employment Protection Act 1978.

[57] Under employment protection legislation, in order to qualify a woman had to have been in continuous employment with the same employer for two years for more than 16 hours per week, or for five years for 8–16 hours per week. The 8- and 16-hour thresholds were abolished in 1995 following the House of Lords judgment in *R v Secretary of State for Employment ex parte Equal Opportunities Commission* [1994] IRLR 176. See ch 2, this volume.

[58] Directive 92/85/EEC.

[59] Art 118a of the Treaty of Rome, which was concerned with the harmonisation of working conditions in the health and safety context.

[60] Preamble, taken from Framework Directive 89/391/EEC of 12 June 1989, OJ L 183, 29.6.1989, 1.

[61] Preamble, taken from the Community Charter of the Fundamental Social Rights of Workers 1989, para 19.

recently given birth or who are breastfeeding as a 'specific risk group in many respects' and referred to their 'vulnerability' as the basis for the provision of a continuous period of maternity leave. Article 8 provided for a period of at least 14 weeks' leave, subject to a 2-week period of compulsory leave, to be allocated before or after childbirth in accordance with national practice. Article 10 expressly prohibited the dismissal of the pregnant worker, save in exceptional circumstances not connected with her condition. The right to receive payment and/or entitlement to an 'adequate allowance' while on maternity leave was provided by Article 11(2)(b). Article 11(3) provided that the amount of this allowance 'shall be deemed adequate if it guarantees income at least equivalent to that which the worker concerned would receive in the event of a break in her activities on grounds connected with her state of health'. Article 1(3) prohibited any reduction in existing standards of protection within Member States, thus rendering any attempts at 'levelling down' untenable.

A comparison of the prior provision in EU Member States and the extent of the measures used to implement the Directive beyond the minimum standards imposed found that the UK was notable for its relative lack of support for working mothers.[62] Until the extension of maternity leave to 18 weeks by the New Labour government in 1999 (see below),[63] the UK's implementation of Directive 92/85/EC was by compliance with the minimum standards possible.[64] Under Lewis's categorisation of welfare states, the UK presented as a 'strong male breadwinner' state,[65] evidenced by the lack of cohesion between the development of policies concerned with employment and parenting through the maintenance of strong divisions between what were deemed to be private and public responsibilities.[66] The provision of formal childcare was largely a matter of private arrangement with the progress of state provision blighted by 'fragmentation of the policy process'.[67]

---

[62] N Busby, 'Divisions of Labour: Maternity Protection in Europe' (2000) 22 *The Journal of Social Welfare & Family Law* 3, 277.

[63] By the Maternity and Parental Leave, etc Regulations 1999 enacted under the Employment Relations Act 1999. Maternity leave was extended to 18 weeks by Regulations 4 and 7 for all employees and Regulation 5 provided a right to extended maternity leave for all those employed for at least one year 11 weeks before the expected date of birth. This was part of a package of measures intended to remove obstacles to mothers' participation in paid work, see Department of Trade and Industry, Fairness at Work (Cm 3968, 1998) 5.1. For critiques of New Labour's reconciliation policies, see Conaghan, 'Feminism and Labour Law: Contesting the Terrain', above n 41, 38; A McColgan, 'Family Friendly Frolics? The Maternity and Parental Leave etc Regulations 1999' (2000) 29 *Industrial Law Journal* 2, 125.

[64] Busby, 'Divisions of Labour: Maternity Protection in Europe', above n 62, 288. For a comprehensive exploration of the UK's regulatory approach to pregnancy and parenting in the workplace and its various shortcomings, see G James, *The Legal Regulation of Pregnancy and Parenting in the Labour Market* (London, Routledge, 2009).

[65] J Lewis, 'Gender and the Development of Welfare Regimes' (1992) 2 *Journal of European Social Policy* 3, 159.

[66] Busby, 'Divisions of Labour: Maternity Protection in Europe', above n 62, 288.

[67] V Randall, 'The Politics of Childcare Policy' in J Lovenduski and P Norris (eds), *Women in Politics* (Oxford, Oxford University Press, 1996).

B. Towards a 'Family-Friendly' Approach

In the domestic context, reconciliation became a policy domain in its own right by virtue of New Labour's focus on 'family-friendly' policy in its 1998 White Paper 'Fairness at Work'.[68] Although the language of 'work–life balance' and 'work-family reconciliation' now seems very familiar, the idea that an individual's home life might be formally recognised as a relevant aspect of workplace regulation was a progressive and, for some, radical idea. This is not to say that sex, or more specifically gender, has not always played a pivotal, albeit implicit, role in the regulation of paid work's organisation and performance. The system of industrial relations in the UK and the means by which individual relationships have traditionally been regulated are deeply embedded in the traditional division of labour within households. Such divisions – between the public and private realms of paid work and unpaid care and between productive and reproductive labour – persist in both normative and empirical terms. As a result, progress in the field of reconciliation has been patchy, with a focus on business needs and the facilitation of a flexible labour market rather than on the needs of working parents. The ideological shift that was instigated by New Labour, ostensibly away from motherhood and maternity and towards shared parenting and 'new fatherhood',[69] has been sustained by successive governments. However, the political rhetoric has not necessarily been matched by a substantive law and policy approach capable of bringing about or supporting a shift in men's behaviour or in workplace culture so that, in practice, much of the legal framework itself and the ways in which it interacts with related policy remains profoundly gendered.

Dominant ideologies relating to both motherhood and fatherhood have been identified as features of both the EU and UK frameworks with the effect that even law and policy specifically intended to assist in the reconciliation of paid work and unpaid care can be shown to perpetuate gendered behaviour due to its ideological framing and practical operation.[70] Before exploring the relationship between ideology and policy further, this chapter will consider the UK's WFB framework (referred to as 'reconciliation' or 'work–life balance' policy) instigated by the New Labour governments between 1997 and 2010. As this analysis shows, the rationale and reasoning underpinning the framework has developed in a piecemeal fashion with its roots firmly embedded in the social and economic arrangements which developed around a fledgling market economy almost three centuries ago. Despite

---

[68] Department of Trade and Industry, Fairness at Work (Cm 3968, 1998).

[69] A Gregory and S Milner, 'What is "New" about Fatherhood? The Social Construction of Fatherhood in France and the UK' (2011) 14 *Men and Masculinities* 5, 588.

[70] C McGlynn, 'Ideologies of Motherhood in European Community Sex Equality Law' (2000) 6 *European Law Journal* 1, 29; James, *The Legal Regulation of Pregnancy and Parenting in the Labour Market*, above n 64; E Caracciolo di Torella, 'Brave New Fathers for a Brave New World? Fathers as Caregivers in an Evolving European Union' (2014) 20 *European Law Journal* 1, 88; N Busby and M Weldon-Johns, 'Fathers as Carers in UK Law and Policy: Dominant Ideologies and Lived Experience' (2019) 41 *Journal of Social Welfare and Family Law* 3, 280.

the subsequent plethora of law and policy development that has taken place in line with social and economic progress, the lack of any clear reconsideration of the underlying premises and rationale has resulted in a framework which lacks a cohesive vision and overarching ideological approach.

IV. New Labour: Continuity and Change

By the 1990s, the demise of the normative male breadwinner/female caregiver family model[71] had been preceded by a number of interrelated factors including increased globalisation and the rise of precarious working relations.[72] The bonds of mutual trust, for long heralded as the cornerstone of the employment contract, had been eroded[73] so that workers were increasingly required to be adaptable and to work more flexibly.[74] Alongside these structural factors, individual aspiration and self-actualisation had grown in prominence so that changes in working patterns and arrangements were increasingly reflective of, and in part driven by, changes in the behaviour, expectations and aspirations of individuals regarding both paid work and the division of labour at the household level.[75] By the end of the decade this combination of structural change and shifting identities[76] was viewed by many as presenting an ideal opportunity for policy formulation in the field of reconciliation. The election of a Labour government in 1997, following 19 years of Conservative rule,[77] looked likely to provide the necessary impetus given that its manifesto pledges had included opting in to the EU's Social Chapter which carried a commitment to implement the Parental Leave Directive (PLD),[78]

---

[71] L Dulk, B Peper and A Doorne-Huiskes, 'Work and Family in Europe: Employment Patterns of Working Parents across Welfare States' in B Peper, A Doorne-Huiskes and L Dulk (eds), *Flexible Working and Organisational Change: The Integration of Working and Personal Life* (Cheltenham, Edward Elgar Publishing, 2005) 13.

[72] J Fudge and R Owens (eds), *Precarious Work, Women, and the New Economy: The Challenges to Legal Norms* (Oxford, Hart Publishing, 2006).

[73] R Sennett, *The Corrosion of Character* (London, WW Norton and Company, 1998).

[74] K Klare, 'The Horizons of Transformative Labour and Employment Law' and M D'Antona, 'Labour Law at the Century's End: An Identity Crisis?' in J Conaghan, R Fischl and K Klare (eds), *Labour Law in an Era of Globalization: Transformations, Practices and Possibilities* (Oxford, Oxford University Press, 2002).

[75] James, *The Legal Regulation of Pregnancy and Parenting in the Labour Market*, above n 64, 271.

[76] ibid.

[77] Referring to the sweeping changes made to the labour law framework and resulting demise of the notion of collective laissez-faire as the central mode of interpretation, Joanne Conaghan has described the legacy of the 1979–1997 Conservative government as including 'inter alia, the almost total collapse of the traditional analytical framework within which labour law had long been understood and interpreted'. Conaghan, 'Feminism and Labour Law: Contesting the Terrain', above n 41, 15; see further H Collins, 'The Productive Disintegration of Labour Law' (1997) 26 *Industrial Law Journal* 295; W McCarthy, 'The Rise and Fall of Collective Laissez-Faire' in W McCarthy (ed), *Legal Intervention in Industrial Relations: Gains and Losses* (Oxford, Blackwell, 1992) 1; B Hepple, 'The Future of Labour Law' (1995) 24 *Industrial Law Journal* 303.

[78] Parental Leave Directive 96/34/EC (now replaced by Parental Leave Directive 2010/18/EC), implemented by Parental Leave (EU Directive) Regulations 2013.

the introduction of a national minimum wage (NMW)[79] and the adoption of a national childcare strategy aimed at planning provision 'to match the requirements of the modern labour market and help parents, especially women, to balance family and working life'.[80]

A. Working Time and Family Time

Regardless of manifesto pledges or political ideology, whichever party had come to power following the 1997 general election would have had to implement the EU's 1993 Working Time Directive (WTD).[81] In rejecting the previous Conservative government's legal challenge to the Directive, the European Court of Justice (ECJ) had held that the WTD had been correctly adopted by majority voting as a health and safety measure under Article 118A of the Treaty of Rome.[82] In its manifesto, Labour had aligned the rights provided by the WTD to those that would be implemented under the Parental Leave Directive[83] thus:

> While recognising the need for flexibility in implementation and for certain exemptions, we support the right of employees not to be forced to work more than 48 hours a week; to an annual holiday entitlement; and to limited unpaid parental leave.[84]

This framing made the important link between working time and family time, albeit through the provision of 'limited' and 'unpaid' leave. The manifesto pledges to enact the right to parental leave and to regulate working time gave the appearance that they had originated at Labour Party level rather than through an obligation to implement EU law. When set alongside the introduction of the NMW, which *was* New Labour's own conception and which subsequently had

---

[79] To be determined, 'not on the basis of a rigid formula but according to the economic circumstances at the time and with the advice of an independent Low Pay Commission, whose membership will include representatives of employers, including small businesses, and employees'. The aims of the NMW were to 'remove the worst excesses of low pay (and be of particular benefit to women), while cutting some of the massive GBP 4 billion benefits bill by which the tax payer subsidises companies that pay very low wages'. The Labour Party manifesto 1997, available at http://labour-party.org.uk/manifestos/1997/1997-labour-manifesto.shtml.

[80] Labour Party manifesto, above n 79. In March 2002 the Department for Work and Pensions proposed to pay grandparents to look after their grandchildren so that parents could work, effectively given official backing to a practice in many families.

[81] Directive on certain aspects of the organisation of working time (93/104/EC). For an exploration of the gendered nature of working time regulation, see A Zbyszewska, *Gendering European Working Time Regimes: The Working Time Directive and the Case of Poland* (Cambridge, Cambridge University Press, 2016).

[82] Case C-84/94 *United Kingdom of Great Britain and Northern Ireland v Council of the European Union*, [1997] IRLR 30.

[83] The 48-hour limit was implemented by the Working Time Regulations 1998 (SI 1833), which came into force on 1 October 1998. The rights to holiday leave and unpaid parental leave were introduced in the Employment Relations Act 1999.

[84] Labour Party manifesto, above n 79.

a significant impact on women's earnings and thus the gender pay gap,[85] these policy strands appeared to offer a genuine political commitment to overcoming some of the structural barriers faced by those combining unpaid care and paid work. Curtailing the long working hours endured by British workers, particularly men, would enable a more equitable division of care and associated tasks within households, whilst guaranteed pay rates would improve the workplace experiences of women. In theory, both parents could benefit equally from the gender-neutral provision of parental leave which, according to the Directive, aimed to 'improve the reconciliation of work, private and family life for working parents and equality between men and women with regard to labour market opportunities and treatment at work'.[86]

B. Parental Rights, Maternity Rights

Despite New Labour's 1997 election manifesto commitment to opt into the European Social Chapter and corresponding obligation to implement the PLD, it did so at the level of minimal compliance.[87] In its defence, the Labour government was firefighting the impact of a long period of resistance to the implementation of any European social law which was a legacy of the previous Conservative administrations: the UK was one of only three EU Member States for which the Parental Leave Directive required implementing legislation (the others being Ireland and Luxembourg).[88] Although, in common with all other Western European countries, the UK had long-standing provision for paid maternity leave, unlike its fellow EU Member States, it had no provision for other types of leave.[89]

The Parental Leave Directive was implemented in the UK by the Maternity and Parental Leave, etc Regulations,[90] which came into force on 15 December 1999. As well as providing an entitlement to three months' (unpaid) parental leave for anyone with responsibility for a child during the first five years of the child's life, the Regulations extended the ordinary maternity leave period from 14 to 18 weeks[91] and the additional maternity leave period from 26 weeks to 29 weeks. The additional period, which had previously only been available to those women who had been employed for 2 years 11 weeks prior to the expected

---

[85] Research from the Low Pay Commission shows that the gender pay gap among the lowest paid fell from 12.9 per cent when the NMW was introduced in 1998 to 5.5 per cent in 2014: see Low Pay Commission, *National Minimum Wage Report*, Cm 9017 (London, HMSO, 2015) 67.

[86] Parental Leave Directive 96/34/EC (now replaced by Parental Leave Directive 2010/18/EC), implemented by the Parental Leave (EU Directive) Regulations 2013.

[87] J Lewis and M Campbell, 'Work/Family Balance Policies in the UK since 1997: A New Departure?' (2007) 36 *Journal of Social Policy* 3, 365, 373.

[88] Busby, 'Divisions of Labour: Maternity Protection in Europe', above n 62, 288.

[89] Lewis and Campbell, 'Work/Family Balance Policies in the UK since 1997: A New Departure?' above n 87, 373.

[90] SI 1999 No 3312.

[91] Regs 4 and 7.

week of childbirth (EWC), was now available to those with one year's continuous service 11 weeks prior to the EWC subject to specific notice requirements.[92] A further right to 'a reasonable period' of unpaid emergency leave (discussed further in chapter five of this volume), also required by the Parental Leave Directive, was introduced by the Employment Relations Act 1999.[93] The right was available to anyone for the purposes of providing assistance or making arrangements for the provision of care for a dependant[94] in the case of an emergency.

The right to payment during maternity leave[95] remained separate from the entitlement to leave, the general rule being that remuneration was not payable during either ordinary or additional maternity leave.[96] A woman on maternity leave was deemed to be in a unique position and therefore unable to claim equal pay and benefits with a man (or a woman) who was working.[97] In the EU context, payment during maternity leave remained the preserve of the Pregnant Workers Directive,[98] which merely provided that maternity pay 'shall be deemed adequate if it guarantees income at least equivalent to that which the worker concerned would receive in the event of a break in her activities on grounds connected with her state of health.'[99] This meant that the UK system of providing statutory maternity pay, subject to certain qualifying conditions, at 90 per cent of earnings for the first six weeks and thereafter at a flat rate set annually in line with statutory sick pay was deemed acceptable. As with all minimum standards provided under EU law, it has always been possible to improve upon this through national measures. The lack of any innovation in this respect, coupled with the complete absence of payment for the period of parental leave, represented a missed opportunity to reconcile the dual goals of improving women's paid work experience and increasing men's engagement with care.

There can, nevertheless, be little doubt that New Labour's promotion of reconciliation policy represented an important moment in terms of the state's recognition that individuals' care commitments should be acknowledged and accommodated within workplaces through legislative intervention. However, whether and to what extent this aspiration was matched by any identifiable change in actual provision capable of heralding a new departure for working families is,

---

[92] Reg 5.

[93] By the insertion of a new s 57A in the Employment Rights Act 1996.

[94] Defined as a spouse or partner, child, parent or someone living with you as part of your family or who relies solely on you for help in an emergency.

[95] See the Statutory Maternity Pay (General) Regulations 1986; Social Security Contributions and Benefits Act 1992. This aspect of the legal framework remains unchanged: to qualify for SMP a woman must be an 'employed earner', ie she must have been employed continuously for a minimum of 26 weeks by the 15th week before the EWC and must be paid at or above the lower earnings limit at which NI contributions are payable. Women who are not eligible for SMP may qualify for Maternity Allowance paid direct by what was the Benefits Agency (now the Department for Work and Pensions).

[96] Reg 9, Maternity and Parental Leave, etc Regulations 1999.

[97] Case C-342/93 *Gillespie v Northern Health and Social Services Board* [1996] IRLR 214 (ECJ).

[98] Directive 92/85/EC.

[99] Art 11(3) PWD.

as the changes introduced in 1999 demonstrate, debatable. The ability of governments to realign law and policy frameworks in line with social change is limited in most contexts: they are not presented with a blank page in any policy field on their first day in power and the institutional architecture of the welfare system makes a fresh start practically impossible.[100] The notion of path dependence,[101] which is used to examine the conditions under which change occurs, tends to result in an emphasis on continuity over change in most circumstances. However, as Lewis and Campbell have noted,

> [i]n the field of family policy in general and of work/family balance (WFB) policies in particular, the case for change would appear to be clear cut. Before 1997, the UK had no explicit commitment to either, but under three successive Labour governments this policy field has come to occupy an important place on the political agenda.

C. Competitiveness and Choice?

In his foreword to Fairness at Work,[102] Tony Blair asserted that its aspiration was to 'change the culture of relations at work' whilst recognising that 'a change of culture cannot be brought about by a change in the framework of law. But a change in law can reflect a new culture, can enhance its understanding and support its development.'[103] This approach relies heavily on an acceptance of the normative power of law to drive change – an approach which has been promoted as being,[104] and shown to be,[105] particularly appropriate in the current context. Political acceptance that the law does have a part to play in the reconciliation of paid work and unpaid care may well have been New Labour's greatest legacy in the field of WFB policy. However, to be truly effective in shifting the division of labour within households, this endeavour requires policymakers to move beyond their comfort zone of instrumentalising women's participation in paid work through childcare provision, employment protection and social security[106] and to intervene more directly in the workplace arrangements of male workers, thus far the preserve of

---

[100] Lewis and Campbell, 'Work/Family Balance Policies in the UK since 1997: A New Departure?', above n 87, 365.

[101] ibid, 378.

[102] Department of Trade and Industry (DTI), Fairness at Work, Cm 3968 (London, The Stationery Office, 1998).

[103] See also DTI, Work and Parents: Competitiveness and Choice, Cm 5005 (London, The Stationery Office, 2000) para 4.12.

[104] S Lewis, '"Family Friendly" Employment Policies: A Route to Changing Organizational Culture or Playing about at the Margins?' (1997) 4 *Gender, Work and Organization* 1, 13; N Busby, *A Right to Care? Unpaid Care Work in European Employment Law* (Oxford, Oxford University Press, 2011); Busby and Weldon-Johns, 'Fathers as Carers in UK Law and Policy: Dominant Ideologies and Lived Experience', above n 70.

[105] L Haas, K Allard and P Hwang, 'The Impact of Organizational Culture on Men's use of Parental Leave in Sweden' (2002) 5 *Community, Work and Family* 3, 319.

[106] J Lewis, 'Gender and Welfare State Change' (2002) 4 *European Societies* 4, 331.

non-interventionism on the part of the state. Perhaps unsurprisingly it was in this respect that the greatest resistance was encountered by both employers and opposition parties leading to a cautious approach by the government in the introduction of new policy.[107]

In an attempt to counter such resistance, the business case, rather than the benefit for families or individual parents, was promoted in the announced expansion of reconciliation policies in the 2000 Green Paper Work and Parents: Competitiveness and Choice.[108] Furthermore, the start of the new decade heralded a change in the framing of New Labour's reconciliation policy which, from 2001, was referred to as 'work–life balance', indicating a more inclusive approach that extended to those without care responsibilities.[109] The focus of the legislation, however, continued to be families, with the right to request flexible working initially restricted to parents.[110] That policy has been widely criticised as amounting to style over substance, with its unrealised promise of flexible working due to its provision of the right to request, rather than on a substantive right to work flexibly.[111] The implementation of the Working Time Directive was also criticised as weak, due to its mismatch with the UK's individualised system of workplace bargaining and the maximum use of the opt-outs proffered by the Directive's permitted derogations in the Working Time Regulations 1998.[112] Despite the stated policy intentions, New Labour's failure to deal adequately with the regulation of working time as a means of reconciling paid work and unpaid care through the imposition of restrictions on employers and increased flexibility for workers stymied progress for working parents, leaving existing practices largely untouched.

In February 2005 the government set out further proposals for developing the legislative and policy framework for working parents in its consultation document 'Work and Families: Choice and Flexibility'.[113] In the document, the government

---

[107] Lewis and Campbell, 'Work/Family Balance Policies in the UK since 1997: A New Departure?', above n 87, 376.

[108] DTI, Cm 5005 (London, The Stationery Office, 2000).

[109] S Macpherson, 'Reconciling Employment and Family Care-Giving: A Gender Analysis of Current Challenges and Future Directions for UK Policy' in N Busby and G James (eds), *Families, Care-giving and Paid Work: Challenging Labour Law in the 21st Century* (Cheltenham, Edward Elgar, 2011) 24; J Lewis, *Work Family Balance, Gender and Policy* (Cheltenham, Edward Elgar, 2009) 1.

[110] Employment Act 2002, s 47. Subsequently extended to all employees who meet certain eligibility requirements by the Coalition Government (Children and Families Act 2014, s 131). Employers must 'deal with the application in a reasonable manner' but can reject requests on a broad range of business grounds – see further ch 5, this volume.

[111] See G James, 'The Work and Families Act 2006: Legislation to Improve Choice and Flexibility?' 35 (2006) *Industrial Law Journal* 2, 272; E Rose, 'Workplace Temporalities: A Time-Based Critique of the Flexible Working Provisions' (2017) 46 *Industrial Law Journal* 2, 245.

[112] C Barnard, 'Recent Legislation: The Working Time Regulations 1998' (1999) 28 *Industrial Law Journal* 1, 61; C Barnard, S Deakin and R Hobbs, 'Opting Out of the 48-Hour Week: Employer Necessity or Individual Choice? An Empirical Study of the Operation of Article 18(1)(b) of the Working Time Directive in the UK', (2003) 32 *Industrial Law Journal* 4, 223–52.

[113] DTI, 'Work and Families, Choice and Flexibility', Government response to public consultation, October 2005: www.dti.gov.uk/er/consultationchoiceflexibility2005final1.pdf. See also DTI, 'Balancing Work and Family Life: Enhancing Choice and Support for Parents' (London, The Stationery Office, 2003), which refers (at 23) to a 'step change in the level of support and choice available to parents'.

articulated its aim as being to widen the choices regarding arrangements for care and paid work available to families and to facilitate fathers' caregiving thus:

> We recognise that families have diverse needs, and are committed to offering choices that respond to the diversity of needs and preferences. The principles of choice and equality underpin the proposal to enable fathers to play a bigger role in caring for their young children.[114]

This was the precursor to the Work and Families Act 2006, which introduced a number of changes and new provisions aimed at enhancing flexibility, including: unconditional entitlement to 52 weeks of maternity leave; the extension of the period of maternity pay to 39 weeks; flexibility regarding the mother's return to work after maternity leave with an eight-week notice period.[115] A number of new provisions were introduced, including the introduction of 'keep-in-touch days', allowing paid work for up to 10 days during maternity leave without losing the right to maternity leave and pay;[116] a right to return to work after full maternity leave on the same terms and conditions;[117] a right to 26 weeks of additional paternity leave; and the extension of the right to request flexible working to carers of adults.

In her critique of the Work and Families Act 2006, James has noted that, although its provisions could be seen as providing working parents with 'further ammunition in the battle for achieving a work/life balance', their overall impact would be limited due to the lack of any underpinning policy shift capable of confronting the concerns facing both workers and employers in this area.[118] Her criticism focused, inter alia, on the piecemeal and incremental nature of the improvements made to the duration of the maternity pay period, which failed to take account of the economic necessity rationale on which most women's decision to return to work following maternity leave was based.[119] Furthermore, the continuation of an eligibility requirement of 26 weeks' continuous employment up to the 15th week before the EWC[120] divided fathers into those with the right to benefit from the provision of paternity leave and those without, which was in stark contrast to all women's entitlement to maternity leave as a day-one right. Taken together, despite the policy rhetoric surrounding New Labour's commitment to shared or gender-free parenting, the nature of the provisions and their interrelationship had 'damaging

---

[114] 'Work and Families', above n 113, para 12.

[115] Reg 11.2(a), Maternity and Parental Leave Regulations 1999 (SI 1999 No 3312).

[116] See G James, 'Enjoy your leave, but "keep in touch": Help to Maintain Parent/Workplace Relationships' (2007) 36 *Industrial Law Journal* 3, 313.

[117] Regulation 18A, Maternity and Parental Leave Regulations 1999.

[118] James, 'The Work and Families Act 2006: Legislation to Improve Choice and Flexibility?', above n 111, 272. For a critique of the treatment of fathers in New Labour reconciliation policy, see E Caracciolo di Torella, 'New Labour, New Dads – The Impact of Family Friendly Legislation on Fathers' (2007) 35 *Industrial Law Journal* 3, 318.

[119] James, 'The Work and Families Act 2006: Legislation to Improve Choice and Flexibility?', above n 111, 273; C Callender, N Millward, S Lissenburgh and J Forth, *Maternity Rights and Benefits in Britain 1996*, Department of Social Security Research Report No 67 (London, HMSO, 1997).

[120] Employment Rights Act 1996, s 80.

ideological ramifications' reinforcing the notion that the mother has (and should have) the main responsibility for childcare and that the father's role is secondary. This represented a 'missed opportunity for fathers who are increasingly interested in caring for their children'.[121]

By lacking a unifying strategy which matched the stated aims of New Labour's reconciliation policy more directly to its provision, the piecemeal approach did not disturb existing arrangements and had little impact on parents' actual ability to choose how to care for their children. In assessing the reconciliation policies of the New Labour governments between 1997 and 2010, Warren et al have high-lighted a strong resistance to time policy innovations.[122] Despite over a decade of reconciliation policy by the end of New Labour's tenure, working hours remained rooted in the male-breadwinner model so that 'men's very long hours make them marginal to unpaid work, while women's short hours make them marginal to paid work'.[123] This is attributable to the fact that, whilst such policies encouraged women's labour market participation,[124] there was a reluctance to 'challenge gender inequalities in unpaid work by intervening in traditional family roles or through regulating paid work time'.[125] Although by 2006 the UK's reconciliation framework had become politically entrenched with even the Conservative opposition having moved towards support for the state taking a role in this area,[126] the UK still retained some domestic peculiarities around issues of time.[127] Maternity leave had been considerably lengthened, rather than a shorter period of paid maternity leave being combined with a more generous paid parental leave, and, unlike many of its Western and Northern European neighbours, the UK provided no right to reduce working time below 48 hours. Despite the apparent regulation of working time, the UK's tradition of legal abstentionism ostensibly continued to shape and influence individuals' relationship with paid work and unpaid care. Although employers were given choices around how best to manage work time

[121] James, 'The Work and Families Act 2006: Legislation to Improve Choice and Flexibility?', above n 111, 275; see further EOC's Response to the Government's Work and Families Bill, October 2005, available at www.eoc.org.uk.

[122] T Warren, G Pascall and E Fox, 'Gender Equality in Time: Low-Paid Mothers' Paid and Unpaid Work in the UK' (2010) 16 *Feminist Economics* 3, 193, 195.

[123] ibid, 212.

[124] UK policy now encouraged one-to-one family-based care during the child's first year with the right to return following extended maternity leave available. In addition, more incentives were offered to mothers to enter the labour market through the development of childcare services and the promotion of flexible work patterns.

[125] Warren et al, 'Gender Equality in Time: Low-Paid Mothers' Paid and Unpaid Work in the UK', above n 122, 212.

[126] See the debates at second and third reading of the Work and Families Bill: Hansard HC Deb 05 December 2005, Vol 440, cols 643–708, available at https://publications.parliament.uk/pa/cm200506/cmhansrd/vo051205/debtext/51205-15.htm#51205-15_head1; 18 January 2006, Vol 441, cols 848–907, available at https://publications.parliament.uk/pa/cm200506/cmhansrd/vo060118/debtext/60118-05.htm#60118-05_head2.

[127] Lewis and Campbell, 'Work/Family Balance Policies in the UK since 1997: A New Departure?', above n 87, 378.

adjustments, individual workers with family care responsibilities found that the way in which such flexibility was manifested in workplace policy merely served to reaffirm and support existing divisions of labour within workplaces and households.

Dominant ideologies of motherhood and fatherhood undoubtedly shape our choices at the household level, exerting a powerful influence over decisions concerning who will provide unpaid childcare and who will participate in paid employment.[128] Reconciliation policy, if it is effective, must challenge and attempt to overcome the underpinning stereotypical assumptions which have their roots in outdated and unsubstantiated essentialist beliefs such as the delimiting effects of pregnancy and motherhood on women's labour force participation. However, academic analyses have shown how such assumptions are themselves embedded in law and policy which serves to reaffirm stereotypical ideals regarding the gendered order within which women are portrayed primarily as caregiver and homemaker and men as breadwinner. This dichotomisation is accommodated within the legal and policy framework to such an extent that even those provisions which are aimed at achieving gender equality by enabling the reconciliation of paid work and unpaid care can actually serve to replicate and further entrench such divisions.[129] The next section will explore the extent to which such dominant ideologies have shaped and continue to shape the UK's framework, which is characterised by its paucity of legal and policy provision aimed at facilitating working fathers' engagement with childcare. Recent attempts have been made to remedy this, and they will be considered by way of an overview of the UK's current provision. The slow move towards recognition, within the framework, that fathers as well as mothers have parental care responsibilities has continued since the earliest reconciliation legislation of the New Labour government in the late 1990s. However, as this brief overview will show, clear distinctions continue to be drawn between mothers and fathers and, in practice, between different categories of fathers with the extent of those rights intended to facilitate caregiving subject to wide variation.

V. The Current Framework

Employed mothers are currently entitled to a maximum of 12 months of maternity leave, nine months of which is paid if certain eligibility requirements are met.[130]

---

[128] A Hattery, *Women, Work and Family: Balancing and Weaving* (London, SAGE, 2001); G James, 'Mothers and Fathers as Parents and Workers: Family Friendly Employment Policies in an Era of Shifting Identities' (2009) 31 *Journal of Social Welfare & Family Law* 3, 271.

[129] C McGlynn, 'Ideologies of Motherhood in European Community Sex Equality Law' (2000) 6 *European Law Journal* 1, 29; Busby and Weldon-Johns, 'Fathers as Carers in UK Law and Policy: Dominant Ideologies and Lived Experience', above n 70.

[130] Social Security Contributions and Benefits Act 1992, s 164(2)(a).

During the first six weeks, payment is 90 per cent of the woman's average wage. For the remaining 33 weeks, those who meet the eligibility requirements[131] are entitled to the lower of either an annually agreed flat rate of statutory maternity pay or 90 per cent of earnings.[132] As is the case for all reconciliation entitlements, individual employers can pay more than the statutory minimum, but cannot go below it. In 2002 leave for adoptive parents was introduced,[133] which mirrors maternity leave apart from the provision that, where there are two adoptive parents, the leave can be taken by whichever parent is nominated.[134]

Both parents have the right to unpaid parental leave. Qualification will depend on employment status and one year's continuous service, and anyone applying for such leave must have responsibility for the child.[135] Under the default provisions, each parent is entitled to a maximum of 18 weeks' unpaid leave per child, subject to a maximum of four weeks per child per year.[136] Leave may be taken in weekly blocks until the child's 18th birthday, thus enabling parents to stagger their entitlement over key stages of their child's life.[137] Despite its gender neutrality and potential to provide parents with the right to spend time with their children during the extended childhood period beyond the year following birth, the take-up rates for parental leave remain low, with only 11 per cent of parents with a child under six taking leave in 2012.[138] The unpaid nature of the leave, alongside its inflexible nature by which it must be taken in one-week blocks, are the most obvious explanations for the low rates. The right to emergency leave for carers[139] is also severely limited in terms of the time that can be taken[140] and so is incapable of providing ongoing support for those balancing paid work and unpaid care.

Fathers' access to work/family rights arises at three key stages of a child's life: the ante-natal period; the post-birth period; and the extended childhood period. During the ante-natal period, all working fathers are entitled to a day-one right to unpaid leave to attend two ante-natal appointments.[141] Immediately following the birth, working fathers with 26 weeks' continuous service by the end of the 15th week before the expected due date are entitled to paternity leave.[142]

---

[131] ie those who have been in the same employment for a continuous period of at least 26 weeks at the 14th week before the expected week of childbirth: Social Security Contributions and Benefits Act 1992, s 164(2)(a).

[132] For the year 2020/21, £151.20 a week.

[133] Under the Employment Act 2002; the relevant provision is now in the Children and Families Act 2014.

[134] Paternity and Adoption Leave Regulations 2002, Reg 2(1), (4).

[135] Maternity and Parental Leave Etc ... Regulations 1999 (MPLR), Reg 13.

[136] MPLR, Regs 14(1) and Reg 16 and Sch 2 para 8.

[137] MPLR, Reg 16, Sch 2, para 7; see *Rodway v New Southern Railway Ltd (Formerly South Central Trains Ltd)* [2005] ICR 1162; EAT decision [2005] ICR 75).

[138] S Tipping, J Chanfreau, J Perry and C Tait, *The Fourth Work–Life Balance Employee Survey* (London, Department for Business, Innovation and Skills, 2012) 6.

[139] Employment Relations Act 1999, s 8.

[140] See *Qua v John Ford Morrison Solicitors* [2003] ICR 482.

[141] Employment Rights Act 1996 (ERA), s 57ZE.

[142] Paternity and Adoption Leave Regulations 2002/2788 (PALR), Regs 4(2)(a) and 8(2)(a); Social Security Contributions and Benefits Act 1992 (SSCBA), s 171ZA.

In order to qualify, the father must also have, or expect to have, responsibility for raising the child or be in a relationship with the mother and have or expect to have main responsibility for the child's care.[143] Fathers who satisfy these qualifying conditions are entitled to a maximum of two consecutive weeks of paternity leave to be taken in the 56 days following the birth of a child[144] and may be entitled to statutory paternity pay at this time.[145] The father may also be entitled to shared parental leave (SPL) if both he and the mother satisfy the eligibility requirements. To qualify, the father must be an employee with at least 26 weeks' continuous employment up to and including the week before SPL is due to start.[146] In addition, the father or mother's partner must have been employed or be a self-employed earner for at least 26 out of the 66 weeks before the EWC and have minimum earnings in the previous tax year.[147] In order to claim SPL, the mother must also satisfy these conditions, or have been entitled to maternity allowance, and must have curtailed her maternity leave.[148] Working parents can share a maximum of 50 weeks in total.[149] Although the default position is that leave must be taken in one continuous block,[150] both parents can take leave concurrently and can request different non-consecutive blocks of leave for a minimum of one week subject to employer agreement.[151] Like mothers, fathers have the right to unpaid parental leave. To qualify, the fathers must be an 'employee' with one year's continuous service and have responsibility for the child.[152]

A. Dominant Ideologies in the UK's Current WFB Framework

The current framework regulating fathers' ability to participate in unpaid care alongside paid work has resulted from law and policy introduced by the New Labour, Coalition and Conservative governments over the past 20 years, which have at their core a shared idea of what fathers should be but no clear strategic approach regarding how best to make that a reality. Furthermore, as academic work has shown, there is a discernible disconnect between the policy ideal and lived experience, in particular, highlighting the key tensions that exist between

---

[143] PALR, Regs 4(2)(b)–(c); 8(2)(b)–(c)).

[144] ERA, ss 80A and 80B; PALR, Regs 4(1) and 5(1).

[145] Paid at the current rate of £145.18 per week, or 90 per cent of normal earnings, whichever is the lesser amount (SSCBA, ss 171ZA–171ZEE; Statutory Paternity Pay and Statutory Adoption Pay (Weekly Rates) Regulations 2002/2818, Regs 2–3.

[146] Shared Parental Leave Regulations 2014/3050 (SPLR), Regs 4, 5 and 35.

[147] SPLR, Reg 36.

[148] Maternity and Adoption Leave (Curtailment of Statutory Rights to Leave) Regulations 2014/3052, Part 2.

[149] SPLR, Reg 6. The Regulations state that 52 weeks are available, but this is subject to two weeks' compulsory maternity leave following childbirth under the Employment Rights Act s 72.

[150] SPLR, Reg 13.

[151] SPLR, Part 2.

[152] MPLR, Reg 13.

the traditional role of fathers and notions of 'new fatherhood'[153] and the rhetoric and reality of government policy in this area.[154] 'New fatherhood' emerged as a policy model in the late 1990s under the New Labour government's promotion of the inclusion and enhancement of the role of fathers within families.[155] New Labour's policy trajectory in this context has sustained up to the present day and this mismatch between rhetoric and policy provision can be clearly discerned in the resulting framework. Despite proclamations regarding the need for men to be more hands-on and involved in their role as fathers, the resulting law and policy framework entrenches stereotypical notions of fathers' absence from the home and thus from unpaid caregiving.

Like the provisions regulating mothers' relationship with paid work, which are predicated by a range of assumptions relating to women's biological state and psychological predilection for care and related domestic work,[156] the provisions regulating men's relationship with care are underpinned by a dominant ideology of fatherhood.[157] This ideology is characterised by paternal absence from care, which arises on two distinct grounds. First, the notion of man as breadwinner or economic provider continues to define conceptions of masculinity and expectations of good fathering. This conception results in limited recognition of caring responsibilities and their impact on paid work. The other assumption on which the ideology focuses is the non-resident father with his absence from the family home used as a means of limiting and penalising his engagement in care.

This idea of fathers' absence from care arrangements being attributable to their role as breadwinners has, as its exemplar, the conception of the 'standard worker model'. The prioritisation of men's role first and foremost as providers is evident in the requirement that working fathers must establish their employment status before their status as fathers is recognised. With the sole exception of the right to time off to attend ante-natal appointments, all other fathers' rights – paternity leave, SPL and unpaid parental leave – require working fathers to be employees with an established employment relationship. Whereas mothers always have the right (and responsibility) to take leave during the child's first year, only fathers who have the requisite paid work connection will be entitled to do so, thus legitimating their absence from childcare. Furthermore, all of the rights exclusively available

---

[153] A Gregory and S Milner, 'What is "New" about Fatherhood? The Social Construction of Fatherhood in France and the UK' (2011) 14 *Men and Masculinities* 5, 588.

[154] R Collier, 'A Hard Time to be a Father?: Reassessing the Relationship between Law, Policy, and Family (Practices)' (2001) 28 *Journal of Law and Society* 4, 520; R Collier, *Men, Law and Gender: Essays on the 'Man' of Law* (Oxford, Routledge, 2010); R Collier and S Sheldon, *Fragmenting Fatherhood: a Socio-legal Study* (Oxford, Hart Publishing, 2008); C Smart and B Neale, '"I hadn't really thought about it": New Identities/New Fatherhoods' in J Seymour and P Bagguley (eds), *Relating Intimacies: Power and Resistance* (New York, St Martin's Press, 1999) 118.

[155] Caracciolo di Torella, 'New Labour, New Dads – The Impact of Family Friendly Legislation on Fathers', above n 118.

[156] Busby, *A Right to Care? Unpaid Care Work in European Employment Law*, above n 104.

[157] Busby and Weldon-Johns, 'Fathers as Carers in UK Law and Policy: Dominant Ideologies and Lived Experience', above n 70; Fredman, 'Reversing Roles: Bringing Men into the Frame', above n 5.

to fathers facilitate short absences from work, usually around or related to the birth, and thus fail to address the longer-term reconciliation of paid work and care responsibilities. It will consequently continue to fall to mothers to renegotiate their relationship with paid work and care. The right to request a flexible work arrangement is gender-neutral[158] but, as case law illustrates,[159] there is no guarantee that the changes sought will be granted or that the reasons given for the decisions made by employers can be challenged.[160] This makes it much harder for fathers to rely on this right in practice than mothers.

The non-resident father is almost completely absent from the legal framework and related expectations of care arrangements. Although working fathers are in principle able to exercise leave rights irrespective of their relationship with the child's mother, the reality is that many of the assumptions relating to fathers and care are rooted in a heteronormative view of the family in which two different-sex parents reside with their birth children who are dependent on them for care. Families falling outside of this normative model are problematised so that they are either overlooked completely or not supported by the provisions.[161] The restriction to one individual who is able to exercise fathers' rights in respect of a child can be particularly problematic for non-resident fathers who will be required to negotiate their involvement with their child or children with the child's mother. If she has a new partner, the father's position may be further complicated by his inability to satisfy the conditions required. In such circumstances the mother remains the gatekeeper to the father's involvement: for example, if she chooses to allow her partner to exercise the rights, the father is left with no means of challenging that decision. The mother's role as gatekeeper has been identified as a consistent factor in determining the nature and extent of paternal care[162] and serves to reinforce the 'care-less' conception of male identity.[163] This stereotype of the absent father and its entrenchment in reconciliation policy can, thus, be seen to legitimate non-resident fathers' absence in care arrangements.

VI. Work and Families: The Call for Change

As chapter two has shown, women's engagement with paid work is fundamentally shaped by the fact that they remain the primary providers of unpaid care

---

[158] Flexible Working Regulations 2014/1398.

[159] *Walkingshaw v The John Martin Group*, Case No S/401126/00.

[160] James, 'The Work and Families Act 2006: Legislation to Improve Choice and Flexibility?', above n 111; James, *The Legal Regulation of Pregnancy and Parenting in the Labour Market*, above n 64.

[161] M Weldon-Johns, 'From Modern Workplaces to Modern Families – Re-envisioning the Work-Family Concept' (2015) 37 *Journal of Social Welfare and Family Law* 4, 395.

[162] H Hauari and K Hollingworth, *Understanding Fathering, Masculinity, Diversity and Change* (York, Joseph Rowntree Foundation, 2009) 7 and 37; C Lewis, A Papacosta and J Warin, *Cohabitation, Separation and Fatherhood* (York, Joseph Rowntree Foundation, 2002) 28–37.

[163] J Herring, 'Making Family Law More Careful' in J Wallbank and J Herring (eds), *Vulnerabilities, Care and Family Law* (Abingdon, Routledge, 2014) 43.

regardless of whether they participate in the labour market or not. This is the case in relation to care provided for children, elders and other recipients; however, it is motherhood that has the greatest impact on women's working patterns, determining if and when women work and, in many cases, the type of work they undertake. This chapter has demonstrated that, despite some relatively recent changes to the UK's reconciliation framework which give men specific and shared entitlements to periods of parental leave, their working lives remain distinct and separate from their roles as fathers, partners or sons. A brief overview of working families within the UK provides some insights into the organisation of paid work and unpaid care at the household level and reveals the lack of impact that two decades of law and policy intended to reorient the gendering of care within families has actually had.[164]

A. Working Families in the UK

According to official data, there are 6.2 million couple households with dependent children in the UK and 1.7 million lone-parent families.[165] Mothers' employment rates continue to rise: in 2018 the employment rate for mothers was 74 per cent – an increase of 5.1 per cent over the previous five years. Employment rates are higher for both women and men with dependent children than for those without.[166] Dual-earner households are now the norm in the UK. In two-parent households, the percentage of both parents working full-time has increased from 26 per cent in 2001 to 31 per cent in 2013.[167] The number of children within the household is an indicator of maternal working hours. In 76 per cent of households comprising different-sex couples with one child and in 75 per cent of those with two children, both parents remain in employment. However, families with one child are most likely to have both parents in full-time employment (40 per cent), families with two children are more likely to split employment so that fathers work full-time and mothers work part-time (41 per cent) and in families with three or more dependent children, 41 per cent have just one parent – usually the father – in employment.[168] As these statistics show, in different-sex couple households, the number of children continues to

---

[164] The following section draws heavily on the disaggregated data provided in the *Modern Families Index 2019* produced by Bright Horizons and Working Families, available at www.workingfamilies.org.uk/publications/mfi2019_full/.

[165] Office for National Statistics, *Families and Households* 2017, www.ons.gov.uk/peoplepopulationand community/birthsdeathsandmarriages/families/bulletins/familiesandhouseholds/2017.

[166] ONS *Families and the Labour Market* 2018, www.ons.gov.uk/employmentandlabourmarket/ peopleinwork/employmentandemployeetypes/articles/familiesandthelabourmarketengland/2018.

[167] S Connolly, M Aldrich, M O'Brien, S Speight and E Poole, 'Britain's Slow Movement to a Gender Egalitarian Equilibrium: Parents and Employment in the UK 2001–2013'(2016) 30 *Work, Employment and Society* 5, 838.

[168] ONS, *Families and the Labour Market* 2017, www.ons.gov.uk/releases/.

impact on women's employment behaviour whereas men's remains unaffected. The persistence of the 'one-and-a-half worker model' among different-sex couples reflects and reinforces gender inequalities in paid work.[169]

The UK's 13 million parents who engage in paid work (employed and self-employed)[170] rely on a variety of workplace arrangements. 853,000 have flexible working hours and 494,000 (the majority of whom are women) work during school term time only.[171] UK fathers' working hours continue to be among the longest in Europe although there has been a slow and gradual decline from an average of 47 per week in 2001 to 45 per week in 2011 due to reductions in weekend and evening working. The proportion of fathers working 48 hours or more declined sharply from 40 per cent in 2001 to 31 per cent in 2013.[172] Mothers continue to perform more routine family activities and be more involved with the care of children than fathers,[173] although fathers' involvement with their children has increased and continues to do so. Men spend an average of 16 hours a week doing unpaid care work (including childcare, laundry and cleaning) whereas women spend 26 hours per week. Women carry out 60 per cent more unpaid work than men on average[174] and are more likely to work part-time (51 per cent, compared with 18 per cent of men). The arrival of children has a marked effect on mothers' and fathers' working hours: 65 per cent of mothers with a child under 11 worked part-time (compared with 47 per cent of all women) and fathers with a child under 11 are marginally more likely to work longer hours than other men – 33 per cent compared to 31 per cent. These working patterns are not unique to the UK but persist, to varying degrees, across every country in the EU.[175]

B. An Alternative Approach to Dependency and Care?

The historical legacy of the early regulatory intervention in the separate spheres of paid work and the family, imbued with fictive and outdated notions of motherhood and maternalism and fatherhood and paternalism, has resulted in the perpetuation of dominant ideologies which, despite over 20 years of targeted WFB law, remain deeply embedded in the current regulatory framework.

---

[169] Warren et al, 'Gender Equality in Time: Low-Paid Mothers' Paid and Unpaid Work in the UK', above n 122, 196.

[170] ONS, *Parents and Non-parents by Sex and Age of Youngest Dependent Child and Different Working Arrangements, UK and Regions* (2018) www.ons.gov.uk/employmentandlabourmarket/peopleinwork/employmentandemployeetypes/adhocs/009340parentsandnonparentsbysexandageofyoungestdependentchildanddifferentworkingarrangementsukandregions2018.

[171] ibid.

[172] Modern Fatherhood (2016), Parental Working in Europe, www.modernfatherhood.org/.

[173] Modern Fatherhood (2013), Fathers' Involvement with Children, www.modernfatherhood.org/.

[174] ONS, *Women Shoulder the Responsibility of Unpaid Work*, http://visual.ons.gov.uk/the-value-of-your-unpaid-work.

[175] H Norman and L Watt, *Why Aren't Men doing the Housework?* (2017), www.workingfamilies.org.uk/workflex-blog/why-arent-mendoing-the-housework.

The resulting dichotomisation of private/public realms and reproductive/ productive work continues to influence and shape individual and household choices and aspirations regarding the division of labour. Rather than challenging stereotypes relating to mothers' and fathers' roles within families, the reconciliation framework mirrors and further entrenches them within the institutions and relationships governing paid work. Change, particularly in relation to men's engagement with care, depends on policy leadership, yet the law and policy framework continues to follow and reaffirm existing arrangements revealing an historical and problematic reluctance on the part of the state to interfere in the 'private' arrangements around the allocation of care. Significantly, policymakers have not been so reluctant to instrumentalise women's relationship with paid work, even when they pay the price of combining this with unpaid care, yet have resisted calls to intervene directly with men's work and family arrangements.[176]

As we have argued in relation to the EU's reconciliation framework, the lack of a unifying strategy and of any clear and cohesive aims and objectives have shaped the WFB policy domain, producing a patchwork of provision.[177] Like its EU counterpart, the UK approach is based on an amalgam of different objectives including gender equality within workplaces and the improvement of mothers' employment rates with its emphasis shifting dependent on external (usually economic) factors.[178] However, whereas EU policymakers have provided leadership in ideological terms backed up by the provision of policy,[179] the UK approach has been largely reactive[180] with the prioritisation of short-term economic goals and associated political agendas.[181] This is despite ideological proclamations, particularly in relation to fathering, about the way things *ought* to be done which have not been matched by any clear policy commitments capable of facilitating those ideas. This largely rhetorical approach has been an enduring feature of

---

[176] S Fredman, 'A Difference with Distinction: Pregnancy and Parenthood Reassessed' (1994) *Law Quarterly Review* 110, 106.

[177] N Busby and G James, 'Regulating Working Families in the European Union: A History of Disjointed Strategies' (2015) 37 *Journal of Social Welfare and Family Law* 295; N Busby, 'The Evolution of Gender Equality and Related Employment Policies: the Case of Work–Family Reconciliation' (2018) 18 *International Journal of Discrimination and the Law* 104. For a full and detailed consideration of the EU's framework, see E Caracciolo di Torella and A Masselot, *Reconciling Work and Family Life in EU Law and Policy* (London, Palgrave Macmillan, 2010).

[178] O Golynker, 'Family-friendly Reform of Employment Law in the UK: An Overstretched Flexibility' (2015) 37 *Journal of Social Welfare and Family Law* 3, 378, 382.

[179] Most recently by way of the Work–Life Balance Initiative (COM/2017/0252 final) introduced under the EU's Pillar of Social Rights, which sets out a comprehensive package of complementary legal and policy measures, including a proposal for a directive on work–life balance for parents and carers (COM/2017/0253 final – 2017/085 (COD). See further https://ec.europa.eu/social/main.jsp?catId=1311&langId=en.

[180] Golynker, 'Family-friendly Reform of Employment Law in the UK: An Overstretched Flexibility', above n 178, 387–89.

[181] N Busby and G James, 'Regulating Work and Care Relationships in a Time of Austerity: A Legal Perspective' in S Lewis, D Anderson, C Lyonette, N Payne and S Wood (eds), *Work-Life Balance in Times of Recession, Austerity and Beyond* (London, Routledge, 2017) 78.

state intervention in parental leave policies since the New Labour government of 1997–2010 and has resulted in the assimilation, through policy headlining, of terms such as 'gender-free parenting' or 'shared care' into the public consciousness without the clarity and commitment required to effect real change. The policy landscape has instead developed through incremental, often complex and restrictive, additions to an already obfuscate framework. The lack of a central core – or any overriding strategy – has resulted in further entrenchment of the enduring gendered coding of care. This has left many women, particularly those in low-paid and low-status jobs, vulnerable to the effects of a deregulated labour market, and given men little choice over their own unpaid care and paid work arrangements.

As chapter two has shown, combining paid work and unpaid care has had and continues to have a negative effect on women's economic stability with pay and conditions for part-time work being particularly poor. Women with care responsibilities are more likely to undertake precarious work with fewer opportunities for promotion and career advancement affecting entitlements to pensions and other work-related benefits so that the impacts are often felt long after the care responsibilities have lessened or disappeared. Meanwhile, fathers in different-sex couple households continue to conform to the male breadwinner model, often working longer hours than their European counterparts. Even where both partners engage in paid work, women continue to bear responsibility for the majority of childcare and other domestic work. Gender role conformity persists within different-sex households despite the detrimental impacts on women's social and economic freedom and the constraints placed on men's ability to participate in childcare. Given the persistence of gendering within families' decision-making around the division of labour, it might be pertinent to ask what an alternative approach capable of shifting current practices would look like.

In the previous chapter, the challenge proffered by vulnerability theory to the standard worker model and its replacement with the vulnerable subject, capable of recognising and reconciling the individual's responsibilities as both worker and carer, giver and recipient of care, was considered. As well as providing a useful alternative to the paradigm model of paid employment by which the efforts and activities of all others are measured and compared, this reimagining is also relevant in the context of the household. The interrelationship between paid work and family life requires a policy approach capable of recognising, uniting and embedding the needs of individuals in relation to both through the regulation of all social and economic activity whilst also acknowledging the fluidity and constant change that occurs over the life course. To be truly effective, this alternative must also provide a challenge to the institutions and relationships which uphold and reproduce current inequalities, be they in relation to women's experiences of discrimination within workplaces or the lack of policy support necessary to encourage and facilitate men's enhanced engagement with care. The final section will conclude with a consideration of vulnerability theory's ability to provide such a challenge.

VII. Conclusions

The dominant model by which responsibility for dependency is allocated is, as this chapter has shown, flawed and serves little purpose beyond maintenance of the status quo. The entrenched system of injustice within families conceals reproductive labour, distinguishing it from its productive paid counterpart. However, one cannot exist without the other and it is this fact that is implicitly overlooked in current WFB policy. The establishment of a false dichotomy between the public and the private forms of work, with policy and legislative attention focused on the former, has re-emphasised the need for a breadwinner/caretaker model as the most efficient way of allocating the division within households. This is despite the lived experiences of most families, which take many diverse forms not easily accounted for under this model. What of the lone parent, the child being raised by same-sex parents, the extended family or families consisting of no blood relatives? As the analysis in this chapter has demonstrated, the current regulatory model fails to reflect the family even in its 'traditional' nuclear form, i.e. consisting of two different-sex parents living with their birth children. In recognition of the changing composition and lived realities of family life, piecemeal adaptations to the policy framework have occurred resulting in an inordinately complex patchwork of provision which is still not fit for purpose and which reproduces dominant ideologies pertaining to the paradigm of the heteronormative nuclear family model.

The application of a vulnerability approach to the division of labour within families enables a reassessment of the outdated and, in many respects, fictive premises on which the current regulatory framework depends. The unquestionable ability of the family as the institution best suited to self-regulate the arrangements under which caregiving and paid work takes place is immediately contested. In her assessment of the welfare system, Fineman challenges the role of the 'mythical, idealized family' within society because of its service on an ideological level as the alternative to collective responsibility for dependants.[182] Misuse of the language of dependency has a divisive and stigmatising impact through its categorisation of individuals as 'the righteous independent taxpayer' and the 'deviant undeserving dependent welfare recipient' which deflects attention from the need for a 'principled inquiry into what should be the nature and extent of state responsibility for the economic and social well-being of all citizens'.[183] The delegation of care to the family detracts from society's shared responsibility for care which should be properly discharged through the fair and equal allocation of resources by the state. This might take place through the provision of state services, taxation, social security or by way of legislation and policy targeted at meeting the needs of the

---

[182] MA Fineman, 'The Nature of Dependencies and Welfare "Reform"' (2015–16) 36 *Santa Clara Law Review*, 287, 288.

[183] ibid, 288.

family, whatever its form, in providing care. In this conformation a responsive state would provide a range of care-centric provision including childcare and a strategic reconciliation policy grounded in the recognition that dependency and care are inevitable components of human existence which require adequate state support and resource.

In considering the gendering of care and the penalties paid by parents through women's labour market discrimination and the lack of opportunity or support available for men's engagement in care, we argue that the allocation of care is not biologically determined but gender-coded. Rather than attempting to unseat such coding, the current law and policy framework reaffirms and further entrenches it. Again, this is wholly reliant on the remnants of a past era in which the labour carried out within and on behalf of families was organised along gender lines. However, the social disadvantages of care are now attached to the status, rather than the sex, of the caregiver.[184] The destabilisation and replacement of the low status afforded to caregivers will only be achieved through a reconsideration of the value of care which must take place at state level. This is an urgent and compelling undertaking without which social and economic progress will continue to be severely hindered and for which careful consideration requires to be given to care, not only in the context of parenthood, but in all its guises. In the next two chapters, we turn our attention to the primary recipients of care to consider their place within the WFB framework, focusing in chapter four on children and, in chapter five, on elderly dependants.

---

[184] MA Fineman, 'Feminism, Masculinities and Multiple Identities' (2012–13) 13 *Nevada Law Journal* 619, 629.

4

Children's Welfare

I. Introduction

Having considered the inclusion of caregivers' experiences and needs in the way working families have been regulated, in the next two chapters focus shifts to include more direct consideration of the primary recipients of their care: in this chapter, children and, in chapter five, elderly dependants.[1] The chapters offer an alternative perspective from traditional academic assessments of labour law's engagement with working families, which have tended to assess the impact of policies on those who provide unpaid care whilst participating in paid work. The perspectives presented in the following chapters, especially when viewed historically, invite us to reconsider our assumptions regarding the purpose and potential of such policies by illuminating underlying tensions in our approach, historically and in the present, to the members of working families who are receiving care, as well as those who provide it.

At its core, this chapter seeks an explanation for how and why children's welfare is not of primary concern to those who seek to regulate working families. As we demonstrate below, put simply, it never has been. Our assessment focuses on a metamorphosis that has occurred over many decades. The main point of entry is the early nineteenth century, mid industrialisation, but rather than assessing the issue chronologically we focus on what, for our purposes, are three key interrelated transformations: the demise of child labour (section II), commitment to compulsory state education (section III) and a growing, but limited, state acceptance of responsibility for child welfare issues (section IV). Overall, we outline how these transformations (re)positioned 'children' as a cohort in society. We demonstrate that this is a journey in which the way 'children' are constructed has undergone a significant metamorphosis from a primary source of labour, key contributor to the family budget/wellbeing and a 'social insurance for parents'[2] to a cohort in need of education and, for some, an 'expensive luxury consumption good'[3] deserving of special treatment and state protection in an age

---

[1] We do not specifically engage with the needs of ill or disabled children/adults here, but many of the conclusions we reach will have implications for these families too.

[2] J Humphries, *Childhood and Child Labour in the British Industrial Revolution* (Cambridge, Cambridge University Press, 2010) xi.

[3] ibid, although, as Humphreys recognises, 'not all children have managed to become the priceless possessions that modernity promises' (at xi).

of paranoid and intense parenting.[4] However, one key consistent characteristic in this development is that children have always been subject to the needs, wants and whims of (adult) others. This marginalisation means that much-needed articulation and consideration of *their* needs have remained largely peripheral, albeit that they have often benefited from obligations placed or rights bestowed upon others. When juxtaposed against broader societal developments through which autonomy has become more highly valued – and dependency increasingly vilified – their metamorphosis from potential or actual economic providers for families and employers to recipients of care has led to an inevitable but problematic decline in their visibility, status and significance. This, as we argue in the final section, is pivotal to our understanding of how children are currently constructed within UK WFB policies. It is here that we also consider the value of an alternative approach, one that is grounded in vulnerability theory, as a means of centralising children's welfare concerns within this area of social policy.

II. The Demise of Paid Child Labour

The exploitation of little children, on this scale and with this intensity, was one of the most shameful events in our history.[5]

The demise of child labour in the UK is significant in the development of a concept of children's welfare because it marks a hugely important departure from what was, for many working-class families, the norm. The 1851 census suggests that more than 24,000 boys under 15 worked in coal mining alone[6] and Tuttle's analysis of data from relevant surveys and inquiries suggested that in 1833 between one and two thirds of all workers in the textile mills were children and young people.[7] The true scope of paid child labour has, however, been disputed by historians[8] and would have varied across time and between industries and geographical location and been sensitive to local cultures.[9] At a basic quantitative level, however, there is general agreement that the Industrial Revolution increased the numbers

---

[4] See, eg, F Ferudi, *Paranoid Parenting: Why Ignoring the Experts May be Best for your Child* (Chicago, Chicago Review Press, 2002) and S Hays, *The Cultural Contradictions of Motherhood* (New Haven, Yale University Press, 1996), discussed further in G James, *The Legal Regulation of Pregnancy and Parenting in the labour Market* (Abingdon, Routledge Cavendish, 2009) 5.

[5] EP Thompson, *The Making of the English Working Class* (London, Victor Gollancz, 1963) 349.

[6] See P Horn, *Children's Work and Welfare 1780–1890* (Cambridge, Cambridge University Press, 1994) 8.

[7] C Tuttle, 'A Revival of the Pessimist View: Child Labour and the Industrial Revolution' (1999) 18 *Research in Economic History* 53.

[8] Horn, *Children's Work and Welfare 1780–1890*, above n 6, 4.

[9] See, eg, P Horn, *Children's Work and Welfare 1780–1890*, above n 6; P Hair, 'Children in society 1850–1980' in T Baker and M Drake (eds), *Population and Society in Britain 1850–1980* (New York, New York University Press, 1982). See also K Honeyman, *Child Workers in England 1780–1820: Parish Apprentices and the Making of the Early Industrial Labour Force* (Aldershot, Ashgate, 2007).

of children in paid labour and meant that greater numbers started (paid) work at a younger age.[10] The exact numbers might be disputed, but there is consensus that during the nineteenth century child labour, whether paid or unpaid, was 'expected' in working class families.[11] This, coupled with the general acceptance of child labour as a morally necessary good,[12] meant that working families and employers operated in a way that belies modern understandings of juvenile vulnerability and parental responsibilities. Within this context, historians have increasingly recognised the contribution this labour made to the family budget and to the economic wellbeing of the country as a whole.[13]

Reasons for the decline in child labour can be attributed to several explanations,[14] but for the most part the decline occurred, as the following discussion of legislative interventions suggests, only when the labour market and economy as a whole had no further need for it. It is the nuances of this development that help reveal how children came to be differentiated from adults in a way that served the purposes of the state, institutions and individuals that benefited from that construction. This is, however, a disjointed historical transformation that is difficult to pin down to a particular time or place. Whilst a society that refuses to employ children is symbolic, denoting a progressive society that values childhood and views children as entitled to be 'cared for' by adults, it is also riddled with messy realities and curious contradictions.

A. Legislative Intervention

Prior to the 1800s the contract of employment, and the assumption of voluntary agreement between worker and employers that it epitomised, governed employment relationships. Urbanisation and industrialisation, the prominence of a dominant laissez-faire attitude and only a limited call for social reforms meant that worker protection per se was not perceived as valuable or necessary. Indeed, it was only when the health and safety of workers was linked to productivity concerns

---

[10] See S Horrell and J Humphreys, '"The Exploitation of Little Children": Child Labour and the Family Economy in the Industrial Revolution' (1995) 32 *Explorations in Economic History* 485, 485.

[11] ibid, 511.

[12] Horn, *Children's Work and Welfare 1780–1890*, above n 6, 1.

[13] See J Humphries, *Childhood and Child Labour in the British Industrial Revolution* (Cambridge, Cambridge University Press, 2010) and K Honeyman and N Goose, *Childhood and Child Labour in Industrial England: Diversity and Agency 1750–1914* (London, Taylor and Francis, 2013).

[14] For example, the impact of technical advances in the labour market made child labour economically unviable in many industries (see P Kirby, *Child Labour in Britain, 1750–1870* (London, Palgrave Macmillan, 2003), who argues that changes in industrial processes and organisation is what caused the decline in child labour). Other factors include the increase in (male) real wages, which may have reduced the need for children to undertake paid work (see C Nardinelli, *Child Labour and the Industrial Revolution* (Bloomington, Indiana University Press, 1990) and also the discussion in H Cunningham, 'The Decline of Child Labour: Labour Markets and Family Economies in Europe and North America since 1830' (2000) 3 *Economic History Review*, 409), and compulsory schooling, discussed below.

that legislation was considered a worthwhile endeavour at all.[15] Hence, the notion of limiting children's participation in paid employment through legislation was not without tension. Child labour was often essential for family survival and key to industrial progress. It was common across many sectors for many decades and, despite the patchy evidence, most historians believe that it is 'best thought of as a kind of mastic holding the early industrial economy together'.[16] It was only when children became irrelevant to the latter, despite remaining important to the functioning of the family unit, that their labour market participation diminished – a gradual and patchy process of demise that was aided by, rather than driven by, and reflected in legislative intervention.

State engagement was, when it first arrived, minimal and specific – directed at a particular industry or circumstance – and enforcement was often very weak. An early example was the focus on climbing boys[17] – chimney sweeps whose horrific lot in life roused concerns by campaigners such as the philanthropist Jonas Hanway, who fought to ban the trade. The conditions of their work were brutal and inhumane: employers often used the youngest and smallest of boys to reach the narrow and crooked flues in the homes of the wealthy and the impact on their health was devastating.[18] Interestingly though, as Horn comments, 'despite repeated campaigns on their behalf … the desire of householders to use their services and avoid mechanical alternatives meant that almost a century elapsed before the trade was *effectively* outlawed'.[19] When legislation came, in 1788, it prohibited apprenticeships for boys under eight, insisted that boys be washed once a week, that they attend church on Sunday and, most telling of all, not be forced to climb a chimney actually on fire! This legislation was not enforced and so it was, inevitably, ignored. In 1834 the minimum age for an apprenticeship was raised to 10; and in 1839 it was raised again to 16 and those under 21 were prohibited from climbing chimneys. Both pieces of legislation were ignored and young children were simply not given an apprenticeship but were still made to climb. In 1864, legislation prohibited boys under 16 from entering houses with a sweep but again this was ignored. It was not until 1875, when it was decided that all sweeps were to be licensed and the police given powers to enforce the 1840 and 1864 Acts that the abuse declined.[20] In reality, as Horn noted, 'only once public opinion had been educated and builders had made changes to allow the safe and

---

[15] P Almond, *Corporate Manslaughter and Regulatory Reform* (London, Palgrave Macmillan, 2013) 97.

[16] Humphreys, *Childhood and Child Labour in the British Industrial Revolution*, above n 13, 6. Nardinelli, however, controversially, disputes that child labour was important in the long term (Nardinelli, *Child Labour and the Industrial Revolution*, above n 14).

[17] Evidence suggests that girls were used to sweep, but not so frequently: see H Mayhew, *London Labour and the London Poor* Vol II (New York, Cosimo Classics, 1861) 347.

[18] See ibid, 338–465, which discusses the lot of chimney sweeps.

[19] Horn, *Children's Work and Welfare 1780–1890*, above n 6, 17.

[20] ibid.

easy sweeping of chimneys by brushes rather than boys, did this brutal form of child employment end'.[21]

Despite such early examples of sporadic legislative interventions,[22] it is the Factory Acts of the 1830s onwards that have become synonymous with attempts to lessen the hardships experienced by working children. With pressure brewing from social reformers, public attention began to focus on the mass of children and women working in horrific conditions in mines and factories whose plight was increasingly intense and had been made more visible as a result of industrialisation.[23] Significantly, industrialisation also prompted a decline in family labour, where children had worked alongside family members, and an increase in individual work – leaving children to 'stand alone in the labour market and workplace'.[24] This nuance is significant from our perspective because it illuminates an important development – a new dimension in the way that children were required to work for the benefit of industry and hence not only for the benefit of their families. Working class children became, on a huge scale, commodities, crucial to the economic development of the country. This new kind of exploitation severed any links, comfort and protection a working child might hitherto have experienced whilst engaging in paid employment, and did so in order to advance the needs of industry at a point in history when this was a national priority.[25]

However, there was still huge opposition against reform – with many arguing, for example, that such regulation was a restraint of trade or that restricting child employment would threaten the economic wellbeing of families, and many challenged the assertion that existing working conditions posed any health risk at all. Nonetheless, a shift of approach occurred: slavery was being questioned, and ultimately ended, in the colonies and comparisons were made between working conditions abroad and at home. At the time reforms, as Horrell and Humphreys explain, were pushed for by mill operatives who wanted a 10-hour day for all, humanitarian politicians concerned with the morality of child labour, 'romantic' pressure groups who hankered after a golden age of rural England and other individuals eager for reform and driven by other concerns – such as the eugenics argument, which focused on the potential impact of harsh working conditions

---

[21] ibid.

[22] See also the Health and Morals of Apprenticeship Act 1803, which imposed a restricted 12-hour working day and responsibility for clothing, accommodation, education and providing medical treatment, but it was poorly enforced and made no significant difference to the wellbeing of those workers (Almond, *Corporate Manslaughter and Regulatory Reform*, above n 15, 97–98). See also the Cotton Mills and Factories Act 1819, which banned the employment of those under 9, and limited the hours of those aged 9 to 16 to a 12-hour day. It was not well enforced, leading to the Cotton Mills Act 1825, which gave magistrates more powers.

[23] See, eg, The Sadler's Committee Report 1833; Children's Employment Committee Report 1842.

[24] Horrell and Humphreys, '"The Exploitation of Little Children": Child Labour and the Family Economy in the Industrial Revolution', above n 10, 487.

[25] ibid.

on future population health.[26] Within this context of very mixed motives, and one of heightened sensitivity to the extension of voting rights, the government commissioned reports and appointed committees to consider the issue of child labour in the mines and the textile industry. Reports were instrumental in raising public awareness of the horrific working conditions and provided support when strong calls for legislative intervention finally came.

The Factory Acts were passed from 1833 onwards, which sought – over time and through a plethora of ad-hoc legislation – to lessen the abuse of children and women (and, later, all workers) in workplaces by, for example, setting minimum working ages and hours and banning children from working at night and insisting on minimum standards regarding ventilation, sanitation and guarding dangerous machinery. For example, the 1842 Mines Act banned women and girls and boys under the age of 10 from working underground. The 1844 Factories Act limited working hours in textile factories for women and those under 18 and insisted that those under 13 work 'only' six and half hours on weekdays and six hours on Saturdays. It also insisted that time keeping be by a public clock and that children and women not be made to clean moving machinery. The 1847 Factories Act introduced a 10-hour day for women and those under 18, and this was extended to men in 1850.

Whilst legal engagement seems substantial in retrospect, especially when starting from such a low base, it is important to note, as Horn does, that 'the passage of factory and mining legislation in the first half of the nineteenth century was designed to regulate but not to outlaw child labour'.[27] This was a slow and awkward intervention. The difficulties often involved in getting the legislation through parliament are testament to entrenched self-interest and an unwillingness to challenge the status quo. It is telling that legislation relating to working hours was only extended to other industries in the 1860s, once its impact was proven to have no negative impact on the profits of textile factories and mills. However, the key to any legislative impact is enforcement and this was notoriously weak. Inspectors were appointed in mills,[28] factories[29] and mining,[30] but their powers of enforcement were limited and the resulting ineffectiveness of the legislation has been widely commented upon.[31] For example, a factory inspector report of 1836

---

[26] ibid.

[27] Horn, *Children's Work and Welfare 1780–1890*, above n 6, 4.

[28] Labour in Cotton Mills Act 1831.

[29] Factories Act 1833.

[30] The Mines Act 1842.

[31] See, eg, Almond, *Corporate Manslaughter and Regulatory Reform*, above n 15; P Bartrip and PT Fenn, 'The Administration of Safety: The Enforcement Policy of the Early Factory Inspectorate 1844–1864' (1980) 58 *Public Administration*, 87; P Bartrip, 'Success or Failure? The Prosecution of the Early Factory Acts' (1985) 38(3) *The Economic History Review* 423; P Bartrip and PT Fenn, 'Factory Fatalities and Regulation in Britain 1878–1913' (1988) 25 *Explorations in Economic History* 60; P Bartrip and PT Fenn, 'The Evolution of Regulatory Style in the Nineteenth Century British Factory Inspectorate' (1983) 10 *Journal of Law and Society* 201; WG Carson, 'The Conventionalization of Early Factory Crime' (1979) 7 *International Journal for the Sociology of Law* 37.

noted how, despite the illegality, children were still found to be working for two days and a night with only meal times and an hour's rest at midnight.[32]

Further ad-hoc regulation was introduced during the second half of the nineteenth century, often as a result of public exposure of a particular social problem or in reaction to an industrial disaster, rather than any deep-seated objection to children working in poor conditions. Often regulation was driven by, or denied because of, commercial considerations which triumphed over child welfare or health and safety priorities.[33] When calls came for change in the coalmining sector, for example, the motivation was to improve literacy and, notably, education was deemed important not because of a child's welfare but due to a greater use of printed materials giving workers instruction.[34] The 1842 Mines Act prohibited the use of boys under 10 so that they could gain an education. In practice, this did not preclude them from working above ground. In 1860, legislation prohibited boys aged 10–12 from working unless they had a certificate of literacy from a schoolmaster. If not, they had to have schooling three hours a day twice a week. Whilst the significance of the legal interventions are huge when viewed as a whole and in hindsight, their impact on the lives of children at the time was not immediate or far-reaching. The factory legislation was, as Horn concludes, 'patchy both in its scope and in its effectiveness'.[35] Very few working children's lives were affected as the legislation focused, especially in the early years, on industries and age groups where child labour was not huge. There were different restrictions laid down, and modified over time, for the various industries but enforcement was fairly weak and so its effectiveness was limited.

The realities of child labour in the UK are indeed 'one of the most shameful events in our history'[36] and its demise was not as dramatic or morally noble as one might have hoped. Legislation did not commit to eradicating child labour but what, in retrospect, the Factory Acts and other relevant legislation during the nineteenth century did achieve was an awakening of public consciousness to the plight of children in paid employment and the movement 'gradually helped encourage acceptance that the State had a responsibility to prescribe minimum conditions of existence for the most vulnerable sectors of society'.[37] The legislative intervention slowly captured, reflected and promoted a new mood – one in which children were, for a variety of reasons, perceived less as labour market commodities and gradually constructed as 'separate' from adults in terms of what labour market engagement might, could and should expect of them. This, whilst a

---

[32] *Factory Inspectors Report*, British Parliamentary Papers 1836, No 353.

[33] See Bartlip and Hartwell's consideration of attempts to regulate the use of lead and phosphorus: P Bartrip and RM Hartwell, 'Profit and Virtue. Economic Theory and the Regulation of Occupational Health in Nineteenth and Early Twentieth Century Britain' in K Hantius (ed), *The Human Face of Law: Essays in Honour of Donald Harris* (Oxford, Oxford University Press, 1997).

[34] Horn, *Children's Work and Welfare 1780–1890*, above n 6, 29.

[35] Horn, *Children's Work and Welfare 1780–1890*, above n 6, 44.

[36] EP Thompson, *The Making of the English Working Class* (London, Victor Gollancz, 1963) 349.

[37] Horn, *Children's Work and Welfare 1780–1890*, above n 6, 45.

sign of progress in many ways, also meant that children came to be differentiated from the 'productive' adult population at a time when autonomy, reflected in the latter, was increasingly idealised.

III. The Importance of Education

During the latter half of the nineteenth century the state's involvement in the education of the masses was established and this had significant, fundamental and permanent repercussions for the concept and status of 'children' in families and society. Prior to this, exclusive schooling was mainly the reserve of the wealthy and so it is difficult to gauge the full trajectory, extent, depth or impact of the growing interest in education during this period:[38] only children of aristocratic or wealthier families were able to attend national fee paying schools on a regular basis and they were, and continued for decades to be, dealt with separately in terms of education policy. Most working-class children needed to work and the half-time system made this feasible for many. Schooling and labour co-existed for a long time and, where schooling was available for working families[39] it was often patchy. Basic education was, in time and as a result of the Factory Acts discussed above, compulsory in some workplaces where children toiled. Workhouses will also have offered some rudimentary schooling under the Poor Law provisions, as did the Industrial Schools, created by the Reformatory and Industrial Schools Acts and designed to manage the large number of homeless juveniles through punitive compulsory education. The overall profile that has emerged, through various studies of autobiographies, is one of inconsistency in individual schooling experiences[40] and evidence of the symbiotic relationship between wealth and education.

[38] See comment on the lack of useful, detailed primary sources relating to schooling in the 18th and 19th centuries: Humphreys, *Childhood and Child Labour in the British Industrial Revolution*, above n 13, 310. Autobiographical studies, such as hers and earlier ones – notably D Vincent, *Bread, Knowledge and Freedom: A Study of Nineteenth-Century Working Class Autobiography* (London, Europa, 1981), have added much to the assessment of the mass of data.

[39] During the first half of the 19th century, there had been a slight, gradual, sporadic increase in schooling opportunities and these had been controlled mostly by voluntary associations and the Church: dame schools, night schools, Sunday Schools and Ragged Schools, for example, became popular – not least because they also provided children with shelter and treats and excursions. Ragged Schools also sought to find work for the children – often in the armed forces or as domestic servants. By 1852, 41 cities and towns had Ragged Schools – and there were hundreds across the country. The schools were not without their critics, who felt they discouraged self-reliance amongst the poor and provided a catalyst for young offenders to mix (See Horn, *Children's Work and Welfare 1780–1890*, above n 6, 48–49).

[40] Reasons for inconsistent schooling include distance to the nearest school, health problems or the costs of schooling: Humphreys cites the case of a young boy who was severely ill and became crippled as a result of having to walk to school 'in the floody times' and sit all day in sodden clothing: Humphreys, *Childhood and Child Labour in the British Industrial Revolution*, above n 13, 311.

Interestingly, within this context, the motivation for state involvement in providing education was multi-faceted: according to Stephens the move can be viewed as a response to increased social unrest, poverty and crime from the 1850s onwards, as a reaction to the threat of commercial competition from countries benefiting economically from state education, and as a reaction to the perception that Prussia's military victories were built upon advantages gleaned from its compulsory schooling system.[41] Crucially, the welfare of the child was not the key reason for implementing the legislation that created and developed the elementary education system. However, the framework that evolved played a huge role in the reconstruction of 'children' and continues to impact upon their lives today. In what follows, we outline and discuss the Education Act 1870, a key legislative milestone in the provision of compulsory education, before unpacking the extent of its impact on transforming children's place in society and the lives of working families.

A. Compulsory Education

The Elementary Education Act 1870, which became known as the Forster Act, was a key turning point for the working classes in terms of educational reform. It marks the beginning of a series of Acts during the latter half of the nineteenth century that introduced compulsory elementary education for children aged 5–13. Whilst voluntary religious schools continued – an 'untidy compromise'[42] reflecting the dual system that emerged after the Act – the 1870 provision introduced a state-centred, publicly funded education system for the first time. Parents were to pay a nominal amount for the schooling, unless they were unable to do so, and religious teaching in the public schools was to be non-denominational and they were to be regularly inspected to maintain standards. The Act was initiated following an investigation by the Newcastle Commission of 1858–61 which unearthed a makeshift, inadequate system of schooling in England. A Select Committee inquiry in 1865 sought to consider in more depth how the situation might be improved,[43] which led to the drafting of the Bill for the Education of the Poor in 1867. This Bill was withdrawn but reappeared the following year as the Elementary Education Bill.

The passage of the Bill was not smooth, highlighting tensions between religious denominations[44] and concerns about the ability to make, and the morality of making, schooling compulsory. The latter had been discussed at various stages

---

[41] WB Stephens, *Education in Britain 1750–1914* (Basingstoke, Macmillan Press, 1998) 78.

[42] ibid, 79.

[43] Education Department Select Committee on Elementary Education 1866.

[44] It is noteworthy, for example, that the Bishop of Oxford and several other clergymen opposed compulsory education as they felt that the Church would be unable to influence such a rise in numbers. See Stephens, *Education in Britain 1750–1914*, above n 41, ch 3.

in the progress of the legislation: the Newcastle Committee Report stated quite clearly that 'if the wages of the child's labour are necessary either to keep the parents from the poor rates, or to relieve the pressure of the severe and bitter poverty, it is better that it should go to work at the earliest age at which it can bear the physical exertion than it should remain at school'.[45] The issue was also evidently of importance during the Bill's readings as also exemplified by the Earl of Shaftesbury when the Bill received its first reading at the House of Lords in July 1870:

> I do not deny that the State has the power – and power is often held to constitute right – to compel the attendance of children at school; but how far would it be just in the exercise of that authority to deprive parents of the earnings of their children, on which they, in so many instances, so largely depend for support? In the case of families with children of 10, 11, and 12 years of age – I am sorry the age has been altered from 6 and 13 to 5 and 12 in the Bill – it would be a very serious infliction to deprive them of the earnings of their children while they would be under the necessity of cloth- ing and feeding them during the time they were being educated. I do not believe it would be possible to bring a system of compulsion into general operation under such circumstances.[46]

Paid child labour did not end immediately upon the enactment of the 1870 Act. The compulsory principle was embedded in the 1870 Act, but it was a permissive power given to School Boards, so dependent on their existence and compliance, and was difficult to enforce. The adjustment in favour of education was patchy and gradual in practice as the realities of life for working families were recog- nised nationally, as suggested above, and locally. In relation to the latter, Stephens provides an illustrative example of how in East Anglia exemptions were often granted by School Boards to children who wished to leave work early and work the land and how the educational opportunities were 'not pursued with any great enthusiasm'.[47] Indeed bye-laws often contained clauses that allowed 'reasonable excuses' for non-attendance and enforcement was, initially at least, quite weak. For many working-class families, schooling was often interrupted when paid work became available: for example, schooling in agricultural communities was often seasonal – 'winter schools' operating when there was less of a need for children to help work on the land[48] – and many accounts report interruptions due to paid work opportunities for the children themselves or to help with domestic chores/ childcare to allow their mother or older siblings to undertake paid work. It is clear that prosperity within the family enabled schooling, but withdrawal was often

---

[45] *Royal Commission on the State of Popular Education in England* (1861) 188.

[46] Hansard, 25 July 1870, para 848. The Duke of Rutland also raised concerns: 'as to the compulsory attendance of children, I believe it to be against the spirit, the wishes, and the feelings of the people of this country. There is an old proverb that one man may lead a horse to the water, but that many cannot make him drink; and I am convinced that it is quite ineffectual to try to force education on the people' (at para 864).

[47] Stephens, *Education in Britain 1750–1914*, above n 41, 93.

[48] Humphreys, *Childhood and Child Labour in the British Industrial Revolution*, above n 13, 310.

necessary for the many families who lived in poverty. This, yet again, underscores the fact that children and their labour were crucial in many working class families' struggle to survive.

Significant legislative intervention followed the 1870 Act, which gradually improved attendance but is indicative of the difficulties facing the government in terms of enforcing attendance and countering the deeply ingrained and often crucial desire for labour market participation. The Sandon Act of 1876 placed a legal duty on parents to ensure that their children attended school and prohibited employment of children under 10 (or eight in agriculture if the authorities thought it necessary). The Elementary Education Act 1880 (the Mundella Act) required that School Boards enforced attendance, set standards in relation to educational expectations and that children in work had to present a certificate stating that the standards expected had been met. Interestingly, employers could be fined if they employed children not holding a certificate.[49] Also key was the 1891 Act legislating that state payments for school fees would be available up to ten shillings per head, making it effectively free and thus reducing the financial burden placed on families. Hence, the compulsory principle that was introduced in 1870 was not a lived reality for many years. It was aided by further legislation but the lives of children only really began to alter in terms of schooling once attitudes toward, and the need for, child labour developed. Significantly, change was also largely driven by a growing conviction in the importance of education for the economic prosperity of the country as a whole. This again underscores that children's needs were not a key motivator for the progress, albeit that they – as the next section demonstrates – were to benefit in the long term.

B. The Long-term Impact on 'Children'

Relevant legislation was, as stated above, enacted amid concerns for the economic efficiency of the country in increasingly competitive times and through a desire to gain social control. Nonetheless, and especially against the backdrop of the inconsistent and inadequate schooling available to the majority of working-class families prior to 1870, it has come to symbolise a significant shift of approach in terms of how children were legislated for regarding education provisions: four interrelated shifts are outlined here. First, at a basic level, it provided a school place for every child which, over time, led to universal compulsory basic education and a key means of enabling future generations to change their position in society. In many ways it was, as Middleton notes, 'the first major measure which did anything constructive for the classes which had been exploited'.[50] Regardless of the

---

[49] Known as a 'dunce' certificate, these continued until 1918. The minimum age was, however, raised to 13.

[50] N Middleton, 'The Education Act of 1870 as the Start of the Modern Concept of the Child' (1970) 18 *British Journal of Educational Studies* 166, 167.

motivations for the original Act, education in Britain became a reality for a greater number of children as a result. The 1870 Act, and the legislation that followed, were thus instrumental in helping to increase the numbers of children accessing education:[51] attendance rates in England and Wales rose from 68 per cent in 1871 to 82 per cent in 1896. In Scotland, by 1901 only 2–3 per cent of children aged 7–11 were not in school.[52] Initially the minimum age of compulsory attendance was 10, but this was raised over the years: to 11 in 1893, 13 in 1899, 14 in 1918, 15 in 1947 and 16 in 1972.[53] Thus, the number of children receiving education and the length of that education was transformed from 1870. This is important from our perspective because it means that 'childhood', if we take it as even partly synonymous with schooling, has expanded gradually but exponentially.

Second, the 1870 Act represented a break with the past, offering a new form of centrally managed educational provision that was not tied to existing structures. Middleton outlines this convincingly, demonstrating how the legislature in 1870 eventually opted for educational reform that had a strong central authority and moved away from existing connections with voluntary societies and frameworks such as the Factory Acts, Industrial Schools Acts and the Poor Law system. In relation to the latter, there was resistance as it was believed that any assistance to parents to pay for their child's education would lead to neglect but, equally, there was a determination not to stigmatise families in this way. Significantly, terminology was altered during the progress of the legislation – 'education of the poor'[54] changed to 'education of the people'. Although the dual system lasted a number of decades, this initial legislation laid the foundations for further state intervention as the influence of the Church lessened, school boards were replaced with Local Education Authorities[55] and the desire grew, especially following two world wars, for greater state involvement in society. Importantly, from our perspective this development in relation to education provided a gradual awareness of, investment in and acceptance of state responsibility for children's welfare; albeit only in conjunction with their education.

Third, and connectedly, Victorian attitudes relating to the responsibility of the state vis-à-vis the welfare of its children were challenged as the compulsion to attend schools laid bare the extent of poverty and illiteracy across the country and drew attention to the raw needs of children and their families. This initial step placed pressure upon governments to then develop schooling so that, during the twentieth century, it became a medium for social reform and welfare provisions

---

[51] Stephens, *Education in Britain 1750–1914*, above n 41, 90–91.

[52] See discussion in ibid, 91.

[53] There was a debate in 2006 regarding increasing the leaving age to 18 and under the Education and Skills Act 2008 it became compulsory, in 2015, for young people to participate in education or training until the age of 18.

[54] The title given to the first Bill introduced in 1867: see Middleton, 'The Education Act of 1870 as the Start of the Modern Concept of the Child', above n 50, 172–73.

[55] Under the Balfour Act of 1902 in England and Wales.

developed as a result: schools 'became the focus of public efforts to improve the general welfare of children'[56] leading, for example, to provisions for meals, physical exercise and medical expertise. Although education has been a site of constant political conflict and continues to elicit a broad diversity of opinions, it has undoubtedly become a permanent matter of public concern and linked, especially following the Second World War, to visions of economic growth and investment in 'human capital'. Indeed, there is an argument that this acceptance of state responsibility, especially within the context of changing expectations around the purpose of education,[57] has in more recent times overburdened schools: Richmond wrote in 1978 that 'they have been saddled with functions and responsibilities which were formerly discharged by other social agencies – family, Church, neighbourhood and work-place'.[58] Growth in responsibility has not, however, been matched by resources. In fact, 91 per cent of schools in England and Wales have had their per pupil funding cut drastically in recent years: by an estimated £7 billion since 2011[59] and crucially important support services, such as the Child and Adolescent Mental Health Services (CAHMS), have also been severely affected by austerity measures.[60] The government has recently promised to increase investment, but not significantly enough to tackle the shortfall created in recent years.[61]

Fourth, the Act of 1870 is thought to be 'the tip of the wedge of universal compulsory education, a wedge which was to alter much of the fabric surrounding the family'.[62] Children had long been principally constructed as a father's property and responsibility and an important form of labour supporting the family and the economy. Children had no legal rights and parental control and authority, which was explicitly gendered, was sacrosanct as the following quote from John Stuart Mill, in 1859, suggests:

> One would almost think that a man's children were supposed to be literally, and not metaphorically, a part of himself, so jealous is [public] opinion of the smallest interference of law with his absolute and exclusive control over them.[63]

Once children were legally entitled to attend school, and more so once schooling was compulsory, this construction of children *within* families changed: for example, 'a child was changed from an asset as a wage earner, to a debit, because school

---

[56] Stephens, *Education in Britain 1750–1914*, above n 41, 91.

[57] See KW Richmond, *Education in Britain Since 1944* (London, Methuen & Co, 1978).

[58] ibid, 8.

[59] See, eg, L Buchan, 'Education Spending Slashed by £17bn since 2011, with 'children paying price for austerity', says Labour', *The Independent*, 14 January 2019.

[60] See, eg, S Neufeld, P Jones and I Goodyer, 'Child and Adolescent Mental Health Services: Longitudinal Data Sheds Light on Current Policy for Psychological Interventions in the Community' (2017) 16 *Journal of Public Mental Health*, 96.

[61] E Busby, 'Boris Johnson Pledges £14bn Boost to Schools over Three Years after "Funding Crisis" Warnings', *The Independent*, 30 August 2019.

[62] Middleton, 'The Education Act of 1870 as the Start of the Modern Concept of the Child' (1970), above n 50, 173.

[63] JS Mill, *On Liberty* (London, Penguin Classics, 1859) ch V.

fees and other expenses had to be met'[64] and parents were expected to facilitate and support their regular attendance. Moreover, recognition of the importance of education at state and individual level and a growth in child-centred[65] education undermined a father's complete dominance over the child as the system provided schools with authority over the children in its care and it took responsibility for child welfare more seriously (see below). In addition, children who became literate would be in a more advantageous position than their illiterate parents, gradually but dramatically shifting the dynamics within families in ways that were not anticipated.

In retrospect, the 1870 Act – and those that followed and expanded the scope of compulsory schooling – impacted a great deal upon children's lives and their place in society. As Rich, writing 100 years later, notes, 'the hopes of 1870 have flowered in a way that could not have been imagined by the politicians of the period'.[66] Provision has expanded to include older children and the number of young adults entering higher education has increased to an all-time high. The focus of education, its perceived purpose, has also changed significantly over the years, often reflecting the particular values of governments.

Overall, the increasing breadth and depth of education policies impacted hugely on the metamorphosis of children that we are articulating here. Childhood has become synonymous with schooling. Compulsory education helped change the place of children in British society and, by default, their role within families altered significantly. The assumption that children would contribute to the family through work, paid or unpaid, unravelled once they had to attend school. Over time, children came to be constructed as entitled to an education and to be cared *for* by their economically independent parents so that their schooling – training that would ensure their autonomy in the future – was supported. The education system has certainly transformed beyond recognition. Arguably, though, throughout the history of educational reforms, children have been, despite the occasional aspirations to be more child-focused, mere pawns in the process of change. Choices made by governments reflect 'deep underlying values about the function of education and the form of society and polity it might help to create'[67] and whilst children have often, in hindsight and as detailed above, benefited from the general evolution of the education system, their best interests were not always the key motivator for change. Economic concerns underscored much of the evolution and even as late as the 1980s the economic function of education was emphasised: the 'Better Schools' White Paper of 1985 stated a government belief that 'the linking of education to training whatever form it takes should have the preparation for employment as one of its principal functions'.[68] It encapsulated

---

[64] Middleton, 'The Education Act of 1870 as the Start of the Modern Concept of the Child' (1970), above n 50, 174.

[65] For discussion, see Richmond, *Education in Britain Since 1944*, above n 57, 25–32.

[66] E Rich, *The Education Act 1870* (London, Longmans, 1970) ix.

[67] S Ranson, *Towards the Learning Society* (London, Cassell Education, 1994) 10.

[68] DES, *Better Schools* (White Paper) (London, HMSO, 1985) 16.

the idea that children are selected for employment opportunities at a fairly young age. This linking of education with the needs of the labour market reminds us how the political function of the education system was, and remains, 'inescapable'.[69]

IV. State Acceptance of (Limited) Responsibility for Child Welfare

The final development that is particularly significant in the metamorphosis of 'children' and their place within the WFB framework is a growth in acceptance of state responsibility for children's welfare. This is the only direct intervention premised upon a clear intention to better support children. It is, however, restricted from the outset as the state engagement is imbued with an overarching reluctance to accept responsibility and directly 'intervene' in the lives of children unless they are at risk of harm and there is no other feasible option. Here we start with a brief discussion of state interventions that laid the foundations for, or are particularly significant in demonstrating, any acceptance of state responsibility for children's welfare. We then suggest that this limited acquisition of state responsibility, framed as it is with the promotion of the liberal self at its core and an inherent belief that the family ought to be primarily responsible for children's welfare, is problematic and inadequate.

A. Interventions

The importance of child welfare as a guiding principle in the UK is very much intertwined with the development of the welfare state, the NHS and social services,[70] but there are early examples of specific national legislation that encouraged, and later reflected, this change in mood. For example, in the wake of the Factory Acts and legal interventions in relation to the education of working-class children, in 1889 the Prevention of Cruelty to Children Act was passed – an early legal milestone which included restrictions on night-time child labour. It also, significantly, threatened to impose fines or imprisonment upon adults who were causing children to break the law and threatened to remove children from the family home if they were mistreated by their parents. This, given the hostility with which any encroachment on the authority of parents (especially fathers) was met, was a radical move. In retrospect, the act is symbolic because it planted the seed for a new era in which abuse of children is not to be tolerated and where the state is more willing to act as a guardian and intervene to protect children when necessary.[71]

---

[69] Ranson, *Towards the Learning Society*, above n 67, 8.
[70] See discussion in ch 1.
[71] See Horn, *Children's Work and Welfare 1780–1890*, above n 6, 66.

Other key relevant legal interventions include the Children Act 1908, which established juvenile courts. Further examples include the Guardianship Act of 1925, which stated that the welfare of the child be the 'first and paramount consideration' before the courts in cases of custody or property; the 1948 Children Act, which established a children's committee and a children's officer in every local authority; and the 1989 Children Act[72] which, importantly, established a broad principle of state protection from child abuse and exploitation and the principle that the child's welfare is paramount in all family law proceedings.[73]

The significance of child welfare has more recently been recognised at EU and international level where a rights-based approach is more prominent.[74] For example, the EU Charter of Fundamental Rights Art 24 provides that children have *a right* to the protection and care necessary for their wellbeing and the Treaty of Lisbon Art 3(3) in 2009 included 'protection of the rights of the child' as a stated objective of the EU. At an international level the 1989 UN Declaration of the Rights of the Child (UNCROC) contains a list of basic rights owed to the child including the right to freedom of expression, thought, religion, health care, and education to develop the child's full potential and the right to play and leisure.[75] The macro-level legal engagement depicts a gradual, broad centralisation of children's welfare as a core political concern. This is also reflected at micro-level, although not until relatively recently in national policy attempts to eradicate child poverty in the UK, as the following example demonstrates.

Historically, there have been very few attempts to tackle child poverty directly, possibly because adult moral agency and individual responsibility have been promoted as the only sustainable and rational solution to poverty in the UK. Improving welfare support for families with children has historically been viewed as a means of encouraging dependency and idleness[76] and this view has prevailed for many decades. There is, however, one notable exception to this general approach. New Labour's commendable historic pledge to end child poverty within

---

[72] Into force in England and Wales in 1991 and in Northern Ireland in 1996.

[73] Section 1: 'When a court determines any question with respect to (a) the upbringing of a child: or (b) the administration of a child's property or the application of any income arising out of it, the child's welfare shall be the court's paramount consideration.'

[74] An approach that can place children, as Cretney et al have noted, 'in a central and powerful place where the value of being the subject and not merely the object of concern is acknowledged' (S Cretney, J Masson and R Bailey-Harris, *Principles of Family Law – Seventh Edition* (London, Sweet & Maxwell, 2003) 494. See also H Stalford and E Drywood, 'Coming of age? Children's rights in the European Union' (2009) 46 *Common Market Law Review* 143; H Stalford, *Children and the European Union: Rights, Welfare and Accountability* (Oxford, Hart Publishing, 2012).

[75] Although not directly enforceable in UK courts, this is a milestone for our purposes in that it demonstrates a political commitment, at international level, to articulating the standards that are to be expected in relation to children.

[76] Indeed, poor relief was refused if a family contained children capable of, but not undertaking, paid work, underscoring early requirements for child labour and the lack of alternative support for families who failed to make use of all available sources of income: see Horrell and Humphreys, '"The Exploitation of Little Children": Child Labour and the Family Economy in the Industrial Revolution', above n 10, 487.

a generation,[77] which was connected to the European-wide agenda and the Lisbon goals of 2000,[78] broke new ground and provided motivation for a vast number of initiatives which attempted to focus attention on those families with children who were most in need. Kenway characterises the approach adopted by New Labour as comprising four main elements: a stress on encouraging parents, especially lone parents, into work; a tax credit system underpinned by the National Minimum Wage to provide financial incentive; a childcare strategy which incorporated state aid (through tax credits) to help pay for it; and a rise in child benefit payments for all families.[79] Other aspects of the strategy included the establishment of the Social Exclusion Unit, increases in the income support earnings disregard, and the Sure Start programme, which was established in 1999 to improve services for children living in the most disadvantaged areas of the UK. The government invested substantial financial resources into the various programmes and aimed to reduce poverty incrementally with targets set and annual monitoring provisions put in place.

This was a bold approach and did place child poverty firmly on the political agenda and, from our perspective, the Child Poverty Act 2010, which received cross-party support, is an example of how 'children' came to be framed, publicly, as deserving[80] of state attention in their own right. It has also proved to be successful in that it made substantial progress.[81] It did, however, attract some valid criticism. For example, New Labour's approach has been criticised for focusing too much on children within lone-parent families,[82] and being unwilling to really tackle the need to redistribute income[83] by remaining, as Goldson put it, 'coy with regard to comprehensively raising state benefits and/or lifting the minimum wage'.[84] In a similar vein, Kenway notes that whilst it 'marked a sharp break with its Conservative predecessors most of Labour government's policies for dealing with poverty [were] an extension of what [had] gone before rather than a

---

[77] See, eg, T Blair, 'Beveridge Revisited: A Welfare State for the 21st Century', speech delivered at Toynbee Hall, 18 March 1999, cited in R Walker (ed), *Ending Child Poverty: Popular Welfare for 21st Century?* (Bristol, Policy Press, 1999) 7–18. See also the Child Poverty Act 2010.

[78] Which saw the European Council agree that Member States make a decisive impact on poverty by 2010: see S Ruxton and F Bennett, *Including Children? Developing a Coherent Approach to Poverty and Social Exclusion across Europe* (Brussels, Euronet, 2001).

[79] P Kenway, 'Social Justice and Inequality in the UK: Eradicating Child Poverty?' (2008) 79 *The Political Quarterly*, 41.

[80] See, however, Goldson's discussion of how not all children were included in this new framing: B Goldson, 'New Labour, Social Justice and Children: Political Calculation and the Deserving–Undeserving Schism' (2002) 32 *British Journal of Social Work* 683.

[81] See, eg, D Piachaud, 'Poverty and Social Protection in Britain: Policy Developments since 1997' (2012) 11 *Journal of Policy Practice* 92; see also G Main and J Bradshaw, 'Child Poverty in the UK: Measures, Prevalence and Intra-Household Sharing' (2016) 36 *Critical Social Policy* 38.

[82] See eg P Morgan, 'Children, Families and the Failure of UK Anti-Poverty Policy' (2007) 27 *Economic Affairs* 32.

[83] B Goldson, 'New Labour, Social Justice and Children: Political Calculation and the Deserving–Undeserving Schism' (2002) 32 *British Journal of Social Work* 684.

[84] ibid, 685.

rupture with it'.[85] Crucially, as Kenway states, it demonstrated Labour's unwilling-ness to alter the paradigm or framework of engagement, which remained firmly rooted in the disputed notion that paid work was the key to eradicating poverty in families:[86] an approach that is firmly rooted in the problematic belief that all adults are, or ought to be, autonomous and rational, independent actors and assumptions regarding the constant availability of paid work.

Ultimately, however, New Labour's attempt to tackle child poverty was derailed; it was mired by the true extent and ramifications of the problem it sought to tackle and then destroyed by the Coalition party's austerity measures, the main losers of which proved to be low-income families with children.[87] Moreover, any progress made was reversed by a change in approach and a re-conviction of deeply entrenched suspicions of welfare support as a viable solu-tion. The latter was viewed by many as destroying ambition for 'work, savings, self-advancement, honesty, mutual care and co-operation' and concern grew that 'the lavish rewards of dependency' would 'ensure that people … work the system on a massive scale'.[88] An interesting study of how poverty is represented in British newspapers shows that media representations during this period often attributed child poverty to poor parenting and suggests this helped remove the problem of child poverty, and any attempt to solve it, from public consciousness.[89] The fall-out of our lack of consistent collective engagement with the issue of child poverty has had, and continues to have, dire consequences for many. Despite the UK being one of the strongest economies in the world, child poverty has increased hugely in recent decades. Whatever form of measurement is preferred,[90] it is clear

[85] P Kenway, 'Social Justice and Inequality in the UK: Eradicating Child Poverty?' (2008) 79 *The Political Quarterly* 41, 41. See also P Lewis, 'Upskilling the Workers Will Not Upskill the Work. Why the Dominant Economic Framework Limits Child Poverty Reduction' (2011) 40 *Journal of Social Policy* 535 and, more broadly, C Hay, *The Political Economy of New Labour* (Manchester, Manchester University Press, 1999); R Heffernan, *New Labour and Thatcherism* (Basingstoke, Palgrave, 2000); and A Callanicos, *Against the Third Way: An Anti-Capitalist Critique* (Cambridge, Polity Press, 2001).

[86] See Kenway, 'Social Justice and Inequality in the UK: Eradicating Child Poverty?', above n 79, 52. See also, eg, Lewis, 'Upskilling the Workers Will Not Upskill the Work. Why the Dominant Economic Framework Limits Child Poverty Reduction', above n 82, 535 where it is argued that 'addressing relative poverty requires an alternative theoretical approach to the neoclassical economics that … underpins policy'.

[87] J Cribb, A Hood, R Joyce and D Phillips, *Living Standards, Poverty and Inequality in the UK* (London, Institute of Fiscal Studies, 2013); H Reed and J Portes, *Cumulative Impact Assessment and Social Research Report by Landman Economics and the National Institute of Economic and Social Research for the Equality and Human Rights Commission*, Research Report 94 (London, EHRC, 2014); and see discussion in Main and Bradshaw, 'Child Poverty in the UK: Measures, Prevalence and Intra-Household Sharing', above n 81, 38.

[88] Morgan, 'Children, Families and the Failure of UK Anti-Poverty Policy', above n 82, 37; sentiments that have been echoed in Coalition policy rhetoric – see Main and Bradshaw, 'Child Poverty in the UK: Measures, Prevalence and Intra-Household Sharing', above n 81, 40.

[89] A Chauhan and J Foster, 'Representations of Poverty in British Newspapers: a Case of 'Othering' the Threat?' (2014) 24 *Journal of Community & Applied Social Psychology* 390.

[90] For a discussion of measurements relating to child poverty see Main and Bradshaw, 'Child Poverty in the UK: Measures, Prevalence and Intra-Household Sharing', above n 81, 41–42.

that 'the enduring and intensifying nature of poverty is inescapable'.[91] In 1979 an estimated 1.4 million children (or 10 per cent) in the UK were living in poverty, in 1999/2000 the numbers had risen to 4.3 million or 34 per cent of children.[92] It was predicted in 2017 that by 2022 over 5 million children (37 per cent of all children) in the UK will live in relative income poverty.[93] A recent report[94] found that child poverty has been rising for those born over the last decade, following improvements in the mid 1990s and early 2000s, so that an estimated 40 per cent of two year olds born between 2016 and 2020 are facing the highest rates of early years poverty in over 60 years. The impact of this poverty is far-reaching and pervades all aspects of children's lives, with repercussions for them in adulthood. Indeed, as a review of qualitative research revealed, 'poverty penetrates deep into the heart of childhood, permeating every facet of children's lives':[95] for example, many thousands of children go to school without anything to eat or drink in the morning;[96] it has a negative impact on children's physical and mental health,[97] life expectancy and cognitive development[98] and educational performance;[99] and, although more research is desperately needed,[100] it is clear that this social injustice impacts disproportionately on the lives of black children.[101]

From our perspective, the lack of development of policies such as this in connection to child poverty, as well as other policies that seek to protect children at risk of harm or bestow particular rights upon them,[102] signposts an important

[91] Goldson, 'New Labour, Social Justice and Children: Political Calculation and the Deserving–Undeserving Schism', above n 80, 684.

[92] *Households Below Average Income* (Department of Social Security, London, 2001), cited in Goldson, 'New Labour, Social Justice and Children: Political Calculation and the Deserving–Undeserving Schism', above n 80, 686.

[93] A Hood and T Waters, *Living Standards, Poverty and Inequality in the UK: 2017–18 to 2021–22* (London, Institute of Fiscal Studies, 2017).

[94] F Rahman, *The Generation of Poverty: Poverty over the Life Course for Different Generations* (London, Nuffield Foundation 2019).

[95] T Ridge, 'The Everyday Costs of Poverty in Childhood: A Review of Qualitative Research Exploring the Lives of Low-Income Children in the UK' (2011) 25 *Children and Society* 73, 73. Or, as Goldson comments, 'poverty and inequality permeates every corner and every crevice of the poor child's social landscape': see Goldson, 'New Labour, Social Justice and Children: Political Calculation and the Deserving–Undeserving Schism', above n 80, 686.

[96] Piachaud, 'Child Poverty, Opportunities and Quality of Life', above n 81, 446.

[97] T Novak, 'Rich Children, Poor Children' in B Goldson, M Lavalette and J McKechnie (eds), *Children, Welfare and the State* (London, SAGE, 1996); S Holterman, 'The Impact of Public Expenditure and Fiscal Policies on Britain's Children and Young People' (1996) 10 *Children and Society* 3; C Howarth, P Kenway, G Palmer and R Morelli, *Monitoring Poverty and Social Exclusion* (York, Joseph Rowntree Foundation, 1999); T Ridge, 'The Everyday Costs of Poverty in Childhood: a Review of Qualitative Research Exploring the Lives of Low-Income Children in the UK' (2011) 25 *Children and Society* 73.

[98] See Child Poverty Action Group, *Poverty: The Facts* 6th edn (London, CPAG, 2018).

[99] I McCallam and G Redhead, 'Poverty and Educational Performance' (2000) 106 *Poverty* 14.

[100] L Platt, 'Child Poverty, Employment and Ethnicity in the UK: the Role and Limitations of Policy' (2007) 9 *European Societies* 175.

[101] B Goldson and R Chigwada-Bailey, '(What) Justice for Black Children and Young People?' in B Goldson (ed), *Youth Justice: Contemporary Policy and Practice* (Aldershot, Ashgate, 1999).

[102] A body of law that has attracted much academic engagement. See, eg, J Eekelaar, 'The Emergence of Children's Rights' (1986) 6 *Oxford Journal of Legal Studies* 237; J Herring, 'The Human Rights

aspect of the metamorphosis that occurred in relation to the construction of children/childhood. Whilst some intervention is better than none in this context, what we have is disperse and far from unproblematic in practice.[103] Although children came to be constructed as worthy of and entitled to some state support, that support has been patchy and reluctantly given. Children are still perceived as the responsibility of the family, often invisible in a society that promotes the interests of those who are already in possession of power and resources – those who are autonomous and self-sufficient. Children's lived realities reveal tensions in the true nature of contemporary state responsibility. In many ways the state has defined its role as one of a safety net for when families 'fail' to provide adequate care. Within this current dynamic 'parents' have often been (re)constructed as potential 'perpetrators of harm'. *Their* failure is presented as what drives state intervention. Hence, state 'responsibility' for child welfare is built upon a narrative of parental failure as a safeguard for children's welfare and it is a narrative that has been favoured recently by political parties and the media: for example, the Coalition government portrayed poor parents as being responsible for poverty, blaming it on bad spending decisions and for transmitting their attitudes and behaviours onto their children.[104] The particular choice of framing of the 'problem' (parents) inevitably means that other issues that impact on children's welfare, such as a family's poverty, ill health and lack of educational opportunities and the responsibilities of others can be conveniently ignored.

V. Children's Welfare in the Current WFB Framework and the Appeal of Vulnerability Theory

The metamorphosis of 'children' is never complete; it is an ongoing process that will be influenced in the future, as it has been in the past, by the priorities of adults.

Act and the Welfare Principle in Family Law – conflicting or complimentary?' (1999) 11 *Child and Family Law Quarterly*, 223; C McGlynn, *Families and the European Union; Law, Politics and Pluralism* (Cambridge, Cambridge University Press, 2006) ch 3; H Stalford and E Drywood, 'Coming of Age? Children's Rights in the European Union' (2009) 46 *Common Market Law Review*, 143; H Stalford, 'EU Law and Children's Rights: A Case Study of EU Family Law' (2010) 10 *Contemporary Issues in Law* 1.

[103] As stated elsewhere, 'deciding what is in the best interests of the child is highly contentious, hugely problematic and not always consistent': see G James and T Callus, 'Child Welfare and Work–Family Reconciliation Policies: Lessons From Family Law' in N Busby and G James (eds), *Families, Care-giving and Paid Work: Challenging Labour Law in the 21st Century* (Cheltenham, Edward Elgar, 2011) 173, 175). See also, for discussion, M Freeman, 'The Best Interests of the Child? Is the Best Interests of the Child in the Best Interests of Children?' (1997) 11 *International Journal of Law, Policy and the Family* 360; F Olsen, 'Children's Rights: Some Feminist Approaches to the UNCROC' (1992) 6 *International Journal of Law and the Family* 192; S Parker, 'The Best Interests of the Child – Principles and Problems' (1994) 8 *International Journal of Law and the Family* 26; C Piper, 'Assumptions About Children's Best Interests' (2000) 22 *Journal of Social Welfare and Family Law* 261; and H Reece, 'The Paramountcy Principle: Consensus or Construct?' (1996) 49 *Current Legal Problems* 267.

[104] See discussion in Main and Bradshaw, 'Child Poverty in the UK: Measures, Prevalence and Intra-Household Sharing', above n 81, 38.

The transformations have, in many ways, been positive as children's lives today are a far cry from the horrors of the workhouses and the industrial revolution. However, the realities of the lives of too many children in the UK demonstrate the limitations of current approaches and how so much more needs to be done to identify and better reflect children's needs. Of particular interest to our project is the fact that children in the UK have come to be constructed as 'inevitably dependent' and, significantly, children are dependent for a long time and the ability of children themselves to reduce their dependency upon others is virtually non-existent. Although the nature of their dependency varies between families and usually diminishes over time, it is important to note that the consequences of this long-term dependency are primarily placed upon the shoulders of their parents or other family members, with state intervention only offered, for the most part, if this is not feasible. The metamorphosis we have outlined above demonstrated how children's needs per se have remained peripheral to those of others – be that individuals, institutions or the state. With this context in mind we now demonstrate how contemporary 'family-friendly' employment laws still fail to adequately reflect children's welfare concerns. In this section we also argue that acceptance of human vulnerability as a foundation for policy development would provide a useful impetus for better identification and inclusion of children's welfare as a core driver for reforms in this field.

A. The Current WFB Framework

The UK package of employment rights available to working parents today, discussed in chapters two and three, was originally premised upon EU work–family reconciliation policies but *at no point* has children's welfare been regarded as important in the formulation or development of these EU provisions. This is despite a broader, commendable, commitment to protecting and promoting the rights of children per se.[105] Similar issues exist in relation to the WFB framework that has developed in the UK. Here, leave entitlements have been a core part of the package of rights available and policy has focused on protecting those workers discriminated against as a result of pregnancy or maternity leave[106] and allowing

---

[105] See H Stalford, *Children and the European Union: rights, welfare and accountability* (Oxford, Hart Publishing, 2012); H Stalford and M Schuurman, 'Are We There Yet? The Impact of the Treaty of Lisbon on the EU Children's Rights Agenda' (2011) 19 *International Journal of Children's Rights* 381. G James, 'Forgotten Children: Work–Family Reconciliation in the EU' (2012) 34 *Journal of Social Welfare and Family Law* 363.

[106] See Equality Act 2010, s 18 and Employment Rights Act 1996, s 99. The fact that these rights are failing to protect women from experiencing such poor treatment has been well documented: see G James, *The Legal Regulation of Pregnancy and Parenting in the Workplace* (London, Routledge Cavendish, 2009); G James, 'Family-Friendly Employment Law (Re)Assessed: The Potential of Care Ethics' (2016) 45 *Industrial Law Journal* 477; EHRC/BIS, *Pregnancy and Maternity-Related Discrimination and Disadvantage First Findings: Surveys of Employers and Mothers*, BIS Research Paper No 235 (London, EHRC, 2015).

mothers, and more recently fathers, to leave the workplace temporarily in order to care for an unborn[107] or newborn baby. The amount of leave permitted has extended over the years[108] and, in addition, the right to request flexible working,[109] discussed in chapter five, provides some potential for supporting care work in the long term. This was initially framed as a right only for parents and then extended to carers[110] more broadly, but has since been reframed as a right for *all* eligible employees, arguably distancing it from any, even implied, association with the promotion of children's welfare. In fact, reflecting the broader historical transformation outlined above, concern for children's wellbeing was never a primary motivator for the development of our modern WFB framework: as stated elsewhere, 'even when recognised by governments as relevant, children's interests are often an afterthought, a consequence of, rather than a motivator for, the rights that are enacted'.[111]

To be clear, it is not that children's wellbeing is not mentioned during the evolution of relevant laws – the 2004 10-year strategy for childcare was premised upon a long-term vision to provide 'choice for parents, the best start for children'[112] and in 2017 the government issued a campaign to 'share the joy' of childcare, encouraging fathers to take advantage of shared parental leave provisions.[113] However, this aspect of the rhetoric cannot mask the underlying premise of the legal frameworks at national and EU level: there have been various reforms in this area, and several amendments to the provisions over the years, and, although packaged and promoted in various ways, they have all had a consistent theme – they aim to provide better support for working parents to undertake *their* responsibilities as opposed to being a means of supporting children's wellbeing per se. The emphasis on working parents assumes that they will (and should), if given adequate choices and flexibility through legal rights and protection, be able to care (well)

---

[107] See Employment Rights Act 1996, ss 55–56. The right to accompany a pregnant partner was extended in October 2014 by the Children and Families Act 2014. For a discussion see G Mitchell, 'Encouraging Fathers to Care: The Children and Families Act 2014 and Shared Parental Leave' (2015) 44 *Industrial Law Journal* 123.

[108] See outline in ch 2 and discussion in G James, 'Family-Friendly Employment Laws (Re)Assessed: The Potential of Care Ethics' (2016) 45 *Industrial Law Journal* 477.

[109] S80F-80I Employment Rights Act 1996, the Flexible Working (Eligibility, Complaints and Remedies) Regulations 2002 (SI 2002/3236) and the Flexible Working (Procedural Requirements) 2002 (SI 2002/3207).

[110] Interestingly, the EU Carers Directive has chosen to limit the right to request to carers (see Commission proposal for a directive of the European Parliament and of the Council on work–life balance for parents and carers and repealing Council Directive 2010/18/EU (COM(2017) 253 Final 2017/0085 (COD)). This is contrary to the approach adopted in the UK.

[111] James and Callus, 'Child Welfare and Work–Family Reconciliation Policies: Lessons From Family Law', above n 103, 174.

[112] *Choice for Parents: The Best Start for Children: A Ten Year Strategy for Childcare* (London, HMSO, 2004).

[113] See   www.gov.uk/government/news/new-share-the-joy-campaign-promotes-shared-parental-leave-rights-for-parents.

for their children *and* undertake paid work without any further state interventions. Legislation also provides individuals with legal rights to enforce, albeit that the system for doing so is flawed,[114] in the event of poor treatment at work. The narrative of 'individual responsibility' for oneself and one's dependants, which is implicit in this legal framework and the enforcement provisions, is based upon and promotes an ideology of individual autonomy and responsibility. This, as Fineman discusses, is 'understood narrowly' and 'is primarily economic in nature'.[115] It underscores the very foundations of the WFB framework and is a core reason why it is incapable, in its current form, of ever adequately reflecting the needs of children and working families as a whole in anything more than a superficial way.

The invisibility of the recipients of the care work that is being facilitated is at best disappointing but there is also a more sinister undertone that needs to be highlighted: often children are not simply absent in the WFB framework but are framed as the essence of the WFB 'problem' – as the main obstacle or 'burden' that prevents parents, women in particular, from participating in the workplace on an equal footing with other, less encumbered[116] workers or as the cause of their absence from work – undermining their autonomy and challenging their ability to live up to the standard worker ideal. Examples of this divisive and unnecessary narrative, which often frames discussions of childcare and related domestic chores as an onerous 'burden' or a 'duty', are found in CJEU decisions, both those considered to be restrictive[117] and more progressive[118] in their promotion of gender equality, as well as in media representations.[119] It is a narrative that constructs children as unequivocally 'dependent' and constructs adult family members as uniquely responsible for managing that inherent dependency if they want to enter and succeed in the labour market. Although the historical transformations outlined above might have resulted, albeit unintentionally, in improving children's welfare, their metamorphosis means that they have come to epitomise 'the problem' to be solved by WFB measures. They became absorbed into a discourse of hierarchical differentiation and one that placed them, because of their inherent lack of autonomy, at the lowest point possible. This is both disempowering for them and for those who are held to be responsible for their wellbeing: parents, and especially mothers. Moreover, constructing children as part of the 'problem' restricts our ability to promote a legal framework that can identify and acknowledge their needs, both as children in their own right, as members of family units and as future adults.

---

[114] See ch 6.

[115] MA Fineman, *The Autonomy Myth: A Theory of Dependency* (New York, The New Press, 2004) 9. See discussion above, ch 1 and below, ch 6.

[116] See above, chs 2 and 3 above.

[117] See, eg, the *Hoffman* Case 184/83 [1984] ECR 3047.

[118] See, eg, *Roca Álvarez v Sesa Start España ETT SA* (Case C 104/09).

[119] See, eg, L Ward, 'Childcare Burden Falls on Families', *The Guardian*, 15 March 2005; and J Bingham, 'British Grandparents Shouldering Childcare Burden', *The Telegraph*, 28 June 2012.

B. Vulnerability Theory and Children's Welfare

Two core and interrelated traits of the vulnerability approach, outlined in the introductory chapter, highlight how it might re-focus our engagement in a way that offers scope to better promote children's welfare in WFB policies. First, at a broad level, because the vulnerability approach challenges the myth of an 'autonomous and independent subject' it undermines the promotion of autonomy in adulthood as the pivotal developmental stage of political subjects – the stage to which all individuals can and should aspire. This latter construction excludes, indeed vilifies, other equally meaningful stages within the lifespan of most people. A child has no capacity to be autonomous. This has always been the case – even at the point in history when many children were required to undertake paid work they did so on behalf of, and under the instruction of, family members. They toiled for the welfare of the family as a whole and, for many, autonomy would also, because of limited opportunities, have been illusory for their entire adult life. Indeed, the aspirational quality of individual autonomy and independence is linked to neoliberalism and the growth of the capitalist market economy. In any event, children are fundamentally incapable of embodying this idealised status. A vulnerability approach, however, does not require or expect them to do so. Instead, it positions autonomy, independence and self-sufficiency as only 'one of a range of developmental stages that an actual human individual passes through in the course of a "normal" lifespan'.[120] It views humans as vulnerable during *all* of these developmental stages and so the focus shifts to how laws might support and encourage resilience in *all* individuals and *throughout* the life course.

The child, in this alternative framing, is viewed as a vulnerable human being at the start of his or her life journey and law's role is key in helping (be it through intervention or non-intervention) to equip her/him to withstand life's challenges so that she/he is capable of meaningfully engaging with and contributing to all aspects of society throughout the life course. This arguably elevates the position of children as they are no longer viewed as the polar opposite of the liberal subject or as an obstacle in the way of those who might otherwise become or remain autonomous, but as human beings equally worthy of support and consideration. Children hold a more central position, on a par with adults, and indeed, could be a primary focus for building the very foundations for resilience, which is at the heart of vulnerability theory.[121] There are different types of resources or assets that social organisations and institutions can provide in order to promote resilience in individuals and, significantly, families are particularly important in providing social assets or resources that are often less tangible than those provided by other institutions and not so easily quantified: as Fineman states, 'the family is a major

---

[120] MA Fineman, '"Elderly" as vulnerable: Rethinking the nature of individual and societal responsibility' (2012–2013) 20 *The Elder Law Journal Vol 71*, 88.

[121] For a discussion, see MA Fineman, 'The Vulnerable Subject and the Responsive State' (2010) 60 *Emory Law Journal* 251, 270.

institution providing social resources, particularly for the young or others in need of care'.[122] Importantly, this task of resilience building, which is central to caretaking even if we don't often construct it in this way, would be better valued, recognised and supported because the nurturing from consistent caregiving and support by family members and others is pivotal to this ongoing endeavour. Fredman's call for us to better value the social function of pregnancy and parenthood[123] is also captured in an approach that would ultimately require and hopefully attract greater support for, and recognition of, care work by the state and, through state means, by employers.

Second, by acknowledging our shared human vulnerability, this approach encourages the reallocation of responsibility for care work and discourages anything that (re)produces gender inequalities[124] but, importantly from the perspective of children's welfare, remains sensitive to the current lived realities of family life and eschews any tendency to position family members as being in opposition to each other. This offers an alternative focus to that historically favoured by those concerned with securing gender equality, which has often ignored, downplayed or misrepresented the parent/child and mother/child relationship. Much feminist engagement has, as Fineman discusses, viewed the family as a site of inevitable oppression or conflict between the individual rights of its members and hence critiqued the disadvantaged position of women in their family roles vis-à-vis men or pitted mothers against fathers and/or children.[125] This focus on individual rights was historically necessary to highlight gender inequalities, especially in the public sphere, but has proved incapable, in isolation, of tackling the dilemmas and difficulties now confronting working families in general, and working mothers in particular. Within much of the traditional feminist literature the 'family is wrongly assumed to be unchanging, an essentialized institution, natural in form and function, that is the repository for dependency'.[126]

It is within this context that narratives of children, discussed above, as 'burdens' requiring 'self-sacrifice' and 'subservience' and restricting women's aspirations in terms of education and careers, have taken hold. Yet this narrative masks an awkward reality; that children need to be cared for and if emancipation can *only* be defined by ensuring women undertake less care work the consequences are likely to be felt primarily, and unsatisfactorily, by children. Indeed, we 'cannot ignore the dilemmas presented by children and others in need of care'.[127] The approach favoured here is to focus less on intimate relationships between adults. Crucially, it must be accepted that the relationship of carer and child is no less legitimate than those between adults. This is not to undermine or ignore

---

[122] ibid, 271.
[123] S Fredman, *Women and The Law* (Oxford, Oxford University Press, 1997).
[124] See ch 2.
[125] Fineman, *The Autonomy Myth: A Theory of Dependency*, above n 115, 149.
[126] ibid, 155.
[127] ibid, 175.

the consequences of motherhood – that 'there is no autonomy to be found in motherhood'[128] – but to demand that, as a result of this fact we do not position the child, or the care work that that child requires, as 'the problem'. Instead we are encouraged to re-imagine how relevant societal institutions can be transformed and accommodations made so that the costs of expectations and behaviours within the family and the workplace are not borne primarily by women; we are encouraged to challenge existing frameworks and allocations of resources and power. The vulnerability approach is capable of being responsive to and challenging the gendered lived realities of working families, rather than playing down this reality. It encourages us to support human interdependency and to better value the caretaker role (whoever undertakes it), rather than construct it as an unrewarding and unchanging obstacle to the 'prize' of autonomy and independence.

VI. Conclusions

Whilst as a whole this chapter has outlined a magnificent and complex transformation in the daily lives of children that is worthy of celebration, it has also raised concerns about the consequences and limitations of that transformation. On the one hand, the metamorphosis has, in Fineman's terms, enabled children's particular vulnerabilities to be recognised: they were not classed as a 'dependent population' at any particular point or because of any particular event in history, but nonetheless came to be constructed in this way. This re-framing, and the almost accidental nature of it, is significant for our purposes as it provides an important context for modern views of children as natural and worthy recipients of care. On the other hand, we have highlighted some of the nuances of that development such as the fact that it was rarely motivated by a significant re-evaluation of *their* needs, how change was often shaped by economic concerns, how their departure from the public space of paid work has led to their marginalisation in the private sphere. We also highlighted a number of ongoing limitations and tensions that continue: how children are often constructed as a 'burden' on adult autonomy and how far too many children, despite the legal changes outlined here, continue to live in poverty and at risk of harm.

Once children were excluded from the labour market they became firmly (re)embedded as a primary responsibility of their parents or wider family units. They had always, of course, been 'dependent' upon their families but the dynamics of the dependency were altered following the transformation outlined in this chapter. Children, once they stopped being productive in the market sense, became invisible to those concerned with regulating employment relationships and this 'invisibility' has remained even within the context of the development of the relatively modern WFB framework. The lack of attention to children's welfare in this

---

[128] ibid, 169.

recent legal context is 'curious'[129] because one might have imagined that a growing interest in formulating 'family-friendly' strategies would have included consideration of children's wellbeing as a significant component of the policies adopted. Children's welfare has become an issue of public concern, in a way that would never have been anticipated prior to the twentieth century, yet it is still assumed to be adequately and easily absorbed by the family, despite changes in the everyday functioning and labour market participation and expectations of the latter.

We suggest above that acceptance of vulnerability as a lifelong condition challenges assumptions upon which historic developments and current social configurations and institutional arrangements rest. It requires individuals, states and employers to accept a greater responsibility because, ultimately, we can no longer assume that families should uncomplainingly absorb all ramifications of dependency.[130] Nor, we argue in the context of this chapter, can we turn a blind eye to the consequences of our actions, or lack of action, for children's welfare more broadly. This needs to be reconsidered and part of that reconsideration requires us to reimagine the WFB framework so that it is redefined as a group of legal tools for reflecting human vulnerability and building resilience within individuals, families and wider institutions. Before embarking upon this, the historical treatment of another cohort whose needs are crying out for greater exploration – elderly dependants – are discussed in chapter five.

[129] James and Callus, 'Child Welfare and Work-Family Reconciliation Policies: Lessons From Family Law', above n 103, 173.
[130] Fineman, *The Autonomy Myth: A Theory of Dependency*, above n 115.

5

Eldercare

I. Introduction

> At any one time there have been conflicting and competing discourses and represen-
> tations of old women and old men. This is so in the present and expresses the varied
> subjective experiences of being old.[1]

In the same way that 'being old' is a subjective experience that defies a single
representation, the experiences of those undertaking eldercare work varies in
nature and scope and often, unlike care for very young children, considered in
chapter four, fluctuates over a fairly wide timeframe and can often be complicated by illness, disability and/or frailty.[2] As stated elsewhere, caring for an older
relative who is dependent can be experienced as a 'journey', the duration or desti-
nation of which is not always clearly defined. It is a journey involving a number
of people, including the recipients of care, relatives, social services and health care
providers.[3] Of course, a growing number of working families may also, whilst
not necessarily undertaking care work themselves, be organising or managing
care work, drawing on personal budgets to provide care in the form of home help
or care homes;[4] and so 'caring' for dependent older relatives takes many forms
and has multi-faceted implications for working families, implications that are
under-researched. Significantly, many carers who are also employed, an estimated
4.87 million in the UK,[5] are often known to experience huge difficulties remaining in paid employment whilst undertaking this type of care work. Indeed, many
reduce their hours and an estimated 2.6 million carers leave paid employment
every year as a result of these difficulties.[6] Evidence also suggests that eldercare
can have detrimental impacts, both financially and on a carer's health and wellbeing. Carers are paid an 'allowance'[7] which is the lowest benefit of its kind in the

---

[1] P Thane, *Old Age in English History* (Oxford, Oxford University Press, 2000) 458.

[2] For statistics relating to health in later life see Age UK, *Later Life in the United Kingdom 2019*
(London, Age Concern, 2019).

[3] G James and E Spruce, 'Workers with Elderly Dependants: Employment Law's Response to the
Latest Care-Giving Conundrum' (2015) 35 *Legal Studies* 463.

[4] ibid.

[5] Carers UK, *Juggling Work and Unpaid Care* (London, Carers UK, 2018).

[6] ibid.

[7] £65.15 a week in 2019/20, for a minimum of 35 hours. Of course, many work over 35 hours a
week – one survey in England suggests that almost 15% of carers care for between 50 and 100 hours

UK: the equivalent of being paid less than £2 an hour. In return carers save the state an estimated £132 billion a year.[8] The personal impact of this financial hardship can be severe for many, with a quarter of carers who have been caring for over 15 years reporting that they have been in debt as a result of care work, and half of this cohort reporting that they have had to cut back on essentials like food and heating.[9] Significantly, 73 per cent of carers feel their work is not understood and is undervalued by the state.[10]

The lack of focused and sustained engagement with the challenges facing families with eldercare responsibilities has been, as we discuss below, reflected throughout history. Yet, the number of people over 85 in the UK is predicted to double in the next 20 years and nearly treble in the next 30.[11] We now live longer: over 1.4 million people in the UK are aged 85 or over and more people than ever are living into their 90s.[12] In fact, there are more pensioners than there are children under 16.[13] This global[14] demographic shift has implications for families but also has interrelated implications for a broad range of social and economic imperatives from the consumer services we provide[15] to the health care provisions we prioritise[16] and, key for this critique, the employment protections and rights we offer.[17] Whilst mindful of the fact that old age does not necessarily mean dependence for all,[18] it can and does create dependency for many and, significantly, poverty and deprivation in old age remains a huge concern in the UK. As many as 2 million pensioners in the UK live in poverty and 1.1 million live in severe poverty with an income less than the 50 per cent threshold of

a week and over a third of carers (36%) are caring for over 100 hours a week (see Adult Social Care Statistics Team, *Personal Social Services Survey of Adult Carers in England 2016–17* (London, NHS Digital, 2017). The allowance is also subject to an earnings cap, which was raised to £123 in April 2019. This can have an impact on working carers on National Minimum Wage: 16 hours paid at National Minimum/Living Wage (£8.72 from 1 April 2020) will pay £139.52, preventing eligibility for carer's allowance.

[8] Carers UK, *State of Caring 2017* (London, Carers UK, 2017).

[9] Carers UK, *Caring for Your Future: The Long-term Financial Impact of Caring* (London, Carers UK, 2018).

[10] Carers UK, *State of Caring 2017*, above n 8.

[11] Office for National Statistics, *National Population Projections 2008-based* (London, ONS, 2009).

[12] Office for National Statistics, *Mid-2012 Population Estimates UK* (London, ONS, 2013).

[13] ibid.

[14] See, eg, A Bookman and D Kimbrel 'Families and Eldercare in the Twenty-First Century' (2011) 21 *Work and Family: The Future of Children* 117, which discusses the USA.

[15] Interestingly, 39% of people aged 65+ think businesses have little interest in the consumer needs of older people: see ICM, *Research Agenda for Life Survey (November 2010)* (London, Age UK, 2011).

[16] In 2007, two thirds of NHS clients were aged 65 and over but received only two fifths of total expenditure (I Philp, *A Recipe for Care – Not a Single Ingredient* (London, Department of Health, 2007).

[17] Research found that 60% of older people in the UK agree that age discrimination exists in the daily lives of older people: Age Concern and Help the Aged, *One Voice: Shaping our Ageing Society* (London, Age Concern and Help the Aged, 2009).

[18] P Mullan, *The Imaginary Time Bomb: Why an Ageing Population is Not a Social Problem* (London, IB Tauris & Co, 2000) 16. See also J Doward, 'UK Elderly Suffer Worst Poverty Rates in Western Europe', *The Guardian* (18 August 2019), which discusses Pension Reforms and Old Age Inequalities in Europe.

contemporary median income.[19] Within this context our justified reluctance to perpetuate damaging stereotypes ought not to detract us from critiquing this lived reality – a reality that impacts on the quality of life for many older people and those who are responsible for their care. Indeed, the length of time at the end of life that individuals need daily care has risen significantly in recent years.[20] This has repercussions for many of us and until our increased capacity to live longer is matched by an increase in satisfactory institutional care or social service facilities for those who require extra support in old age,[21] we need to better understand[22] and address this growing reality: many of us will be confronted by the need to engage directly with the ramification of eldercare, emotionally, practically and financially at some point in our working lives.

We have, in chapters two and three, demonstrated how the interests of working parents – mothers and, increasingly and interrelatedly, fathers – have gradually become a core focus of WFB policies in the UK. The interests of those with elderly dependants are, by comparison, 'the Cinderella of the family-friendly framework'.[23] The main section of the chapter details our engagement with older people per se in relatively recent decades, which is inevitably tied up with developments identified and discussed elsewhere, such as the welfare state and women's participation in paid work. Overall, this chapter reveals how government's attention to the needs of its older citizens has undergone many peaks and troughs but most significantly, in section II, it reveals how the needs of these individuals and the family members who provide unpaid care to dependent older relatives have always been, and by and large remain, invisible, ignored or downplayed. We also argue that the early categorisation, and the ongoing perpetuation of that categorisation throughout recent history, of older people as somehow 'separate' to the rest of the population has restricted our ability to engage adequately with the needs of those experiencing derivative dependency as a consequence of undertaking eldercare. After critiquing the evolution of our approach to eldercare/older generations, we briefly, in section III, critique the limited and disappointing

---

[19] Department of Work and Pensions, *Households Below Average Income: 1994/95 to 2017/18* (DWP, London, 2019) cited in Age UK, *Later Life in the United Kingdom 2019* (London, Age Concern, 2019).

[20] A Kingston, A Comas-Herrera and C Jagger, 'Forecasting the Care Needs of the Older Population in England Over the Next 20 Years: Estimates from the Population Ageing and Care Simulation (PACSim) Modelling Study' (2018) 3 *The Lancet* 447.

[21] Indeed, it has been suggested that we need double the current number of care homes by 2043 if we are to maintain the current ratio of private institutional provisions to community service: see N Lievesley and G Crosby, *The Changing Role of Care Homes* (BUPA and The Centre for Policy on Ageing, London, 2011).

[22] An understanding that also requires us to better explore the realities of living longer for black and minority ethnic populations (see K Bhui, K Halvorsrud and J Nazroo, 'Making a Difference: Ethnic Inequality and Severe Mental Illness' (2018) 213 *The British Journal of Psychiatry* 574) and LGBT citizens (see Age UK, *Later Life in the United Kingdom 2019*, above n 19.

[23] See James and Spruce, 'Workers with Elderly Dependants: Employment Law's Response to the Latest Care-giving Conundrum', above n 2. Perhaps why some academics are keen to explore alternative means of compensating carers for their work – see B Sloan, *Informal Carers and Private Law* (Oxford, Hart Publishing, 2013).

WFB provisions currently available to workers with eldercare responsibilities and show how these provisions are still truly 'lagging far behind our understanding of parenting and childcare issues'.[24] In this final section we also consider the potential of vulnerability theory to improve our engagement for those who require care in old age and for the working families who provide it. The discussion in this section mirrors arguments made throughout the book, pointing to the need for an approach that better accepts dependency because of ageing as one manifestation of our multi-faceted human vulnerability that deserves support, and better facilitates a mutually supportive partnership between individuals, their families, employers and the state.

II. A History of Ageing and Eldercare

This core section of the chapter provides a broad critique of approaches, historically, to ageing and eldercare in the UK. It is presented chronologically to enable certain trends to be revealed, but of course in reality history is not tidy and developments are less linear than this structure might suggest. At the core of the section is a commentary upon where, at any given time, responsibility for eldercare rests noting that, at a fundamental level as suggested in Fineman's vulnerability theory, the less a state is willing to undertake responsibility for the needs of older people or to provide adequate support for families with older dependants, the greater the responsibility for individuals and their families.[25] Our critique exposes the ebb and flow of where responsibility for eldercare, in all its manifestations, is placed at any given time. Although perspectives began to alter beforehand, it is in postwar Britain that older people were increasingly viewed as a separate cohort. We demonstrate that this new narrative was originally useful because it enabled the excruciatingly difficult conditions that many older people were experiencing at that time to be identified and challenged as unacceptable in what was becoming a more prosperous society. In the long term, however, this construction of older people as a separate and particularly vulnerable/dependent population distanced them from more ideal autonomous individuals and provided a convenient mechanism for re-allocating state financial support when economic circumstances, demographics and ideological underpinnings changed, creating the potential for tensions to surface, as they did at later points, between the elderly and other generations. As Fineman puts it, 'the political and popular culture depictions of the generations as distinct social groupings at war with each other reflect a certain understanding of the individual, as well as the appropriate organization of

---

[24] See Carers UK, *The Case for Care Leave: Family, Work and the Ageing Population* (London, Carers UK, 2013) 14. See also James and Spruce, 'Workers with Elderly Dependants: Employment Law's Response to the Latest Care-giving Conundrum', above n 2.

[25] See discussion in the Introduction and MA Fineman, '"Elderly" as Vulnerable: Rethinking the Nature of Individual and Societal Responsibility' (2012–2013) 20 *The Elder Law Journal* 71.

society and the concurrent responsibilities of the individual, the family, and the state and its institutions'.[26]

A. Pre 1940s: Early Ideals of Autonomy

'And the Union workhouses,' demanded Scrooge, 'Are they still in operation?'

'They are. Still,' returned the gentleman, 'I wish I could say they were not.'

'The Treadmill and the Poor Law are in full vigour, then?' said Scrooge.

'Both very busy' ...

'I help support the establishments I have mentioned: they cost enough: and those who are badly off must go there.'

'Many can't go there; and many would rather die.'

'If they would rather die,' said Scrooge, 'they had better do it, and decrease the surplus population.'[27]

The social construction of 'old age', 'the elderly' or 'older people' is generally agreed to have begun following the Second World War. Four key observations can be made about the treatment of older people prior to the 1940s. First, age was not a key determinant of workplace participation. What is clear is that distinctions were made in terms of people's poverty and ill health rather than their age per se, and the core difference, which drove policy interventions, was made between the 'able-bodied', who could work, and the 'infirm', who could not. Overall, evidence suggests that old people struggled to earn a living with many in poverty and this, as Thane notes, 'had always been so'.[28] Those with families able and willing to accommodate their care needs within the family unit were relatively 'lucky' but hidden from public view (and scrutiny) as, of course, were the women who provided the necessary care. Within this context, most working-class people carried on working as long as they were able and were employed in many different types of work, often physically demanding, casualised, marginal and poorly paid – and they would also, as discussed in chapter five, have worked from a very young age.[29]

Second, there was an expectation that a family member who could do so, would and should provide care for any dependants in need of support. Indeed, the Poor Law statute of 1597 stated that 'it is expounded that the great grandfather, grandfather, Father and Sonne upward and downward in lyneall descent or degree shall relieve one another as occasion shall require'. This was amended in 1601 to include female relatives, absolve grandchildren from responsibility and

---

[26] ibid, 84.

[27] C Dickens, *A Christmas Carol* (London, HarperCollins Publishers, 1843/2013) 8–9.

[28] Thane, *Old Age in English History*, above n 1, 279.

[29] ibid, 273–79.

restrict the obligation to those 'being of sufficient ability' to provide support.[30] The 'liable relatives' clause, as it was known, was rarely activated and in reality the poor relief system provided some provision for those shunned by family and unable to work. It was not, however, repealed until 1948 and even then, some politicians expressed regret about its abolition: Osbert Peake, the Minister of Pensions and National Insurance, expressed concern that 'there was no longer any legal liability on children to maintain parents ... all these measures had tended to destroy any sense of family responsibility'.[31]

Third, of those unable to work, and without families able and willing to accommodate them, a poor relief system operated. By deliberately fostering harsh conditions worse than the very lowest paid job, a main aim of the workhouses set up following the enactment of the 1834 Poor Law Amendment Act was to incentivise the able-bodied to find paid work and inhibit recourse to public relief.[32] Many died in workhouses, which provided a means of establishing a compliant workforce, a system of control – a 'necessary ingredient of emerging capitalism'.[33] Many older people who were unable to work, as Townsend comments, 'were submitted to a style of life intended essentially for the able-bodied poor'.[34] Indeed, there are accounts of low-level 'work' being given to older generations as a form of charity, to keep them clear of the law and workhouses by differentiating them from beggars.[35] For the majority, though, poverty was an unavoidable consequence of retirement and old age. Interestingly, given the historical assessment being undertaken here, admission to workhouses was viewed as reflecting a weakness on the part of the individual rather than a weakness on the state to accommodate the needs of the poor.[36]

Fourth, it was only in the context of the industrial revolution and some (limited but new) policy engagement in relation to workplace safety that attitudes towards older people, and the notion that they were in some way to blame for their predicament, began to change. It was at this point that the significance of old age entered the political environment as a 'social problem' in any sense.[37] As Thane comments,

---

[30] 'The father and grandfather, mother and grandmother and children of every poor, old, blind, lame and impotent person, or other poor person not able to work, being of sufficient ability, shall at their own charges relieve and maintain every such poor person, in that manner, and according to that rate, as by the justices ... in their sessions shall be assessed'.

[31] Cited in Thane, *Old Age in English History*, above n 1, 372.

[32] See N Lievesley and G Crosby, *The Changing Role of Care Homes* (London, BUPA and The Centre for Policy on Ageing, 2011).

[33] P Townsend, 'The Structured Dependency of the Elderly: A Creation of Social Policy in the Twentieth Century' (1981) 1 *Ageing and Society* 5, 8.

[34] ibid.

[35] Thane, *Old Age in English History*, above n 1, 275.

[36] Townsend, 'The Structured Dependency of the Elderly: A Creation of Social Policy in the Twentieth Century', above n 33, 9.

[37] See, eg, J Quadagno, 'Generational Equity and the Politics of the Welfare State' in J Quadagno and D Street (eds), *Aging for the Twenty-First Century* (New York, St Martin's Press, 1996) and S Katz, *Disciplining Old Age* (Charlottesville VA, University Press of Virginia, 1996).

'what changed in the later nineteenth century was the emergence of a widely expressed revulsion that old people should be forced to such straits in an increasingly prosperous society ... [and] it came to be accepted conventionally that old people, like young children, should no longer be expected to toil for survival'.[38] This 'revulsion' did not, however, translate into anything resembling a 'strategy' for quite some time. Non-contributory pensions were introduced in the Old Age Pensions Act 1908 but the fact that they were worth only a quarter of a labourer's wage – married couples received a lower rate and those claiming poor relief were not eligible – underlined an approach that favoured limiting the numbers needing public support and encouraging paid employment.[39] This novel approach was also evident in the 1925 Contributory Pensions Bill, but this provision was purposely levelled at a rate 'insufficient by itself to provide a grown man or woman with the necessities for life' so that it would encourage thrift in the population as a whole.[40] In addition to these limited, but key, provisions 'the old' were also being identified as a group worthy of particular focus in studies of poverty and unemployment in Britain.[41]

Overall, prior to the 1940s there were hints of some rudimentary and disjointed recognition that the state ought perhaps to take some interest in the poorest of its older population, but these were countered by ideals of individual autonomy and non-intervention which remained dominant. Concern for those older people who were in need of additional support, in an age of threats to national security and when the very status quo of those who had long since wielded power in society was insecure, remained firmly off the radar until the middle of the twentieth century.

B. 1940s, 50s and 60s: A New 'Discourse of Differentiation'

The construction of 'old age' in the 1940s and 1950s ought to be viewed in the context of a rapidly changing post-war society where technological advances and demands for efficiency were replacing many of the jobs that would have kept older workers in employment. It was also a time when social security reform was increasingly important and the Labour Party and trade unions, spurred on by the pioneering work of Beveridge, were particularly eager to banish poverty

---

[38] Townsend, 'The Structured Dependency of the Elderly: A Creation of Social Policy in the Twentieth Century', above n 33, 9.

[39] This is evidenced in P Clarke, *Britain 1900–1990* (London, Allen Lane, 1996) 56. See also the speech by Lloyd George rebuking suggestions that the age limit should be 65 instead of 70 years old (Hansard, 1908, Vol 190, col 575) cited in C Phillipson, *Reconstructing Old Age: New Agendas in Social Theory and Practice* (London, SAGE, 1998) 110.

[40] ibid.

[41] See, eg, SJ Chapman and MM Hallsworth, *Unemployment: The Results of An Investigation Made in Lancashire and an Examination of the Reports of the Poor Law Commission* (Manchester, University of Manchester, 1909).

in old age.[42] It was during this period that 'older people' really became 'absorbed into a specific discourse of differentiation'.[43] By the 1940s, following the impact of two world wars in terms of the catastrophic loss of human life and economic devastation, the repercussions of population ageing had become a widespread concern in the UK and elsewhere, notably in the US.[44] This concern is evident, for example, in the way that interest in the scientific study of gerontology increased during this period, as did a belief in the power of medicine to tackle the symptoms of an ageing body.[45] This 'biomedical revolution' in turn sparked a growing belief in the potential for a healthier old age[46] and, one can assume, a belief that any physical dependency associated with the ageing process would also decrease. The new construction of old age was also influenced by two other, interrelated, key developments: mandatory retirement and the development of the welfare state.

i. Mandatory Retirement

Following a period immediately after the Second World War of encouraging workers to remain in employment as long as possible, in the 1940s and 1950s retirement was redefined as a distinctive and valued part of life[47] 'beyond gainful employment'.[48] Prior to the introduction of 'retirement' as a life event to be experienced whilst still physically fit and healthy, the transition away from paid work was more gradual and 'typically coincided with the biological transition from fitness to dependency'.[49] During this period, there was a growth in retirement planning and a core industry emerged that promoted the promise of an active and independent lifestyle following workplace participation.

In the 1940s and 1950s the idea of retirement was mooted and slowly but surely, although not without some reluctance and hostility,[50] accepted as a desirable alternative to paid employment later in life. During the 1960s 'the idea of

---

[42] See Thane, *Old Age in English History*, above n 1, 368.

[43] S Katz, *Disciplining Old Age* (Charlottesville VA, University Press of Virginia, 1996) 51. Although, according to Phillipson, the notion of the old as a separate group began at the end of the 19th century – once sickness benefits were replaced by an old age pension: see Phillipson, *Reconstructing Old Age: New Agendas in Social Theory and Practice*, above n 39, 109.

[44] See Thane, *Old Age in English History*, above n 1.

[45] See S Harper and P Thane, 'The Consolidation of "Old Age" as a Phase of Life, 1945–1965' in M Jefferys (ed), *Growing Old in the Twentieth Century* (London, Routledge, 1988) 43.

[46] Phillipson, *Reconstructing Old Age: New Agendas in Social Theory and Practice*, above n 39, 34.

[47] ibid, 112.

[48] T Cole, *The Journey of Life: A Cultural History of Aging in America* (Cambridge University Press, 1992), 223.

[49] Harper and Thane, 'The Consolidation of "Old Age" as a Phase of Life, 1945–1965', above n 45, 43.

[50] Especially as loss of employment was still perceived to be an individual 'crisis' and for many the repercussions were psychological and social as well as financial. See Phillipson, *Reconstructing Old Age: New Agendas in Social Theory and Practice*, above n 39, 56.

constructing an identity within retirement was increasingly emphasised'.[51] Indeed, a 'Preparation for Retirement Committee' was established in 1960 in order to promote the notion of retirement as a fulfilling and positive stage in a person's life.[52] The re-focus on pensioners came after damning reports identified the dire level and extent of poverty experienced in old age: Cole and Utting's Report of 1962[53] found that 'nearly two and a half million old people were living in 1959–60 very near to the poverty line as determined by National Assistance standards'.[54] As an interesting and significant aside, the study reported that 'women were worse off than couples or single or widowed men in every respect', and noted that 'they were less often working; fewer of them had private pensions; and although some of them had large amounts of assets, the majority – and again far more than men or couples – were without any at all or had only negligible sums'.[55] This finding is not surprising: given the historical subordination of women they were, and still are,[56] very likely to experience devastating financial repercussions in old age.

Connectedly, a major part of the response of the government to the poverty experienced by a large number of older citizens, in welfare terms, was the widening of access to pensions[57] and its indexation to earnings ensured pensioners' positions improved during this time. A greater number of retirees gained access to some basic financial assistance from the state during old age and there was, albeit from a low base, a general increase in the living standards of older people. Overall, during this period there is evidence of huge strides forward in relation to the reconstruction of 'old age' as a time in life when individuals could leave paid employment without the risk of dire poverty. By the end of the 1960s, statutory retirement ages were widely acceded and, as Harper and Thane comment, 'it was accepted that the *normal* period of full-time economic employment would cease for *most* of the population at these ages'.[58] Indeed, as a result of the broader approach toward retirement and the growing financial support for the older population, this period was described by some as a 'golden age', when fears about growing old in poverty without access to employment were abated and the reality, for many though not all, was not in reality as bad as they had expected.[59] Indeed Macnicol, who is extremely critical of later developments,

[51] ibid, 115. See also Thane, *Old Age in English History*, above n 1, 20.
[52] Discussed in Harper and Thane, 'The Consolidation of "Old Age" as a Phase of Life, 1945–1965', above n 45, 47.
[53] D Cole and J Utting, *The Economic Circumstances of Old People* (London, Bentley and Co, 1962).
[54] ibid, 102.
[55] ibid.
[56] See Introduction to this chapter.
[57] eg the State Earnings-Related Pension Scheme (SERPS) was introduced by the Social Security Pensions Act 1975 and more people began to draw upon occupational pension schemes (see Phillipson, *Reconstructing Old Age: New Agendas in Social Theory and Practice*, above n 39, 69.
[58] Harper and Thane, 'The Consolidation of "Old Age" as a Phase of Life, 1945–1965', above n 45, 59.
[59] L Hannah, *Inventing Retirement* (Cambridge, Cambridge University Press, 1986).

describes the period 1945–1973 as a time when 'old age was generally viewed in western societies as a stage of life to be protected and the right to retirement remained sacrosanct'.[60]

ii. Welfare State

The second key development of this period, the acceptance of the welfare state as a desired and permanent fixture, counterbalanced the promotion of independent, active retirement by promising state support to those whose independence was threatened by their particular lived reality of poverty in old age.[61] Older people were included within a framework of 'social rights' and 'social citizenship',[62] and society developed a new interest in easing the economic hardships many individuals were known to experience later in life. The extent of this poverty had been highlighted when responsibility for the welfare of old people was transferred to the Unemployment Assistance Board, established in 1934, and the introduction of Supplementary Assistance in 1940. The latter replaced Poor Law Assistance, for which only about 10 per cent of pensioners applied and so the government had predicted that the cost would be relatively small. However, the new provision was taken up by many more pensioners, about one third in 1941, which was 'powerful testimony to the fear and hatred of the Poor Law' and uncovered a need that was far greater than anticipated. The new narrative of 'old age' may have emphasised their potential fragility and risked marginalising 'a perfectly normal group of people in every community in every civilisation'[63] but, as Phillipson comments, this development was 'the price for eroding the distinction between "deserving" and "undeserving" old'.[64] It 'clearly positioned old people as a core group within the welfare state'[65] and this re-categorisation distinguished, for the first time, older people as a cohort whose needs were potentially worthy of economic support *from the state*.

The nuance, given the context of this book, is, however, important here: it was during this period that a shift occurred in terms of the (re)allocation of responsibility for the health and wellbeing of citizens *in general* and it was because older people were included in this general shift that the state accepted responsibility for alleviating some economic hardships and the more common afflictions associated with growing older. This strategy was supported by a deeper development of the

---

[60] J Macnicol, *Neoliberalising Old Age* (Cambridge, Cambridge University Press, 2015) 2.

[61] Phillipson, *Reconstructing Old Age: New Agendas in Social Theory and Practice*, above n 39, 37.

[62] This development of the welfare state was, for Marshall, a key phase in the evolution of social citizenship for everyone: TH Marshall, *Citizenship and Social Class* (Cambridge, Cambridge University Press, 1949).

[63] R Cottam, 'Growing Old' in The National Council of Social Service, *Living Longer: Some Social Aspects of the Problem of Old Age* (London, The National Council of Social Service, 1954) 7.

[64] Phillipson, *Reconstructing Old Age: New Agendas in Social Theory and Practice*, above n 39, 115.

[65] ibid.

welfare state and is regarded as an indication of how society was 'elevated' during this time, because it initiated what Lowe termed a 'deeper sense of community and mutual care'.[66] Significantly, it was during this period that 'the notion of an intergenerational contract' was first introduced; one where 'the young and middle aged supported elderly citizens – partly on a reciprocal basis given their contribution to work and welfare earlier in their life'.[67] Hence, the welfare state epitomised, at its birth at least –although even then imperfectly[68] – a notion that resources ought to be allocated across the life-course from 'cradle to grave'[69] in a way that enabled the economically active/wealthier at any given time to support those cohorts who were, at any given time, disadvantaged or, in Fineman's terms, experiencing hardship associated with their vulnerability as human beings. Certainly, a long-standing strategy of non-intervention, and recourse to Victorian workhouses for the poorest, was challenged by an approach that appeared to favour, albeit in a very limited sense at this time, supporting older people rather than ignoring them or chastising them for their inability to take on paid work. With the introduction of the welfare state and the inclusion of older citizens' needs within this paradigm, the pendulum shifts, ever so slightly, towards a model that acknowledges a role for the state as caregiver. This can be viewed in Fineman's terms as early recognition, albeit unintentional and unpromoted, of our collective vulnerability and strength.

However, whilst this era is one of significant movement towards some state recognition of responsibility for eldercare and is considered to be a 'golden age' for retirees, it would be wrong to portray this period in purely positive terms, as that would somewhat distort the realities of life for many. Hindsight provides us with the opportunity to (re)assess key developments with a different lens. Indeed, the ramifications of promoting retirement in such altruistic terms, as described above, were challenged at the time as lack of employment was largely associated with poor mental health, a reduction in status, loss of friendships and low self-esteem and feared by many as a source of inevitable and impending hardship and poverty. Later, the very ethos of retirement was critiqued in detrimental terms: writing in the late 1970s, Townsend attributed the introduction of retirement to 'changes in the organisation of work and the kind of people wanted for work' and saw it merely as a 'euphemism for unemployment',[70] arguing that it was part of the social manufacturing of dependency of the elderly;

[66] R Lowe, *The Welfare State in Britain since 1945* (London, Macmillan, 1993) 21. See also P Leonard, *Postmodern Welfare* (London, SAGE, 1997) 21.

[67] Lowe, above n 66, 117.

[68] See Thane, *Old Age in English History*, above n 1, 369, who comments on the fact that pensions were introduced only to those already in the 1946 National Insurance Scheme and were set at a level that was inadequate as a means of alleviating poverty.

[69] See discussion in ch 1.

[70] Townsend, 'The Structured Dependency of the Elderly: A Creation of Social Policy in the Twentieth Century', above n 33, 10.

a dependency that he saw as having been deepened and widened over time.[71] Cole, an American writer but whose views resonate in Britain too, suggested that the construction of 'old age' in this period was, rather than an emancipatory evolution symbolising intergenerational solidarity in the aftermath of war,[72] simply a new type of marginalisation, one that 'proceeded on the assumption that most old people cannot contribute significantly to the "real world" (ie the labour market)'.[73] The concerns raised by writers such as Cole and Townsend offer an important contrast to the image, often promoted in the 1940s and 1950s and beyond, of retirement as a 'golden age' for elderly citizens. It is also important to note that the new approach to old age and the welfare provisions that emerged were fundamentally moulded by a deep-seated and widely held conviction that 'the role of the state should be confined to providing the minimum that is desirable and acceptable, supplemented by private efforts in various forms'.[74] This was a period of progress, but that progress remained heavily imbued with the notion of individual autonomy and reliance upon the unpaid labour of families, especially women.

Overall, transformations during this period – in relation to retirement and the welfare state – be they viewed as an emancipation from the horrors of the Victorian workhouses or a 'new type' of marginalisation initiated through paternalistic policies that led to the 'othering' of older people – or both – had a huge impact on the way that age is constructed from this point forward. Whilst engagement with old age per se changes – and overall it changes for the better when compared with the lot of older people who were poor or in need of care prior to this point – it was, however, built upon an assumption of the continuing availability of employment up until retirement. It was also premised upon an ingrained and unspoken assumption about the limits of state responsibility and a belief that the majority of women would not enter the public world of work, at least not for long periods or in a way that would impact upon their ability or willingness to care for family dependants. It was implicitly clear, if unarticulated, that individuals and families would continue to shoulder the majority of responsibility for eldercare, albeit now supported to a degree by the new NHS and welfare state. The significance is the slight, if flawed, acknowledgement of some responsibility and willingness to care for our elderly infirm. Had this been embraced and developed, we may have adopted an approach more sensitive to the needs of older dependants and their carers and more closely reflective of the core values embedded in vulnerability theory. In retrospect, this was the closest we came in the

---

[71] ibid.

[72] See Phillipson, *Reconstructing Old Age: New Agendas in Social Theory and Practice*, above n 39, 39.

[73] Cole, *The Journey of Life: A Cultural History of Aging in America*, above n 48, 233. See also J Macnicol, *The Politics of Retirement in Britain, 1878–1948* (Cambridge, Cambridge University Press, 1998) and A Walker, (ed), *The New Generational Contract: Intergenerational Relationships, Old Age and Welfare* (London, UCL Press, 1996).

[74] Thane, *Old Age in English History*, above n 1, 384.

history of regulating members of these working families to an effective strategy of defamilisation.

C. 1970s and 1980s: The Unravelling of State Support

If the 1950s and early 60s were a 'golden age', it was certainly short-lived because in the 1970s and 80s we witnessed, as Macnicol states, 'increasing attacks from the political right on state provision for old age'.[75] Indeed, from the late 1960s onwards, but particularly in the 1970s and 1980s, state support for older people begins to 'unravel'[76] and this is evident in shifts that occur in relation to political narratives. These shifts in terms of how 'older people' are portrayed and promoted by governments has an impact on political agendas and provides a key indication of whether or not they are likely to be a priority and supported by the state. These are discussed before we outline the impact of neoliberalism and core 'attacks' on state provision.

i. Shifts in Narrative

Three key examples will suffice to demonstrate how, during this period, we witness alternative ways of constructing situations and issues that have a core impact on how older people are portrayed from here on: retirement, pensions and intergenerational equity and responsibility. Retirement, compared to the golden age outlined above, is no longer portrayed as an important provision to secure the welfare of older generations but, as Phillipson remarks, 'the debate shifts, with governments encouraging retirement as a part of the need to restructure and rationalise manufacturing industry'.[77] Retirement, by the 1970s, begins to be viewed as a means of helping to reduce the impact of unemployment – a means of moving large numbers out of the workplace: it starts to have 'a valued social and economic objective'.[78] In blunt terms, industrialisation meant that significantly fewer people were needed for paid employment and the retirement of older workers provided a more palatable 'solution' than the alternatives.

During this period pensions were fundamentally reconstructed as a benefit to be earned as 'employees' rather than an entitlement of all 'citizens' – a personal undertaking as opposed to a social (human) right. Emphasis was placed on the unsustainability of public pension systems – a 'pensions crisis' – in light of population ageing.[79] This 'striking' shift in language, as Phillipson notes, had huge

---

[75] Macnicol, *Neoliberalising Old Age*, above n 60, 2.

[76] Phillipson, *Reconstructing Old Age: New Agendas in Social Theory and Practice*, above n 39, 78.

[77] ibid, 62.

[78] ibid, 65.

[79] See T Moulaert and S Biggs, 'International and European Policy on Work and Retirement: Reinventing Critical Perspectives on Active Ageing and Mature Subjectivity' (2012) 66 *Human Relations* 23; J Grady,

consequences for individuals and their families, particularly in light of the changing landscape of the labour market in the UK. It is a narrative that rejected any
assumption of entitlement to financial support in old age and underpinned the
neoliberal spirit of the Thatcher government, which favoured individual responsibility for wellbeing and resisted public spending.[80]

In relation to inter-generational equity and responsibility, during this period
the notion that the younger generation *ought* to support the older generation, who
had already given so much in terms of their labour, lost its momentum. Instead, the
narrative started to change[81] so that the older generation were perceived implicitly as 'holding back' younger workers or the unemployed. Views of older people
as 'burdens' became more prominent[82] and they were increasingly portrayed as
somehow 'less deserving' and in direct competition for, if not a drain on, increasingly limited public resources.[83] The unfairness of public pensions as a tax burden
on (younger) workers/citizens was highlighted, distancing the political strategy of
this era from the communal 'cradle to grave' narrative upon which the welfare state
had been founded.[84]

ii. Impact of Neoliberalism and Attacks on State Provision

As a whole, this negative narrative was part of a major reprioritisation, part of a
move to outwardly promote industrial and economic concerns above the needs
and desires of older people whilst downplaying our communal responsibility and
capacity to provide for this group of citizens. It reflects a move away from previous, explicitly paternalistic, policies towards more neoliberal concerns. Indeed,
it is during the 1970s and 80s that we witnessed an increase in support for the
neoliberal ideology that explicitly positions individuals in general as responsible
for their own welfare, regardless of wealth or advantage.[85] Of particular interest, given the focus of this book, is the fact that this ideology, whilst not rooted
in the 1970s and clearly evident earlier, became more influential at this time.
Significantly, it has framed most political agendas ever since. It is interesting

'Retirement and Pensions Crisis' in S Manfredi and L Vickers (eds), *Challenges of Active Ageing for
Equality Law and the Workplace* (Basingstoke, Palgrave Macmillan, 2016) 49.

[80] See L Foster, 'Active Ageing, Pensions, and Retirement in the UK' (2018) 11 *Population Ageing*
117, 119.

[81] There is evidence of hostile views of the elderly as a 'burden' in the 1940s – see the 1949 Royal
Commission on Population Report cited in Phillipson, *Reconstructing Old Age: New Agendas in Social
Theory and Practice*, above n 39, 86.

[82] A similar narrative was emerging in the USA – see S Preston, 'Children and the Elderly: Divergent
Paths for America's Dependents' (1984) 21 *Demography* 435.

[83] Phillipson, *Reconstructing Old Age: New Agendas in Social Theory and Practice*, above n 39, 85. See
also Macnicol, *Neoliberalising Old Age*, above n 60, ch 6.

[84] See Foster, 'Active Ageing, Pensions, and Retirement in the UK', above n 80; Macnicol,
Neoliberalising Old Age, above n 60.

[85] This approach is one that is also epitomised in the United States – see Fineman, '"Elderly" as
Vulnerable: Rethinking the Nature of Individual and Societal Responsibility', above n 25, 74.

that one of the central tenets of neoliberalism is its ability to appear 'naturalistic, commonsense and unquestionable'.[86] In terms of its impact on social policy, it is by and large based on a belief that, 'true welfare is best delivered through family, friends and neighbours, charities and private for-profit agencies' and that 'welfare benefits (other than via safety nets for the really needy) tend to worsen the very problems they purport to solve: rewarding idleness and dependency encourages rational economic men and women to choose them'.[87] Hence neoliberal agendas do not offer special protection to what are categorised as 'vulnerable populations' and when this particular conceptualisation became popular, as discussed in the next section, it had a catastrophic impact on the provisions available to older generations.

As a consequence of this new neoliberal agenda, in the late 1970s and early 1980s we began to witness the 'progressive erosion of key elements of older people's welfare state'.[88] The context was set for cutting the provisions available for older people. A key target was the state pension provision. The Social Security Act of 1980, with the aim of reducing public spending, recalibrated the state pension so that the formula for annual increases was linked to prices rather than wages or prices (depending on which was higher). This had the impact of reducing, gradually over time, the relative value of state pensions and was, it has since transpired, an issue that caused internal friction in the Conservative Party:[89] Macnicol has described this reform as 'the most radical and profound change in state pension policy in the post-war period'[90] and the falling value of the pension will have forced people to work longer or reduced their income in later life. State Earnings-Related Pension Schemes (SERPS) were also reduced considerably and the policies promoted during this period caused dire financial problems for older people: during the Thatcher government the proportion of pensioners living below the poverty line increased from 13 per cent to 43 per cent.[91] In addition to changes in the way pensions were set, the government also introduced personal pension plans in 1986,[92] and the regulatory powers of the Occupational Pensions Board – which provided advice on quite complicated pension matters – were reduced in the 1980s and early 1990s. This had, as Thane points out, 'disastrous results' including

[86] Macnicol, *Neoliberalising Old Age*, above n 60, 17. See in particular the discussion of the process of 'cognitive locking' – a term developed by Blythe (M Blythe, *Great Transformations: Economic Ideas and Institutional Change in the Twentieth Century* (Cambridge, Cambridge University Press, 2002) 170) – to explain how social problems are often defined in a way that promotes the notion that there is only one possible solution to that problem.

[87] Macnicol, *Neoliberalising Old Age*, above n 60, 15.

[88] Phillipson, *Reconstructing Old Age: New Agendas in Social Theory and Practice*, above n 39, 118.

[89] See A Travis, 'Ministers Feared 1980 Plan to Cut State Pension Would Cause Riots, Paper Shows', *The Guardian* (30 December 2010).

[90] Macnicol, *Neoliberalising Old Age*, above n 60, 33.

[91] See M Dean, 'Margaret Thatcher's Policies Hit the Poor Hardest – and it's Happening Again', *The Guardian* (9 April 2013).

[92] Financial Services Act 1986.

the misappropriation of pension funds by Robert Maxwell and the mis-selling of private pensions.[93]

Beyond pensions, it was clear that the Conservative government viewed state spending as a core reason for the economic difficulties of the country[94] and Phillipson cites a number of key examples of the 'erosion' of state support that occurred during this period and impacted on older people. We witnessed a substantial reduction in convalescent and continuing care facilities for older people, a reduction in the number of NHS hospital beds available for older people, and a reduction in the number of home helps and 'meals on wheels', domiciliary and district nursing.[95] Funding changes and restructuring of health and social care meant that private care facilities also assumed a much bigger role. Interestingly, local authorities were responsible for most care homes in 1980 but by 2002 the private sector provided the majority.[96] The implications of this are far-reaching not least because privatisation means removal of democratic accountability,[97] taking care providers out of the remit of public concern/responsibility.

The erosion that we witness during this time is of course part of the broader shift in approach to social welfare and public spending generally in the UK, as outlined above. However, in many ways, this 'unravelling' of state support for older people was only possible because, as a group, they had already been constructed as a 'vulnerable population'. This earlier categorisation conveniently placed them in stark opposition to the 'liberal population': a construction that originally met their practical needs and alleviated the worst experiences of poverty. In the late 1970s and 1980s though – when unemployment was high, the economy was unstable, the nature of the labour market was radically altered and the agenda shifted in the way we have described above – the needs of older people were ripe for comparison with (the needs of) others. Moreover, following the privilege afforded to this cohort by the state in the 1940s, 50s and 60s, the possibility of a later shift towards a less age-focused society became 'fraught with dangers'.[98] The ideal of promoting a society that was age-neutral was now fundamentally flawed given the broader changes that had taken place during the intervening decades. Fineman's vision of a society where vulnerability is not aligned with individual or group identity but intrinsic to the human condition, appeared increasingly utopian as the division between rich and poor, old and young was greater than it had been in decades.

---

[93] Thane, *Old Age in English History*, above n 1, 384.

[94] The first White Paper of her government concerning public spending stated that 'Public expenditure is at the heart of Britain's present economic difficulties' (*Public Expenditure White Paper* (London, HM Treasury, 1979)) cited in Dean, 'Margaret Thatcher's policies hit the poor hardest', above n 91. See also Gough, 'Thatcherism and the Welfare State: Britain is Experiencing the Most Far Reaching Experiment in "New Right" Politics in the Western World' (1980) 1 *Marxism Today* 7.

[95] Thane, *Old Age in English History*, above n 1, 119.

[96] See N Lievesley and G Crosby, *The Changing Role of Care Homes* (London, BUPA and The Centre for Policy on Ageing, 2011).

[97] Macnicol, *Neoliberalising Old Age*, above n 60, 19.

[98] See Macnicol, *Neoliberalising Old Age*, above n 60, 1.

D. 1990s to Present

The limited legal provisions currently available to working caregivers are outlined in section III. In terms of general comment, engagement with the needs of older people and their carers has taken two paths since the late 1990s, increasingly so in the new millennium and especially in the wake of the 2008 recession. On the one hand, older people have continued to be detrimentally affected by negative measures, in the form of austerity-motivated spending cuts and a related narrative of hostility, that have resulted in further diminishing the little support they receive from the state. On the other hand, there has been a strong push to further promote individual responsibility for wellbeing in old age. These latest engagements, discussed in turn below, are all part of the same continuing neoliberal agenda which has become increasingly influential in UK policy. Each epitomises, albeit in different ways, the further retreat of state responsibility through a slow and gradual, but thorough and definitive, familisation strategy – a retrenchment of eldercare needs as an individual and private concern.

i. *Spending Cuts, 'Rollback' and a Narrative of Hostility*

The state has continued to 'roll back' and distance itself from the practical realities of fulfilling its legal obligation to meet the assessed care needs of older people. Since the 1990s, there has been a huge reduction in the number of local authorities directly providing care for older citizens as they increasingly contract with commercial care companies or charities: a process started in the later 1980s when the Thatcher government published a White Paper, 'Caring for People' – which led to the 1990 Community Care Act, requiring local authorities to develop an independent sector for eldercare and compulsory competitive tendering for public services.[99] This marketisation of care has added an extra dimension to the overall profile of responsibility for its provision in the UK. Indeed, the majority of state-funded residential and domiciliary care is now provided by the independent sector. Hence, care provision has, during this period, increasingly been provided by organisations that tendered competitively and are, ultimately, part of profit-making industries. This has fundamentally altered the nature of the recipient–provider relationship and its ramifications are reflected in the working conditions of (mostly female) care workers, the low pay associated with care work and the high turnover of staff in the sector.[100]

---

[99] An approach that has been adopted by governments ever since: see D Grimshaw and J Rubery, 'The end of the UK's liberal collectivist social model? The implications of the Coalition government's policy during the austerity crisis' (2012) 36 *Cambridge Journal of Economics* 105.

[100] See L Hayes, *Stories of Care: A Labour of Law: Gender and Class at Work* (London, Palgrave, 2017). For an interesting discussion of how our understanding of how care has been constructed as a consumption of time, see L Hayes and S Moore, 'Care in a time of austerity; the electronic monitoring of homecare workers' time' (2017) 24 *Gender, Work and Organisation* 329.

Whilst public spending had long been inadequate, especially following the 2008 financial crisis, funding for adult social care between 2010 and 2015 experienced an unprecedented hit, with local authorities having to absorb cuts to the tune of 26 per cent.[101] This further withdrawal of state support has meant that local authorities have increasingly been forced to fund eldercare through private sector contractors at ever lower prices, with fallout felt by care workers whose time has become increasingly commodified and rationed as a result.[102] How this impacts upon the quality of caregiving is under-researched but, as Hayes and Moore suggest, stricter monitoring of care work time 'strips care of its interactive flexibility and attempts to deny the relational underpinnings of individual service'.[103]

Cuts to social care provision have also manifested themselves in terms of tightened eligibility thresholds for care support. Age UK estimates that around one third of those who had been entitled to state support became ineligible following the implementation of austerity programmes.[104] Of grave concern, links have been made between austerity cuts and an increase in mortality rates amongst older people as deaths, after a steady decline from the late 1970s onwards, rose from 2011.[105] Even if not life-threatening, the extent and quality of care available to older dependants over this time period has become increasingly dependent upon an individual's financial and family circumstances. Many have been pushed to self-fund their entire care, rely upon others for support or face neglect. Of course, many people experience poor health as they age, often requiring support simply to navigate the 'choices' and 'control' that are now a popular mantra of adult social care 'packages'. As a consequence, the reality is that a large divide now exists between those who have such support and those who do not as well as, from a carer's perspective, those who can and cannot afford to meet the care needs of elderly dependants. As Hayes notes, 'a growing number of people face the consequence of neglect because they are too poor to pay' and, crucially from our perspective, 'family support is either unavailable or insufficient to meet their needs'.[106] Indeed, a recent report suggests that older people in the UK suffer the worst poverty rates in Western Europe.[107]

---

[101] Services for the elderly were the most severely hit of all social services – see Association of Directors of Adult Social Services (ADASS), *Budget Survey 2015* (London, ADASS, 2015) cited in Hayes, above n 100, 5, fn 2.

[102] Hayes and Moore, 'Care in a Time of Austerity; the Electronic Monitoring of Homecare Workers' Time', above n 100. On the commodification of care, see Ungerson, C (1997) 'Social Politics and the Commodification of Care' 4(3) *Social Politics, International Studies in Gender, State & Society* 362–81.

[103] Hayes and Moore, above n 102, 338.

[104] Age UK, *Later Life in the UK* (London, Age UK, 2015).

[105] R Loopstra, M Mckee, SV Katikireddi et al, 'Austerity and old Age Mortality in England: a longitudinal cross-local area analysis, 2007–2013' (2016) 1 *Journal of the Royal Society of Medicine* 109.

[106] Hayes, *Stories of Care: A Labour of Law: Gender and Class at Work*, above n 100, 5.

[107] J Doward, 'UK Elderly Suffer Worst Poverty Rates in Western Europe', *The Guardian* (18 August 2019).

Relatedly, if, as detailed above, the narrative took a negative turn in the 1970s and 80s, in more recent years we have witnessed an even more sinister shift in terms of how old age has been portrayed: described as an economic 'burden', a 'social problem', the old have been portrayed as 'drones feeding off the more productive activities of others'.[108] As Walker demonstrates, this terminology has long been used to justify restraint in social security and health and social services spending,[109] but discourse is especially vicious in the context of the financial crisis, where care for older dependants has been conceptualised as 'a bottomless pit of need and expenditure that threatens to precipitate ongoing economic crisis'.[110] The conflation in political discourse of the burden of an ageing population and the economic crisis creates a mandate for cuts to social care provisions.[111]

Issues of intergenerational 'fairness' are also raised at this time, creating a perception of divisions that are destructive and ultimately enable the state to promote austerity rather than taxation as a solution to the crisis: the latter is portrayed as unfairly placing 'a heavy burden on people of working age',[112] a narrative that undermines the foundations of the welfare state and is emblematic of the deep hold that neoliberal politics has by this period in our history. Any 'appeal to the homogeneity of human experience stands in sharp contrast to austerity's appeal to self-reliance among ageing 'individuals' who are living longer and are required to manage the consequences of their own over-consumption of (life)time'.[113]

ii. Supporting Individual Responsibility, through Paid Employment, for Wellbeing in Old Age

Beyond the withdrawal of state investment and support that was epitomised in the cuts and narrative of hostility discussed above, a different – but equally significant – type of engagement also surfaced during this period: a concerted effort was made to promote individual responsibility for managing wellbeing in old age. This manifested itself in two core ways: first, the introduction of relevant anti-discrimination provisions, which provided individuals with a right to

---

[108] Phillipson, *Reconstructing Old Age: New Agendas in Social Theory and Practice*, above n 39, 120.

[109] A Walker, *Half a Century of Promises* (London, Counsel and Care, 1995) 26. See also AM Warnes, 'Being Old, Old people and the Burdens of the Burden' (1993) 13 *Ageing and Society* 297.

[110] Hayes and Moore, 'Care in a Time of Austerity: The Electronic Monitoring of Homecare Workers' Time', above n 100, 332, who cite Carers UK, *Growing the Care Market: Turning a Demographic Challenge into an Economic Opportunity* (London, Carers UK, 2012). See also P Mullan, *The Imaginary Time Bomb* (London, IB Taurus, 2000); and B Rasmussen, 'Between Endless Needs and Limited Resources: the Gendered Construction of Greedy Organization' (2004) 11 *Gender, Work and Organization* 506.

[111] Hayes and Moore, above n 110, 332.

[112] HM Government, *Shaping the Future of Care Together* (London, Department of Health, 2009) 18, cited in Hayes and Moore, above n 110, 333.

[113] Hayes and Moore, above n 110, 333.

pursue a claim if they felt that they had been discriminated against because of their age. Relevant anti-discrimination provisions, introduced in 2006,[114] protect those denied access to, or ability to remain in, the workplace due to their age. The provisions, now contained in the Equality Act 2010, provide individual protection against direct or indirect discrimination. Interestingly, age discrimination is treated differently from other forms of discrimination in that it is possible for direct age discrimination to be justified by an employer.[115] It is clear that the justifications permitted here are less broad than for indirect age discrimination claims,[116] but the fact that justifications are permitted at all is significant. It reflects that age discrimination per se, as a morally unacceptable practice, is not taken as seriously as other acts of discrimination but is firmly placed at the bottom of a hierarchy of protected characteristics.[117] The importance of this protection has less to do with concern for those who experience age discrimination at work but is prima facie a reaction to changing demographics and state concern about the potential cost implications of that reality. As Fredman has put it, 'emphasis on combatting age discrimination is not, therefore, a result of a sudden appreciation of the need for fairness, but gains its chief impetus from macroeconomic imperatives'.[118]

Despite being placed at the bottom of a hierarchy of discrimination protection, the right to claim age discrimination has nonetheless been used by many individuals to challenge (not always successfully) a variety of discriminatory acts, policies or practices,[119] one of the most significant of which was a managerial policy which, before the abolition of the statutory default retirement age (see below), imposed a mandatory retirement age of 65.[120] This overall protection is an important, albeit flawed, reflection of the mood of this era – one that, in light of demographic

---

[114] The Employment Equality (Age) Regulations 2006 SI 2006/1031, which transposed the EU Framework Directive that had come into force six years earlier (Council Directive 2000/78/EC establishing a general framework for equal treatment in employment and occupation, OJ [2000] L303/16). The relevant protection is now located in the Equality Act 2010, s 5. For a discussion see M Sargeant, 'The Employment Equality (Age) Regulations 2006: A Legitimisation of Age Discrimination in Employment' (2006) 35 *Industrial Law Journal* 209.

[115] Equality Act, s 13(2) states that 'A does not discriminate against B if A can show A's treatment of B to be a proportionate means of achieving a legitimate aim'.

[116] See Baroness Hale in *Seldon* [2012] UKSC ICR 716 at 733.

[117] As argued elsewhere: see M Bell and L Waddington, 'Reflections on Inequalities in European Equality Law' (2003) 28 *European Law Review* 349; M Bell, 'A Patchwork of Protection: The New Anti-discrimination Law Framework' (2004) 67 *Modern Law Review* 465; E Howard, 'The Case for a Considered Hierarchy of Discrimination Grounds in EU Law' (2006) 13 *Maastricht Journal of European and Comparative Law* 443.

[118] S Fredman, *Discrimination Law* 2 edn) (Oxford, Oxford University Press, 2011) 102.

[119] See, eg, *Donkor v Royal Bank of Scotland* [2016] EAT IRLR 268, *Prigge v Deutsche Lufthansa* [2011] ECJ IRLR 1052, *Reynolds v CLFIS UK Ltd* [2015] CA ICR 2010, *Palmer v RBS* [2014] EAT ICR 1288; *Homer v Chief Constable of West Yorkshire Police* [2010] UKSC ICR 704; *Chief Constable of West Midlands Police v Harrod* [2017] CA ICR 869.

[120] *Seldon v Clarkson Wright & Jakes* [2012] UKSC ICR 716. See B Barrett and M Sargeant, 'Working in the UK Without a Default Retirement Age: Health, Safety, and the Oldest Workers' (2015) 44 *Industrial Law Journal* 75; L Vickers and S Manfredi, 'Age Equality and Retirement: Squaring the Circle' (2013) 42 *Industrial Law Journal* 61.

changes, increasingly favours individual self-care for as long as is humanly possible. The importance of labour market participation to facilitate this, and hence avoid recourse to the state for financial support, is underscored.

The second significant manifestation of a strategy that promoted individual responsibility for managing wellbeing in old age was also evident in the promotion of 'active ageing'. This represents 'a vision for a policy in which facilitation of the rights of older people will enable the expanding population to remain healthy (reducing the burden on health and social care systems), stay in employment longer (reducing pension costs), whilst also fully participating in community and political processes'.[121] In the UK, the 'active ageing' agenda has manifested itself in a number of ways including the abolition of mandatory retirement and the rise in the age of state pension eligibility which, together, encourage individuals to work longer and take greater responsibility for their economic security in later years. Statutory default retirement was abolished in April 2011,[122] radically changing the social policy context so that the mandatory retirement policies amount to age discrimination unless they can be objectively justified. In 2008 the government began to raise the state pension age with the aim of increasing it to 68 by 2046. The phased increase has already standardised pension ages for men and women and remains under review.[123] As well as encouraging productivity for as long as possible, the state pension age increases are linked to the cost-cutting measures discussed above – it is estimated that raising the state pension age by one year saves the state around £13 billion.[124]

Reforms to the pensions system during this period have also underscored neoliberal preferences for reducing state provision, encouraging autonomy and self-preservation. They include the UK strategy, introduced in 2005, to encourage individuals to defer their receipt of state pensions and potentially increase their final pension amount by over 10 per cent,[125] and the move toward defined contribution schemes (which offer no guaranteed income but are dependent upon the performance of the investment) as opposed to the defined benefit schemes they replace. Defined contribution schemes move the risk of investment to the individual and their use has risen in workplaces but has long been, and remains, controversial.[126] Other examples include the introduction of auto-enrolment in

---

[121] Foster, 'Active Ageing, Pensions, and Retirement in the UK', above n 80, 120.

[122] Employment Equality (Repeal of Retirement Age Provisions) Regulations 2011 SI 2011/1069.

[123] See www.gov.uk/check-state-pension, where individuals can check – by entering their date of birth – when they might be entitled to a state pension.

[124] See Macnicol, *Neoliberalising Old Age*, above n 60, 63.

[125] It was possible to defer payment by up to five years and increase the pension by up to 7.4% prior to this. Changes were introduced by Labour in the Pensions Act 2004. This was, however, reduced again in the Pensions Act 2014 to 'more closely reflect the value of the income foregone' (Explanatory Memorandum to the State Pension Regulation 2015/173 at para 7.27).

[126] See, eg, C Berry, 'Austerity, Ageing and the Financialisation of Pension Policy in the UK' (2016) 11 *British Politics* 2, 8–19. P Langley, 'In the Eye of the 'Perfect Storm': the Final Salary Pensions Crisis and Financialisation of Anglo-American Capitalism' (2004) 9 *New Political Economy* 539.

2012, which enrols eligible individuals without workplace pensions, into a pension scheme,[127] and the introduction in 2015 of a new single-tier pension which combines the basic and earnings-related pensions.[128]

Overall, the state's more recent pensions strategy is, as Berry remarks, 'a subtle form of welfare retrenchment through which the state withdraws from any attempt to provide a genuine income-replacement benefit for pensioners'.[129] It is a strategy predicated upon what Foster terms a 'productivist version of active ageing' and is flawed not least because it assumes that the demand side of the working relationship is unproblematic – ie secure with abundant opportunities for older workers.[130] It also rests upon the myth that choices about labour market participation are made by 'rational economic actors' within a fixed and flexible, naturally occurring reality. In practice, decision making is influenced by an array of complex but often predictable life course trajectories[131] including, of particular relevance here – the implications of growing old. Moreover, the individual's 'choices' are confined by the strategy of familisation outlined in this chapter which is epitomised in a lack of options and a lack of state support. Often, eldercare responsibilities, when placed upon working families, result in little alternative but to leave employment before eligibility for state pension is secured.[132] Pension contributions are also implicated by such 'early' departures and this inevitably has gendered repercussions.[133]

---

[127] In 2014 4.8 million people were enrolled and less than one in ten opted out. See discussion in S Webb, 'What Sorts of Pensions and Savings Delivery Models are Likely to be Viable and Fair Across Generations?' in B Franklin, C Urzi Brancati and D Hochlaf (eds), *Toward a New Age: The Future of the UK Welfare State* (London, The International Longevity Centre, 2016) 69–74. Concerns have been raised about the ability of the scheme to deliver adequate pensions and the potentially negative impact on women, whose careers are less predictable: see, eg, J Grady, 'Gendering Pensions: Making Women Visible' (2015) 22 *Gender Work and Organisation* 445; and J Ginn and A Macintyre, 'UK Pension Reforms: is Gender Still an Issue?' (2013) 12 *Social Policy and Society* 91.

[128] The government introduced changes following an impact assessment in which concerns were raised about the low levels of savings and intervention deemed necessary because of 'concern that the current state pension will not provide a clear foundation to support people in taking greater personal responsibility for saving for their retirement' which, despite automatic enrolment, reform was needed to 'provide a clear foundation for individuals in making savings decisions' and 'to ensure the cost of the system remains sustainable': DWP, *The Single Tier Pension: A Simple Foundation for Saving* (London, DWP, 2013).

[129] Berry, 'Austerity, Ageing and the Financialisation of Pension Policy in the UK', above n 126, 16.

[130] See Foster, 'Active Ageing, Pensions, and Retirement in the UK', above n 80.

[131] ibid, 123; and D Price, K Glaser, J Ginn and M Nicholls, 'How Important are State Transfers for Reducing Poverty Rates in Later Life?' (2015) 1 *Ageing and Society* 1.

[132] Price et al, above n 131.

[133] Implications that were unsuccessfully challenged in a High Court action by women born in the 1950s, claiming that the rise in retirement age is discriminatory because they were not given adequate time to make adjustments to compensate for the years without a state pension: see *R v Secretary of State for Work and Pensions* [2019] EWHC 2552 (Admin). For a broader discussion see Ginn and Macintyre, 'UK Pension Reforms: Is Gender Still an Issue?', above n 127; and L Foster and M Heneghan, 'Pension Planning in the UK: A Gendered Challenge' (2018) 38 *Critical Social Policy* 345.

III. Current WFB Rights for Working Carers and the Appeal of a Vulnerability Approach

Having outlined a history of strategies and solutions promoted over the years in relation to the elderly, we now turn our attention to legal engagement with workers who care for elderly dependants. Once we have critiqued the limited WFB rights available, we suggest how a vulnerability approach encourages us to reconsider the WFB framework in a way that can improve engagement with working carers and older dependants.

A. The WFB Provisions

It is hugely significant that eldercare was an afterthought which was added to the 'family-friendly' framework quite late in the evolution of this body of rights. As outlined in chapters two and three, the New Labour government came to power in 1997 and unveiled a package of 'family-friendly' employment rights. The significance of this important recognition that workers with caregiving responsibilities needed support to enable them to undertake unpaid care and paid work has been discussed. There was, however, very little in this original package for workers with eldercare responsibilities, the focus being largely on childcare for pre-school children. This is both unfortunate and telling: unfortunate because it leaves increasing numbers of working carers unsupported, and telling because it reflects a long-standing reluctance to impose obligations on employers vis-à-vis facilitating what is still considered to be a private endeavour. The ramifications of the lack of legal provision and support for these families and individuals is huge – especially in the light of the historical development outlined above, which demonstrates clearly how the state has accepted very little responsibility vis-à-vis eldercare in the UK.

Legal provision for working carers with older dependants was introduced in December 1999. The right to time off for dependants[134] is an EU provision[135] that allows carers to deal with an emergency involving a dependant (which includes a child, parent or grandparent or someone else who depends on him/her for care). It allows 'reasonable' unpaid time off work to deal with an unexpected incident, such as a sudden injury or where care arrangements break down. In terms of eligibility the UK emergency leave provisions are to be commended for incorporating a wide range of dependants, including someone living in the same house or someone who reasonably depends on the employee for care.

---

[134] Employment Rights Act 1996, s 57A.
[135] PLD, discussed in ch 3.

Often thought of as the poorest leave provision available to working parents,[136] it is important to note that this emergency right is the only *leave* provision currently available to those workers caring with older dependants.[137] As such, the fact that the provision is so flawed has particularly profound ramifications for those working carers with eldercare responsibilities. Principally, the leave is of limited use because it is unpaid. To be of pragmatic use, short-term leave provisions of this nature need to be financially supported. Only then can it minimise the direct financial burden often imposed upon individual working carers who need to be absent from the workplace for a limited period to respond to an often unforeseen and potentially traumatic (for the recipient of care and for the carer) event. As discussed elsewhere, there are several ways that leave provisions can be financed but the sources of funds are usually, as Yang and Gimm comment, either worker-carers themselves, employers or general revenue measures imposed on the population as a whole.[138] In the UK, the latter is likely to be the most effective and would help to re-tilt the current approach towards a more collective, cross-generational responsibility. Whilst the delicate balance involved in resource allocation at state and employer levels needs to be acknowledged, reluctance to source revenue from state funds means that working carers themselves are forced to carry the financial burden of eldercare. The UK right is also fundamentally flawed because of its incredibly restrictive nature: it is no more than a right to arrange alternative care, rather than a right to care for the dependant oneself; and the duration of leave permitted, defined as 'reasonable' time off, reflects the tight boundaries imposed.

In the UK, there is no leave entitlement for those with medium-term, non-emergency, caregiving responsibilities for older dependants. An employee whose parent falls and breaks a leg can use the emergency leave provision to accompany her to hospital but not to provide medium-term or intermittent care whilst she recovers. There are many incidents that cannot be dealt with in a matter of hours or days but will not necessarily result in the long-term dependency that might require a permanent alteration to workplace engagement.[139] These situations can cause untold work–life conflict and yet, a worker has very little support in such cases.

---

[136] See, eg, G James, *The Legal Regulation of Pregnancy and Parenting in the Labour Market* (London, Routledge Cavendish 2009), 50.

[137] It is noteworthy, however, that the new EU Carers Leave Directive (Directive of the European Parliament and of the Council on work–life balance for parents and carers and repealing Council Directive 2010/18/EU) provides opportunities for workers to be granted leave to care for relatives. The details of implementation are left to Member States, who will have three years to implement the legislation, but the main provision allows for carers five working days per year. See N Busby, 'The Evolution of Gender Equality and Related Employment Policies: the Case of Work-Family Reconciliation' (2018) 18 *International Journal of Discrimination and the Law* 104.

[138] T Yang and G Gimm, 'Caring for Elder Parents: A Comparative Evaluation of Family Leave Laws' (2013) 41 *Journal of Law, Medicine and Ethics* 501, 507 discussed in James and Spruce, 'Workers with Elderly Dependants: Employment Law's Response to the Latest Care-giving Conundrum', above n 2.

[139] For alternative approaches see Belgium and Germany – discussed in James and Spruce, 'Workers with Elderly Dependants: Employment Law's Response to the Latest Care-giving Conundrum', above n 2.

It was not until 2006 that the UK offered any truly pragmatic legal support for these carers and it is noteworthy that even at this later juncture, it was not originally introduced with this cohort of workers in mind – they were in many ways an afterthought. The right to request flexible working was first introduced in the UK in 2002[140] but was not extended to include those with caring responsibilities for adults until 2006 (Work and Families Act 2006)[141] (discussed in chapter three). Under this provision, eligible workers – an employee with caregiving responsibilities and 26 weeks' continuous employment history at the date of the application – were able to request flexible working to facilitate caregiving responsibilities. Although only a right to *request* flexibility, employers are under an obligation to consider the request and must have procedures in place for doing so. There have, however, always been broad grounds upon which refusal is deemed reasonable, including the burden of additional costs and detrimental impact upon work quality. An employee cannot, if an application is refused, re-apply for 12 months.

More recently, in 2014, changes were introduced which extended the right to request to all employees with 26 weeks' continuous employment[142] and the statutory procedure under which employers consider flexible working requests was replaced with a duty to deal with requests in a reasonable manner, and within a 'reasonable' period of time. Employers are now also supported with best practice guidance in the new ACAS code of practice on how to handle temporary changes to working patterns, and the right to request flexible working applies to all businesses regardless of their size. As commented elsewhere, 'a right to request flexible working arrangements is key to providing malleable options that can cater for the plurality of circumstances experienced by working carers'[143] and hence, its flaws are disappointing in this context. However, as also argued elsewhere, to be effective such rights need to provide leave provisions that are financially supported, provide adequate coverage in terms of eligibility and scope and a meaningful entitlement to short- and long-term flexible working.[144] The right is limited because it is not located within a framework that encourages employers to seriously engage with workers in order to reach mutually acceptable plans that enable the caregiving and the work roles to be carried out. The scheme in the UK (and Australia and New Zealand) allows the employer to refuse the request for very broad business-related reasons, the substance of which is not open to appeal/review, and the 12-month bar from bringing another request reflects the failure of policymakers to engage with the complexity of caregiving relationships

---

[140] By Employment Act 2002, s 47.

[141] See discussion in G James, 'The Work and Families Act 2006: Legislation to Improve Choice and Flexibility?' (2006) 35 *Industrial Law Journal* 272.

[142] The Children and Families Act 2014. See outline of the legal framework and policy in the House of Commons Briefing Paper No 01086 on Flexible Working (3 October 2018).

[143] James and Spruce, 'Workers with Elderly Dependants: Employment Law's Response to the Latest Care-giving Conundrum', above n 2.

[144] ibid.

in contemporary societies. The current approach restricts the ability of workers to instigate negotiations and to effectively challenge the strict boundaries of rigid workplace norms. Moreover, the UK allows for only permanent changes to be made to the employment contracts and does not provide opportunities for re-assessment over time. A better approach would be one that enables workers to modify arrangements on a temporary basis (as in New Zealand) and provides, where needed, mechanisms for regular ongoing monitoring of agreements, which provide opportunities for both parties to discuss and where relevant revise, the adjustments that have been made. It is also arguable that the right is diluted by its expansion to include all employees regardless of caregiving responsibilities.[145]

B. A Vulnerability Approach to Eldercare

Fineman has defined and problematised three core state 'responses' to eldercare relevant to vulnerability theory and these have since been discussed and usefully categorised by Mattsson and Katzin.[146] The first is the response of 'non-intervention', which appears to be fairly neutral but is highly problematic quite simply because non engagement undervalues care work and/or, particularly in recent years, overvalues the contentious notion of freedom of choice. It fails to appreciate the connection between autonomy and security, views human dependency as a private concern but ignores the inequalities that exist within the private sphere.[147] The second response to the care needs of older dependants is to pursue a policy that endorses 'privatisation and derivative dependency'. This approach explicitly places eldercare, or decisions surrounding how best to organise and pay for eldercare, within the confines of the family. In doing so it forces families, and mostly women within families, to experience widespread 'derivative dependency' and lets the private sector and the state 'off the hook'[148] in terms of accepting any responsibility for some of the most common manifestations of human vulnerability.

The third response is 'marketisation and freedom of choice'. This approach involves the 'deregulation of eldercare or incentives for the development of a market

---

[145] Indeed, it is interesting that the new EU Carers Directive is limited to carers, a move that might have caused tensions had we remained in the EU (Directive of the European Parliament and of the Council on work–life balance for parents and carers and repealing Council Directive 2010/18/EU). It is, however, disappointing that the Directive is willing to allow Member States to 'decide whether to provide a payment or an allowance for carers' leave' although 'they are encouraged to introduce such a payment or an allowance in order to guarantee the effective take-up of the right by carers, in particular by men' (see para 33). This contrasts with the parental and paternity leave provisions, where some form of payment or allowance is compulsory.

[146] These are discussed in T Mattsson and M Katzin, 'Vulnerability and Ageing' in A Numhauser-Henning (ed), *Elder Law: Evolving European Perspectives* (Cheltenham, Edward Elgar, 2017) 113, 122–26.

[147] Fineman, '"Elderly" as Vulnerable: Rethinking the Nature of Individual and Societal Responsibility', above n 25.

[148] Mattsson and Katzin, 'Vulnerability and Ageing', above n 146, 125.

of privately provided eldercare.[149] At the centre of this approach is a problematic belief in the importance of individual preference and personal responsibility: problematic because it assumes a level playing field that does not, in reality, exist. As a result, this risks promoting the wellbeing of those who have resources, for example economic, social, bodily resources – that enable them to negotiate this market, but leaves the least resilient in society in a weaker position. In brief, it fails to recognise, let alone challenge, underlying social inequalities and, as with the previous responses, does not encourage states to be more responsive to, and responsible for, the wellbeing of their citizens.

Each of these approaches is problematic and they have been reflected in the historical approaches to older people and their carers. For example, non-intervention has been a key response to the needs of working carers – whose issues have been ignored by policymakers until relatively recently. Whilst privatisation of care was explicit in the Poor Law provisions referred to above, it has remained implicit in the ethos and approach to eldercare ever since – because the mantra has always been that it is families who often provide the best care for those who are older and infirm. Deregulation has, especially since the 1980s, been a key feature of any formal care provision, which has – as outlined above – been outsourced so that it is no longer the day-to-day responsibility of local government.

To the three potential responses outlined above, it is, in view of the UK approach charted in this chapter, also possible to add a fourth approach – that of 'paternalism' – which is often the state's knee-jerk reaction in determining how to deal with 'vulnerable populations'. Fineman's theory of vulnerability is useful in this context because it helps us reconcile the contradiction between 'a genuinely individualistic/autonomy approach and a more societal – and thus easily paternalistic – approach'.[150] Such an approach is evident in the availability of a winter fuel allowance, free public transport provisions or TV licence concessions for older people. The problem with paternalism as a response, although superficially appealing in that it appears in the first instance to accept that the state has a responsibility towards the wellbeing of its older citizens, is that it positions old age as 'a separate category of human existence' rather than viewing it as 'one end of the continuum of the life of a human being'.[151] This, in turn, can lead to stigmatisation and the perpetuation of stereotypes that 'other' older people and facilitate and promote competition between generations.[152] It is also an expression of vulnerability open to withdrawal in times of economic hardship. Overall, approaches that are overly paternalistic do not reflect difference and diversity and

---

[149] ibid.

[150] A Numhauser-Henning, 'The Elder Law Individual Versus Social Dichotomy – A European Perspective' in A Numhauser-Henning (ed), *Elder Law: Evolving European Perspectives* (Cheltenham, Edward Elgar, 2017) 70, 110.

[151] Mattsson and Katzin, 'Vulnerability and Ageing', above n 146, 129; and see Fineman, '"Elderly" as Vulnerable: Rethinking the Nature of Individual and Societal Responsibility', above n 25.

[152] See ch 1.

can often fail to create a space for recognising the positive aspects of vulnerability. Such approaches can also hinder the fostering of relationships and structures that help build resilience during the life course. The latter is particularly key in order to better recognise and support the potential needs of all of us as we age. It is with this in mind that we consider the potential of an approach that has the notion of 'vulnerability' at its core.

In the UK 'older people', regardless of capability, have been differentiated in society and this separation has been promoted for decades. Originally, the motivations were morally sound and part of an agenda aimed at improving the quality of life of older people. However, older generations are now, according to Fineman, 'not seen as sufficiently autonomous and independent actors' and are therefore 'herded together' and designated, alongside children and 'the disabled' or 'the infirm', a 'vulnerable population'.[153] Constructed as the antithesis of the 'liberal self' the old, like other 'vulnerable cohorts', lack agency and are often, albeit to varying degrees, viewed as dependent on others. Yet, whilst sidelined alongside other so-called 'vulnerable populations' 'we may not be comfortable demanding they conform to the mandates of self-sufficiency and independence'[154] and hence we ask – indeed require – that, when necessary, this vulnerability be absorbed by others. In the UK, the 'others' are family members and predominantly women, except when that is practically impossible and the state then offers minimal support.

This categorisation or 'othering' of the old is challenged by Fineman because she espouses that vulnerability and dependency are universal, a construction that alleviates the stigma that is often attached to the terms. Vulnerability is, in effect, 'ageless' although some forms of physical or developmental dependency are, within this universally applicable theory, 'inevitable' for us all. However, whilst '*all* of us were dependent as children' and '*many* will become so as we age', the extent of dependency is not as 'inevitable' within older generations: indeed, '*many* within that category are physically and mentally able'.[155] With this in mind Fineman advocates that we should avoid the trappings of the 'idealized stereotype of the liberal subject',[156] which provides little space for critiquing the vulnerability that we can all experience during our life course, because it anchors attention on the very problematic trait of autonomy.[157] Adopting 'a vulnerable subject' as a replacement enables new explorations and critiques because its starting point is one of acceptance of the premise that 'every actual adult human being, no matter how strong and independent he or she may seem, is both presently and has been in the past reliant on others and on social institutions'.[158] It recognises that 'the elderly,

---

[153] Fineman, '"Elderly" as Vulnerable: Rethinking the Nature of Individual and Societal Responsibility', above n 25, 84.

[154] ibid, 85.

[155] ibid, 86, italics added.

[156] ibid, 88.

[157] ibid, 110.

[158] ibid, 88.

like everyone else, are situated beings who live with the ever-present possibility of changing needs and circumstances in their individual and collective lives'.[159]

Relatedly, it is significant that Fineman views all care work as a 'collective or social debt', views all individuals as obligated by that debt and insists that 'social justice demands a broader sense of obligation'.[160] This, importantly given the particular hostility that has been evident regarding pensions and eldercare-related social services, challenges any system that allows taxpayers to detach themselves from those who are struggling in society. The responsibility or social debt is shared by all citizens – not just institutions (such as workplaces) or the state – and requires us all to support, perhaps simply through the payment of more taxes or an acceptance of a new way of organising work, the unpaid care work undertaken every day: 'lack of involvement or rejection of responsibility for the needs of others in … society should not be an option'.[161] From our perspective this requires a broad commitment to supporting (or at the least not increasing the burden upon) older people or carers whose capacity to engage in paid work might be limited.

Regardless of how older people are portrayed at any one point in history, when care *is* needed, as it inevitably is at some point in the adult lives of most humans, individual dependency and the derivative dependency[162] of the carers has, for the most part, been and remains, unless warranting emergency medical intervention, framed as a private concern for families. As discussed in the Introduction to this chapter, this familisation strategy, especially in light of the growth in dual-income families, has resulted in growing conflict between the demands of unpaid eldercare and the demands of paid work.[163] Research also highlights the gendered nature of eldercare work and hence the gendered consequences of this conflict need to be recognised: in particular, (female) carers are at risk of being 'under-pensioned' because they have not been able to pay into a pension scheme, leaving them increasingly susceptible to poverty in old age.[164] The limitations of our current WFB framework as a means of helping to resolve existing conflicts without a fundamental shift in approach towards greater recognition of our shared and inescapable human vulnerability is clear.

IV. Conclusions

The current approach to eldercare, as demonstrated in this chapter, is firmly grounded in neoliberal foundations that promote a myth of autonomy, valuing

[159] ibid, 110.
[160] MA Fineman, *The Autonomy Myth: A Theory of Dependency* (New York, New Press, 2004) 47–48.
[161] MA Fineman, 'The Vulnerable Subject and the Responsive State' (2010) 60 *Emory Law Journal* 251, 260.
[162] See discussion of this term in ch 1.
[163] See discussion in the introduction to this chapter.
[164] See Carers UK, *Caring for your Future: The Long-term Financial Impact of Caring*, above n 9, 11.

the liberal self and 'encouraging' individuals, with carrots and sticks, to continue in paid employment for as long as possible, placing the onus on self-support in old age. Promoting a system that relies so heavily upon kin to shoulder the core responsibilities of eldercare reflects a familisation strategy that contradicts the ethos of the original welfare state and undermines the improvements made to pensions in the mid-1970s, when there was a glimmer of hope that poverty in old age might at some point be eradicated. An approach that places the 'vulnerable self' at its core exposes the hierarchies and inequalities permitted and promoted by decades of inadequate investment in adult social care followed by the sweeping cuts to key services upon which older people and their carers depend. If the pendulum of responsibility was ever swinging, even slightly, toward the state, the most recent approach provides no doubt as to where successive governments, since the late 70s, have placed the onus of responsibility. Vulnerability theory forces us to reflect upon this strategy and its implications and to acknowledge how our current system, bolstered by the myth of self-sufficiency and independence,[165] is problematic. We have failed to frame responsibility of caring for those whose bodily or mental functions are impaired at a particular stage in their lives, as a collective endeavour. We have as a result, ultimately, increased pressure on individuals and families – most often their female members – to facilitate individually negotiated and tailored 'solutions' when those care needs arise. This current crisis in terms of the lack of state support perpetuates harm to carers and, potentially, those in need of care. What this historical assessment reveals most prolifically are the limits of *any* approach constructed around the stereotype of the autonomous liberal self, and a strategy of strict familisation, to alleviate that harm.

In the concluding chapter, we draw together the various discussions from throughout this book and (re)imagine how replacing the current WFB framework with a vulnerability approach would shift the parameters of possibility and better engage with, recognise the lived experiences of, and ultimately support all families in their endeavours to care and provide for each other. As Fineman puts it,

> In breaking down the conceptual barriers that accompany thinking of the generations separately, as potentially at odds with each other, it becomes possible to reconsider how society should realistically and fairly apportion responsibility for human vulnerability and dependency across the life-course among the individual, the family, and the state and its institutions.[166]

---

[165] See Fineman, '"Elderly" as Vulnerable: Rethinking the Nature of Individual and Societal Responsibility', above n 25.
[166] ibid, 111.

6

Conclusions: Strains, Stereotypes, Strategies and Solutions

I. Introduction

As the analysis presented in this book has shown, although the explicit regulation of working families is a very modern concern, at least as far as it is reflected in the contemporary framing of 'work–family balance', many of the central premises on which the current framework is based have been around for decades, and in some cases, centuries. The use of an historical perspective has enabled us to reveal the remnants of previous eras, to explore their influence on current arrangements, and to conclude how the past and present combine to impact on how families, whatever their form and their individual members, live their lives today. Only by tracing the various strands of law and policy over a longer timeframe are we able to deconstruct the law and policy framework in order to fully understand its constituent parts and their multi-level interactions. This process reveals how the prioritisation of various interests – through claim staking and policy framing – have privileged some and disadvantaged others.

As this analysis reveals, the resulting inequalities are now hardwired into the WFB framework because of its continued reliance on stereotypical notions of what families and their constituent members are and its embeddedness in existing structures and institutions. This reliance on stereotyping is largely rooted in prior assumptions concerning lifestyles and decision making at the individual and household levels, which may have originated from fact or mere imagination, but which are nonetheless outdated and obstructive to future development. As well as their acceptance of unreliable modelling, the provisions themselves result from political decision making based on perceptions of the wider social and economic circumstances of particular eras and subsequent attempts to control, coerce or shape the lives of specific social groups and their individual members on the grounds of their particular characteristics, including gender, age, level of dependency and class. The weaknesses and flaws inherent in the current framework reveal a multitude of strains and stresses in a system – or set of systems – which has developed incrementally in order to serve a myriad of disjointed and incompatible policy goals at different times in history.

In this final chapter, we will bring together some of the critiques presented throughout the book to provide a broader consideration of what is wrong with the current approach. As the selection of subjects for the individual chapters themselves illustrate, state approaches to the universal problem of reconciling unpaid care and paid work have given rise to separate policy areas based on individual characteristics, so that caregivers and recipients appear as distinct legal subjects, each with their own competing needs and preferred strategies. Due to its emphasis on difference and distinction, this approach will never provide an adequate solution to the unsolved conflict between paid work and unpaid care which sits at the heart of the work–family debate. As we have argued throughout this book, the interests of all of those who give and receive care coalesce around a single unifying feature – our humanity. We are all caregivers and recipients to varying degrees over the life course in line with our changing needs and capacities. However, the use of stereotypes as a means of developing social policy has given rise to unyielding and unrealistic social expectations. Society places an expectation on women to provide a disproportionate amount of care on the grounds of their personal characteristic of sex. Although originally related to childbearing, this is a socially constructed anomaly that requires correction through targeted state intervention as a means of ensuring distributive equality, and preventing further harm,[1] in all spheres of life. This is the basis for applying a vulnerability approach. It provides a simple yet profound explanation for what has led us to where we are and what has gone wrong along the way, as well as offering an alternative vision for how things might be done very differently in the future.

This concluding chapter is structured as follows. Taking the constituent parts of an alternative vulnerability approach, introduced in chapter one, we will examine each in turn using examples from the various regulatory strands examined in each of the chapters above. Section I will focus on the identification of the subject of law's attention, which, as Fineman contends, should rightfully be conceptualised as the vulnerable subject in place of the liberal subject.[2] How this alternative framing would be of benefit in the current context will be considered. Section II interrogates the relationships and institutions that have historically interacted to operationalise the current law and policy framework. The institutions to which responsibility for regulating working families has traditionally been allocated – which include the family, the state in its various guises, the third sector, employers and the civil justice system – are all socially constructed and so provide potential sites of resilience. However, they are all in themselves vulnerable in a multitude of different ways. This vulnerability has been variously harnessed and exploited for different purposes by state actors over time. In more recent years, responsibility for social and economic ordering has ostensibly been

---

[1] MA Fineman, 'Injury in the Unresponsive State: Writing the Vulnerable Subject into Neo-Liberal Legal Culture' in A Bloom, D Engel, and M McCann (eds), *Injury and Injustice: The Cultural Politics of Harm and Redress* (Cambridge, Cambridge University Press, 2018).

[2] MA Fineman, 'The Vulnerable Subject: Anchoring Equality in the Human Condition' (2008–09) 20 *Yale Journal of Law and Feminism* 1.

ceded to the market which, it is claimed, will produce the fairest allocation of resources so long as state interference is minimised. However, markets are also socially constructed entities, heavily influenced and manipulated by a variety of state actions including regulation which, in themselves, privilege some and disadvantage others. Section III considers the role of the state and the shift in the notion of state responsibility that has occurred in the post-war era. The dominance of 'free market' economics has enabled and justified the long liberal tradition of selective state intervention via a combination of laissez-faire, regulation and deregulation. In section IV the proper role of the state will be explored through a consideration of the grounds for and nature of its responsibilities in the current context. In section V, we argue that the application of an alternative vulnerability approach to the area of unpaid care and paid work has the capacity to resolve any conflict between these two fundamental aspects of human existence. Although the emerging vision would be radically different to the current WFB framework and associated law and policy, its adoption offers a viable and reflexive strategy for regulating working families.

II. The Subject of Regulation

Throughout this book we have considered the narrowing of the scope of the various laws and policies relating to the regulation of work and families, noting the restriction of their purview through the process of policy framing that has taken place over time. The choices made by governments regarding who should benefit from state intervention and on what grounds stem from decisions made about whose interests should be privileged and in what ways those interests should be served. These decisions may vary over time depending on social and economic conditions and political persuasions. Nonetheless, the central question of whose interests the relevant law and policy serves is a critical one. The chapter choices are, thus, not ours but are related to varying degrees to the specific targets of relevant policy over the last century or so.

In chapter two we argued that, from the earliest days of its current incarnation, the state focused its attention on the liberal ideal of the autonomous being. This unencumbered paradigm served as the normative model with any deviation from it constructed as an alternative 'other'. Woman's subjugation through marriage and childbearing delegated her to a subsidiary position so that it was man through the normative model of the standard worker who was ordained as the primary subject of state attention. Industrialisation further emphasised the division between unpaid care and paid work, the latter's worth enshrined in the machinery of industrial relations and valorised though the contract of employment. The demands of care meant that women's work, even when marketised, could not conform with the standard model of full-time permanence expected by employers and, even when this gave way to a more fluid, flexible model, the arrangements under which women worked continued to be defined by their atypicality which further entrenched the gender coding of care. By this process of othering, the state was able to manipulate women's relationship with paid work through their unyielding need to provide high levels of unpaid care, primarily but not exclusively for children.

In chapter three, the various demands and expectations placed on women and men in their roles as mothers and fathers were considered in the context of the development of the WFB framework. While women have been the focus from the earliest days of state activity in this context, the nature of law's intervention has been to accommodate care needs, as far as possible, within the existing contractual nexus to enable an apparently seamless transition to motherhood leaving workplace arrangements unaffected. For men, the law's largely non-interventionist stance has left them outside of the work–family frame.[3] In recent years the ideological approach on which law's accommodation of maternity and maternalism within workplaces has always been founded, has been extended to ideas connected with men's role as fathers.[4] Notions of 'new fatherhood' and what it means to be a 'good dad' have started to colour the policy debate. Unfortunately, these ideals have not been met with any specific provisions capable of shifting man's role as breadwinner, through compliance with the standard worker model, towards a more hands-on and engaged worker-carer model. Those fathers able to comply with certain eligibility requirements related to their employment as well as with living arrangements based closely around traditional notions of the nuclear family have been given certain restricted rights to parental leave beyond which the expectation of compliance with the unencumbered standard worker remains.

As chapters four and five illustrate, even when the state acknowledges its responsibility for certain social groups on the grounds of their perceived specific vulnerability, the ways in which that responsibility is discharged further exacerbate difference and distinction. Through a combination of neglect and excessive paternalism, state measures have failed to provide adequate support for some of those most in need. Children's welfare provided the focus for chapter four and, as our analysis clearly shows, children's interests have been marginalised over time through the choice of the family as the preferred site in which those interests should be met. The privatisation of the family through law's reluctance to intervene in its arrangements has often resulted in the subsumption of children's interests by those of their adult family members. This development can be traced back to the end of children's existence as marketised individuals with the demise of child labour during the late nineteenth and early twentieth centuries.

---

[3] S Fredman, 'Reversing Roles: Bringing Men into the Frame' (2014) 10 *International Journal of Law in Context* 4, 442.

[4] N Busby and M Weldon-Johns, 'Fathers as Carers in UK Law and Policy: Dominant Ideologies and Lived Experience' (2019) 41 *Journal of Social Welfare and Family Law* 3, 280.

Once children ceased to be categorised as potentially economically productive beings, their dependency was exposed and the arrangements for their care and wellbeing was even more firmly embedded in the family, whatever its fortunes and prospects. Although the WFB framework provides leave periods intended for the care of (very young) children, it does so, as outlined above, by privileging mothers which, as well as overlooking the needs of other caregivers including fathers, further re-entrenches women's over-association with all things care-related and reaffirms notions of the continued relevance of the nuclear family model. Moreover, children have come to be constructed as an obstacle to adult autonomy. Of course, in practice, albeit because of the limitations of state acceptance of responsibility for their care, their presence *does* often impact on the potential of their adult carer's, most often their mother's, ability to undertake paid work or to progress at work.

Chapter five considered state responses to the need to care for older people at the end of their productive lives. The endowment of a state pension, although a critical provision in the fight against poverty in old age, has been used as a political touchstone by successive governments leaving those reliant on it subordinate to the changing ideologies championed by the state over time. The provision of care for older people (beyond the purely financial) has also been subject to the waxes and wanes of a host of shifting socio-economic preoccupations since the advent of the welfare state. Although, as with childcare, the overriding assumption is that such care will be provided within the family where it is predominantly performed by women, no state provision exists for such worker-carers beyond a short period of emergency leave and/or the right to make a permanent change to working arrangements. There is, thus, a complete failure by the state to acknowledge the various demands such care may place on its individual provider and/or the changing complexity of the needs of its recipient. The policy response to the growing need for eldercare has been the privatisation of social care, thus casting it adrift and exposing its susceptibility to the vagaries of the market, which too often results in inadequate provision for those at the receiving end and the exacerbation of poor working conditions and rising precarity for those paid carers who provide it. Like children, elders have been largely neglected as the specific targets of the WFB strategy, although the delegation of their care to the public domain has resulted in its problematisation so that the focus is on how the 'ageing population' might be cared for in the most economically efficient way.

A. The Fictive Liberal Subject

Despite the changing face of the state and its agencies considered in the various contexts explored throughout the book, one factor remains static and unchanging and that is the assumption that the liberal subject, unencumbered by ties of dependency, is the correct normative model against which all targets for legal and policy intervention should be judged.[5] The foregrounding of productive labour as paramount and the workplace as the primary site of all valuable human activity has valorised the liberal subject in its various guises: 'homo economicus' with his focus on rationality; the 'standard worker' and his ability to provide unyielding loyalty to the cause of production. It is in the interests of the liberal subject that the state acts and this has been the one constant throughout the time period interrogated in this book. Yet, as Fineman contends, and as we have illustrated throughout the book, the liberal subject is a fictive construct which, unlike some of the most commonly utilised stereotypes, has no grounding in lived experience as no one is truly unencumbered and all of us have benefited from the ties that bind us to others through relationships of care.[6]

Rather than redrawing the subject of its focus, law's response to the inability of so many to comply with this model has been the development of the anti-discrimination framework and, more recently, in recognition of the need for caregiving alongside paid work albeit in a very narrowly defined context, the WFB framework. Both are necessary but, if the law is to be truly effective, these frameworks need to be extended and reconciled so that they are mutually reinforcing in more positive and proactive ways. At present they act against each other: anti-discrimination law operates post facto so that, in the case of sex discrimination, women are compensated for discrimination based on their inability to conform with the standard worker norm whereas the rights associated with WFB, although intended to operate proactively, are restrictive and create further hierarchies of worker-carers without fully providing the necessary support for any one group. Although of critical importance in the fight for equal pay and conditions, the framing of sex discrimination legislation disadvantages fathers – and other men – who wish to provide unpaid care alongside paid work. They are outside the frame and thus lack the (relative) privilege it bestows on women in their role as mothers. Within the narrow confines of the WFB framework, mothers are again ostensibly privileged through the relatively enhanced provision of positive rights, although this brings with it the detrimental impacts arising from women's over-association with caregiving.[7] Fathers who do not reside with their children are disadvantaged in comparison to those who do and may find themselves completely excluded from the WFB framework. Furthermore, those who provide care beyond the parent–child relationship, as traditionally defined, are further disadvantaged. This includes a whole range of worker-carers such as those who provide care for their parents – either during childhood or in the form of eldercare outlined in chapter five; grandparents caring for grandchildren; spouses, partners

---

[5] MA Fineman, 'Cracking the Foundational Myths: Independence, Autonomy and Self-Sufficiency' (2000) 8 *The American University Journal of Gender, Social Policy and the Law* 13.

[6] MA Fineman, *The Autonomy Myth: A Theory of Dependency* (New York, New Press, 2004).

[7] N Busby, *A Right to Care? Unpaid Care Work in European Employment Law* (Oxford, Oxford University Press, 2011).

and others with no marital or blood ties to the recipients of their care. The focus of the framework on heteronormative gender distinctions means that, despite the obvious absurdity, same-sex couples are required to comply with a binary 'mother/father' model in order to benefit from the same rights and protections as different-sex couples. This insider/outsider approach creates and reaffirms a hierarchy of worker-carers, some of whom are eligible for state support and others who are not on the grounds of arbitrarily drawn boundaries based on personal characteristics or the assumed nature of the relationship between carer and recipient, but regardless of the circumstances of the care relationship itself.

Perhaps the most obvious and pernicious effects of this approach are discernible through the state's instrumentalisation of women's relationship with both paid work and unpaid care which has been used to include and exclude them from labour law's reach over time, to restrict both their ability to participate in paid work and to limit the legal protections available to them depending on socio-economic circumstances rather than the pursuit of sex equality for its own sake. However, this process of 'othering' is not confined to women in their roles as mothers. Themes of 'deserving' and 'undeserving' (in/out; subject/other) colour the whole policy landscape which has been imbued with such distinctions over time leaving its provision heavily reliant on stereotyping in its conceptualisation of particular social groups and their individual members. 'The lone mother',[8] 'the absent father',[9] 'the neglected child',[10] 'the aged parent'[11] are all, under a traditional liberal typology, variously 'vulnerable' as measured by their degrees of difference from the unencumbered liberal subject. All have in common their stigmatisation, which arises through their inability to conform and which is further endorsed by the perceived particularity of their vulnerability. Through the process of stereotyping, individuals and the groups to which they belong are dehumanised and reduced to situational objects, conceptualised within the policy framework as 'social problems'. The stigmatisation of vulnerability as individually ascribed, negative, undesirable and largely self-imposed is, as well as being socially damaging, wholly unfounded.

The mythology of the liberal typology and the danger that it poses to the reconciliation of paid work and unpaid care can be illustrated with reference to its most valorised subject – the male breadwinner or working father. On the face of it, the working father embodies the liberal subject and appears as the greatest beneficiary of liberalism: a free-market actor who can operate freely and rationally (in the purely economic sense) without consequence and reap the financial and other rewards for so doing. He is not identifiable by his vulnerability but rather by his independence and autonomy. In reality, his vulnerability is exposed and perpetuated by the operation of the WLB framework, which provides him with little

---

[8] See ch 2.
[9] See ch 3.
[10] See ch 4.
[11] See ch 5.

support in respect of his ability to spend time with his children, partner, parents and anyone else with whom he shares a bond of care. This detracts greatly from his lived experience by denying him the opportunity to share in the benefits of caregiving or to experience solidarity with others like himself: traditional notions of 'masculinity' and 'paternalism' laud and celebrate 'strength' through detachment from care and vilify and reject dependency as 'weakness'. The elevation of the liberal subject, which denies fathers little more than a superficial opportunity to engage in caring, benefits nobody in the long run. The liberal subject, in all its guises, is perhaps the greatest stereotype of all.

III. Institutions and Relationships

As highlighted throughout the book, despite its location as the prime site for caregiving which takes place in private and beyond the reach of 'public policy', the family is the site of various inequalities based on gender,[12] age, dependency and economic contribution. As well as being reproduced within the family, such divisions have been created, affirmed and entrenched by the law and policy framework itself based on perceptions of personal autonomy and confirmed by the all-pervasive market. In the context of care, resulting categorisations are used to inform judgements concerning a group's or individual's 'worthiness' in relation to state support, as illustrated, for example, in chapter five in the context of older people's categorisation at the beginnings of the welfare state, or in relation to the reduction/elimination of child poverty under New Labour as discussed in chapters three and four. Whether grounded in benevolence or paternalism, such value judgements are based on the 'giving' of something in return for what is conceptualised as undeserved or blameless suffering, casting those who are less deserving outside of such provision. The institutionalisation of dependency that occurs through this process is unhelpful if the state's ultimate goal is to provide a solution to the unresolved conflict between paid work and unpaid care. In contrast, an approach based on vulnerability recognises dependency – be it experienced during childhood, old age or at any point throughout the life course – not as an unexpected anomaly or an exception to the normalised state of autonomy, but as an inevitable and positive consequence of the human condition.

A. The Vilification of Dependency

In its current formulation, as a variable determinant of the appropriate level of state support, dependency is conceptualised as a 'burden' on the state,

---

[12] C Pateman, *The Sexual Contract* (London, Polity Press, 1988).

measurable by the costs of pensions, benefits and commodified social care – be it for children, elders, disabled people or the infirm. Children and other 'dependants' are reduced to a cost expected to be met by families who have a primary responsibility to ensure that they are able to do so. Those who fail must face the wrath of public opinion and state punishment meted out through the disadvantage suffered by limitations imposed through the benefits system, for example, on the number of eligible children per family.[13] There is no apparent market value in providing high levels of good quality care over a long time period, so its availability depends on services which have been contracted-out to the profit-focused private sector under short-term arrangements with no long-term investment. If vulnerability and dependency are personalised and problematised in this way, located within the market and viewed through the lens of commodification, the only option for those who cannot meet the costs is re-familisation of caregiving supported, where possible, by the non-profit-making sector.

Just as reproductive work is undervalued, in terms of both its gift and receipt, productive work is valorised so that the caregiver's inability to conform is viewed as a sign of weakness which must be compensated for: vulnerability is written right through the WFB framework, but it signifies individual weakness, not common humanity. Although the civil justice system has largely replaced collective bargaining as the main site of workplace dispute resolution, enforcement of the individual rights which underpin such provision may all too often prove evasive. The application of free market principles to the labour for wage exchange gives the illusion of a laissez-faire approach by the state. In fact, as discussed in chapter two, labour market policy is a highly regulated area. The particular approach adopted by successive UK governments epitomises the extent to which public policy has become subsumed by ideology, narrowing regulatory choice and stunting institutional imagination. The emphasis on statutory rights and the concurrent contraction of access to those rights is part of a wider political strategy grounded in neoliberal ideology driven, in recent years, by an increasingly coercive state through dominant government policy aimed largely at suppressing conflict. Where disputes *are* acknowledged – through employee-led claims – they are viewed as contractual in nature and thus a matter of private settlement, increasingly by non-legal means, and/or attributable to unreasonable expectations on the part of the complainant.

Like the stigmatisation of those deemed 'dependent', be it on state benefits or care arrangements, the characterisation of individuals seeking to assert their rights before the employment tribunal as 'vexatious litigants' has been used by policymakers to vilify those in need of support and solidarity.[14] Employment rights,

---

[13] Under the current system for assessing Universal Credit, the number of children eligible for support is limited to two children per family (born on or after 6 April 2017).

[14] N Busby and M McDermont, 'Fighting with the Wind: Claimants' Experiences and Perceptions of the Employment Tribunal' (2020) *Industrial Law Journal* forthcoming, available at https://academic.oup.com/ilj/advance-article/doi/10.1093/indlaw/dwz018/5550867.

where invoked, are dealt with by an adversarial approach aimed at compensating the victims of unlawful actions *post facto* rather than as a basis for reimagining the policy landscape.[15] Most litigation takes place once employment has ended and where litigation does result in a remedy, be it an order for unpaid wages or compensation for unfair dismissal or discrimination, weak enforcement mechanisms mean that there is a high chance it will go unpaid or require further court action.[16] Even this unsatisfactory, but nonetheless independent, avenue for legal redress is being shut down. The imposition of claimants' fees in 2013[17] – subsequently deemed unlawful by the Supreme Court[18] – and imposed restrictions on eligibility for rights such as the increase in the qualifying period for unfair dismissal from one to two years[19] have seriously impeded individuals' ability to assert their legal rights and to access justice.

IV. The Role of the State

The introduction and development of the welfare state has been charted throughout this book. The allocation of state resources from 'cradle to grave' encapsulated in Beveridge's original vision[20] is a powerful notion. However, the rights-based approach which predominates the anti-discrimination and WFB frameworks is not an appropriate means of achieving this. Pensions and other 'benefits', including payment for and/or time off to provide care for one's children, which rely on qualification – be it through prior contributions and/or length of service requirements – merely perpetuate existing disadvantage. This approach is based on the (fictive) notion that we are all equally situated and are thus able to plan for and ultimately to take responsibility for our (future) vulnerability and that of our dependants: that we as individuals or family units should bear the risk.[21] However, if in order to benefit from a compensatory payment or to access a right including the most basic level of employment protection, an individual must

---

[15] E Barmes, *Bullying and Behavioural Conflict at Work: The Duality of Individual Rights* (Oxford, Oxford University Press, 2016).

[16] Research conducted by the Department for Business, Innovation and Skills (BIS) in 2013 revealed that, of the 1,200 successful claimants surveyed, fewer than half (49%) received their awards in full, with a further 16% paid in part. Only 34% of those who received their awards did so without taking further enforcement action. See www.gov.uk/government/uploads/system/uploads/attachment_data/file/253558/bis-13-1270-enforcement-of-tribunal-awards.pdf.

[17] The Employment Tribunals and the Employment Appeal Tribunal Fees Order 2013, SI 2013/1893 introduced fees of up to £1,200 for claimants from July 2014.

[18] *R (on the application of UNISON) v Lord Chancellor* [2017] UKSC 51.

[19] The Unfair Dismissal and Statement of Reasons for Dismissal (Variation of Qualifying Period) Order 2012.

[20] Discussed in ch 1.

[21] MA Fineman, 'Injury in the Unresponsive State: Writing the Vulnerable Subject into Neo-Liberal Legal Culture', above n 1.

have *been able* (ie properly situated) to accrue whatever is necessary, measured in time or money, those most in need are likely to be excluded. Although the rights-based approach may give the illusion that access to a right or a resource has been individually 'earned', as the analyses in this book show, the opportunity to accrue such benefits is not and never has been available to all.

As well as reaffirming and embedding existing inequalities within relevant relationships and structures, this approach further institutionalises them because, as we have argued throughout the book, policy framing, in itself, has always privileged some and disadvantaged others, thus creating and perpetuating a social model consisting of insiders and outsiders with the parameters of each, as the examples of child welfare (chapter four) and older people (chapter five) illustrate, malleable over time. The illusion of fairness and equality in this system of allocation has recently been reaffirmed by the political dogma of neoliberalism which has now become deeply embedded in public consciousness as the natural, commonsense and rational approach to welfare provision. State intervention is minimised as the individual is responsible for her own wellbeing and that of her dependants: we are the entrepreneurs of ourselves[22] and I am 'the CEO of me'.[23] Within the parameters of this problematic framing, the safety net envisaged under the 'cradle to grave' notion of the welfare state is merely a means of rewarding idleness, which is epitomised by dependency.

A. The Mythology of the Market Order

The marketised approach to state provision enables those in control of public resources to shift responsibility for decisions regarding their allocation to the apparently mysterious forces at play. In the aftermath of the financial crash of 2008, the notion of 'crisis' has been used to justify austerity policies[24] which, as our analysis shows, have exacerbated and deepened existing social and economic inequalities. This is itself the result of policy framing and political choice. In the competition for scarce resources, which has been caused and worsened by state reliance on the market, generations are pitted against each other (see chapters four and five) with, among the working-age population, a striver/skiver dichotomy used to differentiate the 'hard-working tax payer' from the 'benefit recipient'. Again, dependency is vilified and autonomy is valorised. State expenditure arises through a process of political choices made by government and not as a natural consequence of an uncontrollable market order.[25] Yet, in reality, rather than the

---

[22] M Foucault, *The Birth of Biopolitics: Lectures at the College de France 1978–1979* (Basingstoke, Palgrave, 2010).
[23] E Kossek, *CEO of Me: Creating a Life That Works in the Flexible Job Age* (London, FT Press, 2007).
[24] S Walby, *Crisis* (Cambridge, Wiley, 2015).
[25] See J Clarke and J Newman, 'The Alchemy of Austerity (2012) 32 *Critical Social Policy* 3, 299.

free-wheeling determinants of our future prosperity or poverty, markets are human constructs controlled and constrained by the decisions made by those in power. What then should the expectations be concerning the state's involvement in the regulation of work and families? In the final section we turn to vulnerability theory in order to answer this critical question.

V. The Application of a Vulnerability Approach

As the analysis presented in this book has shown, the current resolutions offered by law in response to the unsolved conflict between unpaid care and paid work are framed by existing paradigms: employment law, family law, welfare law, tort, contract law and so on. Reform is thus reactive and limited by the separation of existing silos within which the legal system currently operates. If our aim is fundamental reform, we need to resist the constant revisiting of pre-existing approaches and, in their place, construct an alternative model based on radical thinking. For the reasons presented in the foregoing discussion, the starting point must be the relationship between the state and the individual. Specific areas in which legal reform is necessary can only be identified and tackled once the wider conceptual questions about institutional and individual relationships have been posed and answered. Although our focus is on the UK's WFB framework, the institutional functions of law and policy are consistent across societies and across jurisdictions and should, thus, be the focus of any critique.

The application of a vulnerability approach accomplishes this task.[26] Its assumption that the state is always active compels us to question in whose interest the state acts.[27] This accords with our analysis which shows that, through the long-term process of claim staking and policy framing, the focus of state activity has been co-opted, constrained and incrementally narrowed so that, even in the context of WFB, it coalesces around the normative paradigm of the liberal subject. As we have shown, this is a wholly unsuitable target for policy provision in the current context, in short because it has no basis in lived experience and is predicated upon a completely negative discourse concerning vulnerability. Fineman's suggested replacement of the normative liberal subject with the embodied vulnerable subject provides the means to overcome this fundamental conceptual flaw by reducing humanity to its most basic common denominator: our universal vulnerability.

Vulnerability's location in the body means that the vulnerability approach does not offer a normative model but one that is empirically grounded. It is not a

---

[26] For a thorough consideration of the evolution of her work from an early critique of the anti-discrimination approach up to and including vulnerability theory, see MA Fineman, 'Vulnerability and Inevitable Inequality' (2017) 4 *Oslo Law Review* 133.

[27] MA Fineman, 'The Vulnerable Subject and the Responsive State' (2010) 60 *Emory Law Journal* 251.

variable trait or personal characteristic but represents *the* human condition and, as such, provides an ethical mandate for the state to be responsive in its attempts to build resilience as a means of countering any consequences arising from our universal vulnerability. Justification for acting in the interests of the vulnerable subject is unnecessary: in contrast to the liberal subject and the array of other stereotypes confronted in this book, it is not a normative model but a descriptive and observant one representative of the human condition. There is no 'invulnerability' and no alternative term that captures the concept. The stigma associated with vulnerability arises because of the negative associations accorded to it which arise from valorisation of the liberal subject. In contrast, vulnerability theory positions autonomy, independence and self-sufficiency as only 'one of a range of developmental stages that an actual human individual passes through in the course of a "normal" lifespan'.[28] It views humans as vulnerable during *all* of these developmental stages and so the focus shifts to how laws might support and encourage resilience in *all* individuals and *throughout* the life course.

State action which is taken in the interests of the vulnerable subject thus benefits each and every one of us. Based on a shared and negotiated set of values which provide the foundations for building resilience in whatever form it is needed, such action should be taken in order to construct a society in which we can *all* prosper regardless of temporal factors such as age or life stage, personal characteristic, level of dependency or status as caregiver or recipient and in spite of our personal identities. In Fineman's analysis, care work is viewed as a 'collective or social debt' and all individuals are obligated by that debt. The achievement of social justice, thus, 'demands a broader sense of obligation'.[29] This, importantly, challenges any system that enables the 'hard-working taxpayer' to detach himself from the poor or struggling in society. The responsibility or social debt is shared by all citizens: 'lack of involvement or rejection of responsibility for the needs of others in … society should not be an option'.[30] In the current context, a vulnerability approach thus calls upon us all to stand in solidarity and to accept responsibility for the impact of our decisions on the capabilities of others: 'because we are part of and benefit from society, we must be attentive to responsibilities that extend beyond satisfying one's own personal and familial needs'.[31]

In order to arrive at an appropriate response to the unsolved conflict between unpaid care and paid work, a series of political choices must be made by the state in its various guises. This will include civil society and its wider constitution of mediating institutions with specific interests, which are themselves engaged in the prioritisation of values. Although the state may contract out its responsibilities via

---

[28] MA Fineman, '"Elderly" as Vulnerable: Rethinking the Nature of Individual and Societal Responsibility' (2012–13) 20 *The Elder Law Journal* 71, 88.

[29] Fineman, *The Autonomy Myth: A Theory of Dependency*, above n 6, 47–48.

[30] Fineman, 'The Vulnerable Subject and the Responsive State', above n 27, 260.

[31] ibid, 261.

third sector bodies, such as trade unions, charitable or religious entities, or state funded non-governmental organisations, the responsibility for all areas of law and public policy ultimately rests with the responsive state.

The application of a vulnerability approach does not provide a catalyst for change in the current or indeed in any context. Its requirement of a different ethical framework arising from difficult choices concerning the identification of the most appropriate values and its operationalisation through institutional arrangements and structures which have at their heart a concern for the interest of the vulnerable subject mean that its absorption and adoption is a long-term project. This, ultimately, demands a different political settlement between the state and the individual. The scale and complexity of its ambition should not be underestimated but the necessary shift can, and should, be led by legal intervention. As the analysis in this book has shown, law is a powerful engine of change but, under its current demarcation, its gaze has for too long been fixed on certain static categories such as gender, childhood, disability, old age, with little or no recognition of the fluidity and constant development of the human condition. The action necessary to unseat current arrangements will take time but, as the historical analysis presented in this book shows, their questionable foundations have clearly run their course. Recognition of our shared vulnerability is the means by which the many apparent conflicts concerning the reconciliation of paid work and unpaid care can be resolved. Only by accepting our mutual dependency and individual need and desire for support and solidarity within the context of our personal relationships, wider institutions and a truly responsive state can we all appreciate the value of care. This is the only way in which our common interests can be met through the future regulation of work and families.

INDEX